HOMOSEXUALITY AND AMERICAN PUBLIC LIFE

HOMOSEXUALITY AND AMERICAN PUBLIC LIFE

Edited by
CHRISTOPHER WOLFE

Introduction by
WILLIAM KRISTOL

SPENCE PUBLISHING COMPANY · DALLAS
1999

Published in the United States by
Spence Publishing Company
501 Elm Street, Suite 450
Dallas, Texas 75202

Library of Congress Cataloging-in-Publication Data

　　Homosexuality and American Public Life / edited by Christopher Wolfe
　　　p. cm.
　　Includes bibliographical references and index.
　　ISBN 1-890626-11-2
　　1. Homosexuality—United States—Psychological aspects. 2.
Homosexuality—Law and legislation—United States. 3. Homosexuality—
United States—Religious aspects. I. Wolfe, Christopher.
HQ76.3.U5 H645 1999
306.76'6'0973—ddc21   98-40750

Printed in the United States of America

Contents

vii

PART II
MORAL NORMS

PART III
LAW

PREFACE

Christopher Wolfe

A MILWAUKEE RADIO TALK SHOW HOST recently devoted a segment of his show to a discussion of advertisements placed in national newspapers that highlighted some homosexuals and lesbians who had successfully made the transition to a heterosexual orientation. Some of his callers were homosexuals who said that they had made good-faith efforts to change, but that it had not been possible. Nature or God, it seemed, had just made them that way. Other callers were deeply religious people, who contended that the Bible shows homosexuality to be wrong and many of whom argued that homosexuality was, fundamentally, a choice.

The host himself captured the ambivalence of many Americans today. He believed that homosexual acts are wrong, but he also thought that it is likely that homosexuality was not really a choice, but rather a condition rooted in genes or biology. Like many other Americans, some religious and some not so, he seemed impatient with those who base their opinion on the Bible, because not everybody accepts the Bible and, in any case, there are varying interpretations of Scripture (though he had no doubt himself that the Bible condemns homosexual acts). While believing that those who had placed the advertisements unquestionably had a right to do so, he thought that homosexuality was not really a matter in which government should intervene.

The talk-show discussion was fairly representative of "middle-American" attitudes about homosexuality. The issue seems to devolve into a debate between homosexuals, who contend that they are simply made the way they are, and Bible-based Christians, who argue that the homosexual lifestyle is a perverse human choice. A majority are most likely in the middle and have reservations about important elements of both positions: they think that homosexuality is perhaps in some sense "natural"—a result of genes or biology—but that it is still "abnormal" and unfortunate, and perhaps even that homosexual acts are morally wrong, though not the concern of government.

Note that this is the situation in proverbial "middle America." In the world of intellectuals and academics, homosexuality is an issue on which there is precious little genuine intellectual exchange these days. There is a considerable body of ideologically-inspired "scholarship," most of which claims to disprove traditional notions that homosexuality is "abnormal," and much of which advocates a radical re-thinking (and perhaps "reconstruction") of gender and sexuality in light of new perspectives on homosexuality.

It is partly as a result of this scholarship, or at least by the way it is reported in the media, that many ordinary citizens believe that homosexuality is the result of immutable genetic or biological factors. Nature, it is said—or even God—"made them that way." Given the general, and increasing, acceptance of nonmarital heterosexual activity (and perhaps even of the assumption that it is not natural to go without sexual satisfaction of some sort), the growing acceptance of the legitimacy of homosexual activity, as simply one among a diverse array of forms of sexuality, is not surprising. At the very least, many believe that, even if homosexuality were to be considered "abnormal," homosexual activity is not a matter of public concern, and should be tolerated.

The contributors to this volume are generally united in certain fundamental claims about homosexuality. First, homosexuality is indeed a "disorder" and is therefore an affliction for those who suffer from it (whether they realize it or not). Second, the causes of homosexuality are quite complex, but no fair scientific analysis of them shows that homosexuality is genetically or biologically determined. Indeed, third, the practical experience of many therapists and support groups suggests that a homosexual orientation may, in many cases, be reversed. But, fourth, whether the orientation is settled or not, engaging in homosexual activity is not the right answer for those who experience same-sex attraction. This is true both because homosexual acts are morally wrong and because—as is so often the case with moral wrongs—pursuit of the illusion inherent in those acts will not lead to human happiness. Finally, homosexuality is definitely a matter of public concern, since attitudes regarding it are intimately intertwined with profoundly important convictions about the nature of marriage, family, and sexuality.

Homosexuality and American Public Life elaborates and defends these claims by investigating the causes of homosexuality, the morality of homosexual acts, and the appropriate social and political response to the effort to legitimize homosexuality. Part I deals with science, medicine, and homosexuality. Jeffrey Satinover provides a detailed review of the scientific literature on the biology of homosexuality, placing it in the context of what we know about the biology and heritability of other disorders, and shows that there is little convincing evidence for a biological explanation of homosexuality. The influence of the assumption that homosexuality is biologically determined appears wide, but Dr. Satinover's analysis of this assumption is trenchant.

George Rekers provides a broad and balanced survey, based on research and clinical experience, of the common developmental influences or pathways associated with a homosexual orientation. Richard Fitzgibbons draws on his clinical experience, which began with treating the problem of excessive anger and led him to treat a large number of homosexual patients, and describes ways in which same-sex attraction disorder may be prevented and healed. Joseph Nicolosi proposes a socioanalytic view of the formation of gay identity, based on many years of treating homosexually-oriented men, suggesting that self-deception, and therefore the need to transmit that deception to society, is a key element of gay indentity.

Patrick Derr rounds out the scientific discussion by putting AIDS in a global context, describing the magnitude of the pandemic and the way that "AIDS exceptionalism" (from both the right and the left) has distorted our response.

Part II examines natural law arguments regarding the moral status of homosexual acts. Janet E. Smith provides an account of a classic natural law argument against homosexuality in the work of Thomas Aquinas, partly in response to mischaracterizations of Aquinas's position by a contemporary historian, John Boswell. Aquinas, she argues, judges homosexual acts of sexual intercourse to be objectively disordered because they are not ordered to the goods naturally embedded in sexual intercourse. Robert P. George argues that the moral judgment at the heart of traditional sexual morality is the possibility of marriage as a one-flesh communion of persons, which makes marital acts differ fundamentally in meaning, value, and significance from the only types of sexual acts which can be performed by same-sex partners.

Part III turns to the question of why homosexuality should be a matter of public concern. Hadley Arkes argues that the law cannot be neutral or detached on the question of sexual orientation (as the case of pedophilia shows). Following an analysis of several constitutional arguments, he concludes that the law should refrain from promoting and encouraging homosexuality, since it constitutes an understanding of sexuality that is severed from a responsibility for begetting and nurturing the next generation.

Michael Pakaluk undertakes to show why legal prohibitions of discrimination based on sexual orientation and the acceptance of same-sex marriages would undermine the family and society at large. Gerard Bradley discusses the attempt to legitimate same-sex "marriages" by establishing it in one state and then compelling other states to recognize such marriages through the Full Faith and Credit Clause of the U. S. Constitution. He provides a strategy for resisting this attempt. David Coolidge finishes the section with an extended argument regarding same-sex marriage, identifying the deeper issue as the question of what marriage is.

Fr. Richard Neuhaus provides the conclusion for the book, asking "where do we go from here?" He reviews the history of the gay rights movement, and concludes that 1993 may have been the high-water mark of the movement. Recent events suggest that it is not the unstoppable countercultural juggernaut it might have appeared. While Americans may tolerate and have compassion for homosexuals, they have resisted the call to affirm homosexuality.

This book is based on papers delivered at a conference sponsored by the American Public Philosophy Institute at Georgetown University Conference Center in June 1997. It is the first of two projected volumes, the second of which will include accounts of being healed from homosexuality, discussion of religious teachings and homosexuality, descriptions of various aspects of the campaign to legitimize homosexuality, analysis of various public policy issues (for instance, employment and housing non-discrimination, military service, and adoption), and consideration of the appropriate public rhetoric for dealing with homosexuality issues.

The reason for both conference and books is the APPI's conviction that our nation's answer to the question of the public status of homosexuality will greatly affect fundamental aspects of its public philosophy. Are the nature and ends of marriage, the family, and sexuality defined simply by private choice? Or are the nature of marriage, the family, and sexuality objective realities that transcend human (personal or political) choice? Is human freedom realized by defending the autonomy of individual human wills in such matters? Or is freedom achieved by means of our capacity to know and to act in accord with the truth about human life?

It is not too much to say that these questions are at the heart of a civilizational crisis at the end of the second millennium. A "cold war" between East and West has given way to a "culture war" within the West. If this latter war is to be concluded as favorably as the former, the weapons used must be those of reason—a reason that deliberates not merely upon the means to achieve arbitrarily posited human desires, but also upon human ends as well, and a reason that is not willfully closed to transcendent realities.

We offer this book as a contribution to reasonable discussion of this key issue, confident that we can provide a sound intellectual framework and many particular insights to our readers. In all candor, we have pursued this topic, at least in part, because we recognize that others who have shared our general views have oftentimes failed to make their case reasonably and with civility. At the same time, we also recognize that, lamentably, many people are likely to refuse to seriously consider or discuss the reasons that we offer, replying instead with indefensible accusations of bigotry, hatred, and "homophobia." On an issue that touches people's personal identities, perhaps this is to be expected. Whatever the obstacles, however, public deliberation shaped by reason rather than emotion is essential if our nation is to gain ground in the difficult and painstaking effort to resolve such important questions.

MAJOR PORTIONS of George Reker's essay were excerpted, revised, and adapted from his chapter, "The Formation of a Homosexual Orientation," in the book *Homosexuality and Hope*, ed. P. F. Fagan, (Washington, D.C.: Free Congress Research and Education Foundation, 1988), and are used with permission of the foundation. An earlier version of Robert P. George's essay appeared as "Marriage and Moral Neutrality" in T. William Boxx and Gary Quinlivan, eds., *Political Order and Culture: Towards the Renewal of Civilization* (Ann Arbor, Michigan: Eerdmans, 1997), and is used here with permission.

INTRODUCTION

William Kristol

I REMEMBER, in early 1993, when I had just left government, I was invited to lunch with the *New York Times Magazine* editorial board. The issue of gays in the military was in the headlines. The attitude of the *Times* editors was not so much fervent support for the gay rights cause—though they were supporters—but rather a distaste that this issue was being debated at all. How foolish of our polity to be distracted by this kind of dispute, they thought; we should be debating the budget deficit, health care plans, tax policy, and all those serious, grown-up issues that serious people like to write long and tedious articles about. As I recall, I reacted by suggesting that it struck me as perfectly reasonable that people would be more interested in gays in the military than in other, more respectable, topics, especially since the question of gays in the military opened up into the broader question of the status of homosexuality in our country. After all, this question really is important for the future. It will affect the country our kids grow up in much more than whether the capital gains tax is 28 percent or 20 percent, or exactly how HMO's are regulated, or the other issues that serious policy analysts like to debate. Hence, one reason this book of essays is useful is that it brings home to us that the question of homosexuality and American public life is a serious one, important to be discussed and appropriate to be debated.

Now debating this issue is, unfortunately, divisive. Americans really are divided on this question and on other, related issues of sex and gender. In nineteenth century Great Britain, people spoke of two nations, rich and poor, who barely knew each other because they were so different, because their paths crossed so little. One has the sense that America today is perilously close to two nations in the sense of two cultures, each of whose adherents can barely understand the concerns and the beliefs of the other's.

This is not a healthy thing. We might wish it had not come to this. We might wish that a "don't ask, don't tell" policy, which in effect was the general attitude towards homosexuality for decades or even centuries, still prevailed. But it does not. And we cannot shove this topic back into the closet once it has come out; it would be pointless to try. We cannot avoid the debate.

It will be a political debate; and political debates are not always the kindest or gentlest or calmest of debates. So we have to be ready for what will at times be divisive and bitter arguments. Obviously, I think it is important to try to conduct these debates civilly and with respect for those with whom we differ. But one cannot deny that in the coming years and decades in America we are going to have fundamental debates that cut close to the bone, in the course of which people will offend each other.

These will not simply be debates between liberals and conservatives. Indeed, these arguments will exacerbate divisions among conservatives. As a conservative, this is not something I would normally welcome. On the whole, it is better for a political movement to be more or less united: it is more likely to win. On the other hand, there can be no unity if there really are fundamental differences; they need to be argued and fought out. And the issues that surround homosexuality, and sexuality in general—the whole complex of cultural, social and moral questions of which the question of homosexuality in public life often seems to be at the center—these issues increasingly divide the conservative movement.

Libertarians, at least some of them, have moved to a position not just of live-and-let-live, but to an aggressive defense of a kind of pure libertarianism, a denial of any public right to uphold moral standards. Conservatives whose conservatism is morally based, who think that there is a place for morality in the public sphere, find themselves increasingly far from such libertarians. It is a big question whether the conservative political movement, the conservative political party—right now the Republican party—should or will become a "leave-us-alone" party (the term coined to describe the Republican coalition from a libertarian point of view) or an "upholding-moral-standards" party. That fight will take place over the next few years. Lots of politicians will spend lots of time nervously wishing that this battle were not taking place and earnestly imploring everyone to avoid it. But in fact it is unavoidable; and, I believe, at the end of the day, if there is going to be a serious conservative political movement in this country, and a serious conservative political party, the "upholding-moral-standards" side must prevail. The view that "if only we can get rid of big government, all else would be well" is simply not credible, I think, as an intellectual argument, and it is not politically compelling enough to create a governing conservative movement. And it is not true.

What is more, the more one thinks about it, the clearer it is that any serious consideration of homosexuality leads to a consideration of sexuality in general; thinking about questions related to homosexuality in the public sphere, and about judgments to be made in public policy and public morality about homosexual acts and homosexual behavior, requires one to come to broader judgments about sexual mores and the sexual revolution. History may well record this revolution as the most fundamental social movement of the latter part of this century. The whole question of the relation of sex and procreation, of sexual desire and the ends of desire, of sex and children, of whether there is any natural teleology to sex—these are all deep questions. They are not the kind we usually debate in politics. But the question of homosexuality in American public life is going to force an explicit discussion of all those issues. That is not something to which Americans are particularly accustomed. One can make the case that it is something to which we should once have been happy we did not have to be accustomed. But—more directly than almost any of the other liberation movements of the last thirty years, more than the attempt to secure the unbridled right to abortion, more than feminism—the homosexual rights revolution forces a consideration of whether there is any ground in nature for saying that certain human activities are to be preferred to others. It forces us to decide if there is any guidance in nature that for private or public behavior. This debate should be healthy for us. For we need to come to grips with the fundamental question of whether there is a natural standard for human happiness, whether there are natural ends for human desires, and whether public policy has, at least in certain ways, to take into account those natural ends or standards.

Practically, where do we go from here? If I had to summarize my thoughts in four words, it would be "theoretical boldness, practical incrementalism." Practically speaking, you need to win over waverers, if you want to use that term, people who are uncertain what they think about homosexuality in the public sphere, who are wary of the homosexual rights movement—but who are also wary of some of those who put themselves forward vigorously to oppose that movement. And so one has to be politically prudent, one has to try to build coalitions and figure out how to begin making progress on the broader front of rethinking sexuality in the public sphere, and not just homosexuality in the public sphere. This is not going to happen quickly and it is not going to happen easily, but it is not hopeless, either. One of the lessons of the last fifteen years, after all, is that all kinds of things that one could not have believed would happen have in fact happened. The collapse of the Soviet Union is the most obvious example. So practical incrementalism can produce major results.

Let me mention three aspects of a strategy of practical incrementalism informed by theoretical boldness:

(1) In order both to resist the gay rights movement and to advance a traditional agenda in the area of sexuality and public life, one must first of all resist the imperial judiciary. One must resist the courts' attempt to seize control of the fundamental issues of birth, life, and death. It is very important, I think, to make the case that citizens of this self-governing country are entitled to make those decisions. That is both a principled and popular position to take. It allows one to build broad political alliances. It also means one has to

accept, for the time being, the legitimacy of the decisions that our fellow citizens make in these areas—decisions that will fall short of what many of us would like.

(2) We must embrace federalism. New York has always had different mores than other parts of the country. Fine. I think it is important to make clear that we conservatives do not envision an America with conservative mores dominant in every municipality in every state in the land. But we do believe citizens should have the right to have their mores inform public policy in their states and localities. A federalist agenda in the area of public morality will bear fruit in a reasonably short time. For instance, one can imagine an America in which, in most public school systems, homosexual unions are not presented as equally desirable to the traditional family. In a political movement, if what you seek seems utterly unattainable, it is very hard to persuade people to fight and work for it. Federalism is good for many reasons, but one of those reasons is that it helps make an ambitious political task manageable—and also less threatening to those who live in enclaves like New York or Hollywood.

(3) We need to speak for parents. Parents would like to bring their children up in a manner more consistent with their own views than with the views of the enlightened and politically correct. If you look at political debates over the last twenty years, you could simplify them in this way: The conservatives had the clever idea of becoming the party of the family—"family values" as it was called—through the 1980s and early 1990s. That trumped the Left, who were the party of individual autonomy and self-expression, because the American people did sense that the family was an important institution, and that the Left's agenda was either anti-family, or at least did not give any special respect to the family. The Left's comeback to this in the 1990s has been to wrap itself in the mantle of children, and so Bill Clinton has talked endlessly about children. He knows that defending individual autonomy against the family is a loser politically, but that defending children is a winner. But conservatives should not be scared of fighting on the grounds of whose policies are better for our children. That is a fight we can win. And parents are crucial in waging that fight.

So self-government, federalism, and parents can all be elements of a challenge both practical and bold to the dogmas of the sexual revolution. Such a challenge is more important than the elites believe. It is also more powerful than many now think, and the essays that follow establish a foundation for this effort.

PART I

SCIENCE

The Biology of Homosexuality: Science or Politics?

Jeffrey Satinover

SERIOUS RESEARCH on the biology, innateness, and genetic determinants of homosexuality has only just begun. Contrary to what the public is being led to believe, the research that has been done thus far suggests that genetic factors play at most a small role in the development of a homosexual orientation. J. M. Bailey and R. C. Pillard, two of the major researchers most widely credited with having demonstrated that homosexuality is genetic, were forced by the results of their own research to admit otherwise: "These studies were designed to detect heritable variation, and if it was present, to counter the prevalent belief that sexual orientation is largely the product of family interactions and the social environment. . . . Although male and female homosexuality appear to be at least somewhat heritable, environment must also be of considerable importance in their origins."[1] Given the results of such research, it is interesting to note the changes in public attitudes toward homosexuality, how they have occurred, and how current research can be used or misused to effect these changes.

In 1992, two psychologists published a study entitled "Effect of Reading a Summary of Research About Biological Bases of Homosexual Orientation on Attitudes Toward Homosexuals." In the course of this study,

105 volunteer subjects from college classes were exposed to one of three treatment conditions. Subjects in the experimental group read a summary article of current research emphasizing a biological component of homosexual orientation. Subjects in one control group read a summary article of research focusing on the absence of hormonal differences between homosexual and heterosexual men. Subjects in another control group were not exposed to either article. All subjects completed the Index of Attitudes Toward Homosexuals. As predicted, subjects in the experimental group had significantly lower scores[2] than subjects in the control groups.[3]

The operative word here is *summary*. The psychologists tailored the summaries, like the research paradigm itself, to demonstrate the effect on people's attitudes of judiciously selected biological arguments about homosexuality—in the minds of the authors a socially desirable effect.

What this study really demonstrates is the astonishing impact of "scientific" information, especially when it is crafted, condensed, and cleaned up to conceal weaknesses or contradictions in the science. The impact is particularly profound when the readers—in this case college students who are intelligent, but critically naïve about research design, relevance of opposing arguments, and so on—are unable to make their own independent critiques of what they read. The strong but fair word that describes the selective use of science for the explicit purpose of altering opinion is *propaganda*.

But in many ways the public displays remarkable common sense and conservatism. Another 1992 article, published in the *Journal of Homosexuality*, documents the effect of the activist campaign on public attitudes toward homosexuality. Using data from the General Social Surveys (a government-sponsored data collection effort focusing on a wide range of social attitudes), the authors found that between 1973 and 1988 the public became steadily less willing to endorse restrictions on the freedom of homosexual expression. But the authors also found something they could not readily explain: "Paradoxically, negative moral attitudes toward homosexuals did not decline." Nevertheless, the authors continued, "concerted efforts to educate the public on this subject [its moral attitude toward homosexuality] can have an important and rapid effect."[4] Yet the conflation of fact and morals, under the rubric of education, reveals that what they propose is not truly education, but what in other countries has come to be known as *reeducation*.

I

Let us now turn to the actual science and the answers it gives to the questions: Is homosexuality biological? Innate? Genetic?

The Genetics of Major Mental Illness

The most common diagnosis among residents of psychiatric institutions used to be "General Paresis of the Insane," the madness to which Friedrich Nietzsche eventually succumbed. Many decades after Nietzsche's death, scientists discovered that a syphilitic infection of the brain causes this illness. With the discovery of penicillin, it has almost entirely disappeared. General Paresis of the Insane was the first important example of a mental condition, long thought to be a "software" problem, that instead proved to be a "hardware" problem, and a reparable one at that. But until very recently, other instances of commonplace mental conditions with known and treatable biological causes were exceedingly rare.

Most mental states, normal or not, have long been presumed to be of psychological origin, because in the vast majority of cases we have not been able to understand, let alone affect, the biology. We simply have not had the technology to treat an apparent disease of the brain whose primary manifestations are psychological. But neuroscience research techniques have proliferated. We can now distinguish, on the molecular level, at least some of the specific biological mechanisms that play a role in many conditions previously thought to be purely psychological. This kind of research has already produced many dramatic benefits (for example, in psychopharmacology). But we are far from knowing all the various steps involved in the causation of any psychiatric condition.

Consider what is required to demonstrate biological causation even of those conditions with which we are very familiar. In almost all instances, even those where there is no dispute over what constitutes serious pathology, high-quality research is extremely complex and multifactorial, requiring literally hundreds or even many thousands of funded projects and the efforts of many thousands of researchers yearly.

Schizophrenia

In the case of schizophrenia, research has only now, after forty years of effort, begun to yield somewhat reliable results. The first major gathering of researchers on the subject, called "The First International Congress on Chemical Concepts of Psychosis," convened in 1958 in Geneva, Switzerland. (Somewhat ironically, given his reputation as rather more a mystic than a scientist, the conference was chaired by C. G. Jung.) Yet the major questions—What causes schizophrenia? How does it affect the nervous system? What environmental cofactors are critical to its appearance? What interventions might be curative?—remain almost entirely unanswered.

Demonstrating that a behavioral condition is not only biological, but genetic as well, is even more complex. Even heritability estimates (that is, "How heritable is it?") remain wildly divergent because of the uncertainties inherent in techniques of genetics research. With respect to schizophrenia, different studies claim to show anywhere from 40 to 90 percent heritability. Researchers have made numerous claims to have found a meaningful genetic linkage to a particular chromosome, only to retract them.[5] The vastly more complex problem of finding the genes themselves, among the millions on the chromosome, for so complicated a behavioral state, has been compared to finding a needle, not in a haystack, but in the ocean. Hence, sophisticated researchers have long seen the significance of findings of heritability as, at best, dubious: "The concern is not just with the trivial question of measuring 'heritability'"[6] Yet, on the basis of a handful of studies, precisely the opposite is now being heatedly argued with respect to homosexuality.

Bipolar Disorder

The story of the genetics of Bipolar Disorder (also known as manic-depression) is even more instructive because the promise of the research seemed at first to have been so bright. As with schizophrenia, the amount of rigorous research on Bipolar Disorder, underway continuously for over twenty years, greatly exceeds the research to date on homosexuality. Between 1991 and 1993 alone, 103 studies purely on the genetics of Bipolar Disorder were published in major scientific journals. In general, because of the enormous resources expended on this research, especially by the National Institutes of Health, even the poorest current research on Bipolar Disorder in America alone is far more sophisticated and of higher quality than the best research on homosexuality.

In 1987, to great public fanfare, researchers "found the gene" for Bipolar Disorder in an extended Amish family. The article in *Nature* that started the frenzy was confidently titled "Bipolar Affective Disorders Linked to DNA Markers on Chromosome 11."[7] In spite of the cautions raised by more level-headed experts in the field,[8] both scientists[9] and the media made grand predictions that genetic engineering would soon lead to a cure.

Shortly thereafter, to no similar media fanfare, such predictions were abandoned, as contrary evidence poured in from laboratories around the world. "Manic Depression Gene Put in Limbo," the normally staid and oft-quoted (though not this time) *Science* put it.[10] Somewhat more optimistic, *Nature* headlined its retraction "False Start on Manic Depression."[11] If nonprofessionals remember this episode at all, they most likely remember only the sadly overblown original claim; the retractions have faded from public memory. Not only has the original research study proven "a false start," so have all those that followed in its wake.[12]

All of this does not mean that Bipolar Disorder does not have a heritable component or components. Rather, it has three main implications. First, actual genetic linkages are extraordinarily difficult to identify. Because the human genome is so vast, when we scan it for correlations to complex behavioral traits, we will inevitably find some. But these kinds of findings can rarely be repeated and mean little. They are similar to the kind of finding that appears when a battery of blood tests is done. A few blood values show up abnormal just from anomalies in the testing procedure. Such findings are meaningless and disappear when the sample is retested. Given the inherent degree of uncertainty in all blood testing, physicians expect that about one out of every twenty blood values will be abnormal.

Second, Bipolar Disorder may not be a single condition. Clinically, at least five different types of manic-depression exist. These may have entirely different genetic backgrounds with varying degrees of genetic influence; some may have no genetic background. Genetic studies are extraordinarily difficult to perform reliably even when the condition does not show this kind of variation; the difficulty and uncertainty of the outcome is compounded exponentially when it does. Hence, with respect to homosexuality, many of the more careful researchers in the field, usually nonactivists, refer to "homosexualities."

In fact, almost all psychiatric disorders are composites of different conditions. Our ignorance of the brain and the nervous system[13] has forced us to classify "mental illness" not on the basis of underlying pathophysiology (the functional changes that accompany a disease), but on the basis of how symptoms seem to cluster together. This method is on a par with calling a "bellyache" a disease, a classification we would be forced to employ were we unable to know anything about or distinguish between "appendicitis" and mere "flatulence."

Third, any single type of Bipolar Disorder may itself be polygenic, like height or temperament. If a trait or condition is linked to tens or even hundreds of genes or gene variations (and again, for complex behavioral traits this kind of polygenicity is more likely the case than not), there will likely be a continuum of the traits' expression. Only if certain thresholds are crossed—how many and which of these genes are inherited and which environmental factors are present—will the associated symptoms manifest themselves. The nature of genetic linkage studies invariably limits their usefulness in studying complex behavioral traits that come in multiple forms and are probably caused by multiple genes and gene variations. Genetic linkage studies are more useful in studying hypothetical, simple, monogenic physiological traits.[14]

Aggression and Violence

Studies of violence and aggression provide another example of how fraught with difficulty are attempts to identify the genetic bases of behavior. In this case, the lessons are slightly different and socially even more complex than in the previous two cases. For aggression is a somewhat one-dimensional trait compared to a major mental illness, let alone to an entire way of life such as homosexuality. High levels of aggression are a common symptom of schizophrenia,[15] which implicates hundreds of dimensions of human behavior. In examining aggression, therefore, we look at merely one element of the behavioral complexity of schizophrenia, which in turn is one element in the behavioral complexity of an entire way of life. (Somewhat analogously, just as high levels of aggression are routinely a feature of schizophrenia, high levels of sexual activity are routinely characteristic of homosexuals, especially males. [See, for example, "The Social Organization of Sexuality" [16],[17]]. We might, therefore, anticipate greater success in locating a genetic basis for a more limited aspect of homosexuality, say, sexual urgency, than for something so multidimensional as "the gay lifestyle." Nevertheless, it should be noted that men in general seek more sexual partners than women and tend to be more accepting of "casual" sex—this is, more plausibly than homosexuality, a biological, sex-linked trait.[18] The promiscuity of the gay lifestyle may also in some measure reflect the fact that with "mating couples" composed of two males, there is no "female" restraint on "natural" male promiscuity.)

The biological bases of aggression are much better understood than those of schizophrenia. For one thing, aggression is a trait that not only can be identified and quantified in many different species, but bred for as well (for example, in fighting cocks and pit bulls). These so-called "animal models" open the door for a kind of research that is impossible for schizophrenia or homosexuality. Because the diagnosis of schizophrenia is based on clinical phenomena, such as verbalizations and reports of internal states, there are no animal models. For other, equally obvious reasons, a species of exclusively homosexual animals does not exist, at least not for long. But most species demonstrate "bisexuality" or "polysexuality," which is a "loosening," as it were, of the absoluteness of sexual object choice.[19]

The available research on aggression is probably thousands of times greater than that on homosexuality. The genetics of aggression has been worked out extensively to varying degrees in, among others: fruit flies,[20] fish,[21] poultry, cattle, pigs, and dogs,[22] Japanese quail,[23] foxes,[24] mice,[25] domesticated rats,[26] sows,[27] monkeys,[28] and humans.[29] Even so, our understanding of just how, and to what extent, innate biological factors contribute to aggressive behavior in human adults remains highly speculative at best.

Physical Illnesses

The genetic background of even relatively straightforward physical illnesses is not nearly so easy to identify as we are often led to believe. In 1989, molecular geneticists claimed to have identified the gene responsible for cystic fibrosis.[30] This terrible illness of the pancreas, which affects the lungs, inevitably kills its victims in childhood, adolescence, or young adulthood. Funded in large part by the many donations of a major foundation, enormous resources were given to scientists seeking its cause and a cure. The cystic fibrosis gene was heralded as the first major triumph in what was sure to become a major national screening effort for many genetic illnesses.[31]

Four years later, on November 16, 1993, the science section of the *New York Times* published the following sad retraction: "Cystic Fibrosis Surprise: Genetic Screening Falters." As the science writer reported, "Human genetics . . . turns out to be far more complicated than expected. Biologists have found more than 350 points at which the [cystic fibrosis] gene can be mutated, and more are appearing almost weekly.[32] At the same time, scientists are finding that many people who inherit mutated genes from both parents do not have cystic fibrosis.[33] . . . the researchers are finding that combinations of different mutations produce different effects." This picture could be even more complicated if, as some researchers suspect, other genes alter the way different mutations of the cystic fibrosis gene are expressed. Thus, a pair of mutations inherited by one person might behave differently from that same pair inherited by another person, depending on the state of a third, regulatory gene.

INHERENT LIMITATIONS OF BEHAVIORAL GENETICS

Dr. Norman Fost, a pediatrician and ethicist at the University of Wisconsin, observed that, as the evidence from cystic fibrosis research points out, "there is, in fact no such thing as a single-gene genetic disorder. . . . One of the worst things that Mendel ever did was work with this plant that was either tall or short [that is, 'dimorphic']. Not a single gene in human biology works that way."[34] Attempts to associate particular combinations of mutations with particular outcomes in the general population "have been almost totally unsuccessful," admitted Dr. Barbara Handelin, a medical geneticist at Integrated Genetics in Framingham, Massachusetts.[35] Similarly, *Science* reported that "[t]ime and time again, scientists have claimed that particular genes or chromosomal regions are associated with behavioral traits, only to withdraw their findings when they were not replicated. 'Unfortunately,' says Yale's [Dr. Joel] Gelernter, 'it's hard to come up with many findings linking specific genes to complex human behaviors that have been replicated.'" This pattern continued into the 1980s, with scientific reports linking reading disability to genes on chromosome 15, schizophrenia to chromosome 5, psychosis to chromosome 11, and manic depression to chromosome 11 and the X chromosome. All these reports were announced with great fanfare; all were greeted unskeptically in the popular press; all are now in disrepute.[36]

Brian Suarez, a psychiatric researcher at Washington University School of Medicine in St. Louis, calculated what would be required to replicate a genetic finding to provide confirmatory evidence of what otherwise could only be considered a meaningless fluke. He

> projected that if the trait [in question] was 50 percent heritable and each family in the [initial] study had ten members (4 grandparents, 2 parents and 4 children), detecting one of the genes would require studying 175 families that is, almost 2000 people. Replicating that finding [so as to capture the vacillating effects of a nonlinear genetic contribution] would require studying 781 families, another 8000 people. To find and confirm each additional gene (for a polygenic trait), researchers would need to go through the whole business again. "Suddenly you're talking about tens of thousands of people and years of work and millions of dollars."[37]

None of the initial studies of the genetics of homosexuality have come even remotely close to studying as many subjects as in this hypothetical study.

II

In the case of the hypothesis that homosexuality is biological and genetic, research is in its absolute infancy. There have been a mere handful of studies conducted only in the past few years. Nonetheless, from these few studies, the general parameters we might have anticipated from our knowledge of other conditions have already begun to emerge, parameters which do not lend themselves to the gross oversimplifications of politics.

First, like all other complex behavioral and mental conditions, homosexuality is multifactorial. It is neither exclusively biological nor exclusively psychological, but results from an as-yet-difficult-to-quantify combination of genetic predispositions, intrauterine influences (some innate to the mother and others incidental to a given pregnancy), postnatal environment (parental and sibling behavior), and a complex series of reinforced choices occurring at critical phases in development, which will be explored later.

Second, their similarities notwithstanding, male and female homosexuality are probably different conditions that arise from a different combination of influences.

Third, "homosexuality" itself is very poorly defined. Even more than the still vaguely defined term "schizophrenia," the spectrum of sexual orientation (not to mention the simplistic dichotomy, "homosexual" versus "heterosexual") is largely a social device. It obscures a complex set of mental, emotional, and behavioral states caused by differing proportions of distinct influences, resulting in a broad spectrum of only loosely related outcomes. The widespread use of the term "homosexuality" itself tends to create the impression of a reality far more uniform than truly exists. Indeed, one of the chief characteristics of the gay lifestyle is its efflorescence of styles and types of sexuality.

Neuroanatomic Research

In 1991, newspapers primarily on both coasts trumpeted the discovery of a brain difference between homosexuals and heterosexuals. Although the finding of the research itself was reported fairly accurately, the accounts universally concluded that the discovery had social policy implications. Commentators triumphantly claimed that the discovery would remove any remaining uncertainty that homosexuality was either a choice or a consequence of factors in upbringing. Therefore, they claimed, to continue to support anything less than full acceptance of homosexual behavior would be proof positive of prejudicial hatred.

What precipitated this reaction? In August of 1991 a San Francisco neuroanatomist, Simon LeVay, published an article in *Science* reporting his finding that a localized cluster (a "nucleus") of cells in the brains of "homosexual" men was, on autopsy, twice as large by volume as in "heterosexual" men.[38] "Homosexual" and "heterosexual" are in quotations here because in this particular study the definitions of each were extremely imprecise, nor, since the subjects were dead, was there any way of verifying sexual orientation.

But this was not the first such discovery. One year before a group had reported in *Brain Research* that they had found a similar difference in both volume and number of cells in a different brain nucleus.[39] The media did not report this first study because *Brain Research*, unlike *Science*, is read only by neuroscientists. And unlike journalists, the neuroscientists themselves genuinely understood the research and its limitations and saw no reason to make grand pronouncements.

More recently, yet another difference in another part of the brain was reported, also in a prestigious publication, the *Proceedings of the National Academy of Science of the United States of America*. This study claimed that a difference between male homosexuals and heterosexuals was found in the anterior commissure, a structure that divides the left and right halves of the brain. The authors found that the anterior commissure was larger in women and homosexual men than in heterosexual men. This was a group statistical difference, however. The size of the anterior commissure in twenty-seven of the thirty homosexual men fell within the range of sizes found among the thirty heterosexual men. Like LeVay, these authors used brain samples obtained for the most part from men who had died of AIDS, introducing another uncontrolled variable into their work.[40]

The only other study to examine morphological differences in the anterior commissure, published in 1988 and not mentioned by the press, found, in part, precisely the opposite, namely, that the anterior commissure was larger in men than in women.[41]

Even if actually present, however, the discovery of brain differences is, in itself, on a par with the discovery that athletes have bigger muscles than non-athletes. For though a genetic tendency toward larger muscles may make it easier to become an athlete, and therefore more likely that one will become an athlete, becoming an athlete will certainly give one bigger muscles.

The layperson, encouraged by press accounts, is apt to assume that brain differences must be innate and unchangeable, especially differences in the number of cells, as contrasted with the simple volume occupied by a collection of cells. We tend to think of the mind as "software" and the brain as "hardware," the former plastic and changeable, the latter fixed at birth. We have used this analogy to good advantage already.

But the analogy breaks down at a certain point. Various processes go on throughout life: the selective death of brain cells in response to training or trauma, the establishment of new connections between cells, dramatic increases or decreases in the "thickness" of connections between cells as a result of learning, the loss of interneuronal connections through "pruning." Unlike modern computers, the brain's software *is* its hardware.

We know from animal studies that early experience and especially traumatic experience (this has special pertinence to the childhood histories of many homosexuals, as we will discuss later), alters the brain and body in measurable ways. Infant monkeys who are repeatedly and traumatically separated from their mothers suffer more or less permanent alterations in both blood chemistry and brain function.[42] A similar piece of research on homosexuals with a similarly indeterminate meaning is the recent discovery of a protein, an Alpha1-Antitrypsin variant, in the blood of homosexual, but not heterosexual men. Again, we have no way of determining whether this is an innate or an acquired difference, or whether it is even replicable.[43]

There is a major current theory about the developmental causes of depression and the interaction of genetics with development. It claims that under conditions of early trauma, a genetically based susceptibility to stress creates a greater vulnerability to intense stress-responses later in life.[44] Furthermore, this "vulnerability" is represented physiologically as measurable alterations in the brain. Because what constitutes "stress" depends on one's subjective interpretation of events, the brains of individuals with the same genetically determined biology may respond quite differently. One may demonstrate no brain changes; another may demonstrate very significant changes.[45] Likewise, in individuals who became blind as adults and then learned Braille, the part of the brain governing the right index finger became progressively enlarged. And just this year, researchers reported measurable increases in brain tissue associated with learned sexual activity in rats.[46] With this background, we may understand the comments of the editor of *Nature* on the LeVay research: "Plainly, the neural correlates of genetically determined gender are plastic at a sufficiently early stage. . . . Plastic structures in the hypothalamus allowing the consequences of early sexual arousal to be made permanent might suit [those who claim an environmental origin to homosexuality] well."[47]

Of course, all this presumes that the research itself was of high quality. Was it? Writing in *Technology Review*, published at the Massachusetts Institute of Technology, two prominent geneticists commented on the quality of the LeVay research. According to Paul Billings and Jonathan Beckwith, LeVay "could not really be certain about his subjects' sexual preferences, since they were dead."[48] Further, his "research design and subject sample did not allow others to determine whether it was sexual behavior, drug use, or disease history that was correlated with the observed differences among the subjects' brains."[49] Indeed, LeVay's very method of defining homosexuality was very likely to "create inaccurate or inconsistent study groups."[50]

More rigorous findings than these are nonetheless sure to be forthcoming because all aspects of human behavior are influenced by our genetic makeup. All such findings are potentially of value in our attempt to understand how the brain and behavior influence and correlate to each other. Nevertheless, they tell us nothing about origins or the range of freedom we have apart from influencing factors. While we can presume that we probably will find genetic factors that correlate with homosexuality, we should not call such factors "an innate predisposition." In the proper and precise language of science, they are merely "risk factors." But we can be more precise in our discussion of such risk factors by examining what has proven to be one of the most powerful avenues of research into the genetics of behavioral conditions, namely, twin studies.

TWIN STUDIES

The basic strategy of twin study research is fourfold. First, we consider the differing proportions of identical genes between two non-relatives (very little similarity), two biological siblings with the same parents (some similarity), two dizygotic fraternal twins (same degree of similarity as non-twin siblings), and two monozygotic identical twins (one sperm, one egg: 100 percent similarity). Second, we compare the degree of genetic similarity between members of a given pair to the degree of behavioral similarity between members of a given pair. Third, if possible, we control for similar environmental influences acting on both twins. This is done by examining only twins in which both were adopted away after birth into different families.

The fourth strategy applies when adoption studies are not possible. It is extraordinarily difficult to locate both members of a pair of identical twins where at least one has the trait in question, where the trait is relatively uncommon, where both have been adopted away, and where both are willing to participate in a study. Hence, the fourth strategy is to examine differences between biological siblings and adopted siblings to assess the independent influence of family environment.

The third strategy, examining adopted-away identical twins, demonstrated a significant (though far from 100 percent) genetic component to schizophrenia. This struck a fatal blow to the many theories that previously held this illness to be entirely psychological in origin and caused by the nasty habits of selfish parents, especially mothers. No meaningfully large studies of homosexuality in adopted-away twins have yet been performed. All studies of sufficient size to date have examined twins raised in the same household, thus confounding the potential genetic factors with uncontrolled environmental ones. For identical twins are often raised more similarly than non-identical twins.

If homosexuality were 100 percent genetic, the concordance rate—the incidence of both members of a pair of monozygotic, or identical, twins being homosexual or both heterosexual—should also be 100 percent. That is, the concordance rate should reflect perfectly their genetic identity, even if the twins were adopted away from their birth families into different adoptive families. In short, in all cases of a group of monozygotic twin pairs, both twins would either be homosexual or both would be heterosexual; there would never be a discordant pair, a pair with one homosexual and one heterosexual. Such a finding would constitute evidence that, as the media continues to put it, "homosexuality is genetic."

Homosexuality and Emotional "Illness" in Twins

In 1952 a study by Franz Kallmann arrived at this finding of a 100 percent concordance rate for homosexual orientation among identical twins.[51] His study, however, was not on adopted-away twins. In every case the homosexual proband (in the language of genetics research the "proband" is the identified subject, the one being studied or "probed") had a homosexual brother; none were discordant for sexual orientation. Not surprisingly, this study is repeatedly cited as the first evidence that sexual orientation is genetic.

But the Kallmann study is seriously flawed. Kallmann's sample of homosexuals was drawn almost entirely from mentally ill and institutionalized individuals. Kallmann himself later speculated that his finding was an "artifact."[52] A similar flaw afflicted the Kinsey studies on sexuality from the same era. Alfred Charles Kinsey made generalizations to the population at large from a sample drawn largely from prisoners, including sexual offenders. Even though convicted male criminals constitute less than one percent of the U.S. population, they made up 25 percent of Kinsey's sample. Furthermore, respondents were coached to provide the "correct" answers. In 1972, Wardell Pomeroy, a psychiatrist and researcher who assisted Alfred Kinsey in his now thoroughly debunked and largely fraudulent studies on sexual behavior, admitted that "We assumed that everyone had engaged in everything, and so we began by asking when he had first done it. . . . Look [I'd say], I don't give a damn what you've done, but if you don't tell me the straight of it, it's better that we stop this history right here. Now, how old were you the first time this or that happened." While a normal respondent might have promptly told the interviewer where to get off, these were often prisoners; and if the interview were terminated they would have to go back to their cells and would not receive the free candy, soft drinks, and cigarettes offered to those who completed the interviews.[53] Pomeroy, incidentally, was one of the members of the American Psychiatric Association (APA) committee who voted in 1973 to normalize homosexuality. Yet his and Kinsey's questionable research gave rise to the false statistic that 10 percent of the population is homosexual, which homosexual activists used at the APA meeting to argue the naturalness of homosexuality.

In the aftermath of the 1973 APA decision some researchers might be tempted to dismiss the significance of this kind of sample bias in Kallman's study. After all, if homosexuality is not an illness, what difference would it make that the population studied was mentally ill?

But Kallmann's conclusions raise two major concerns. One, rather obvious, is that perhaps homosexuality *is* an illness, or at least a cluster of behaviors that are common to a variety of mental syndromes, whether genetic or psychological. (Another example of such a cluster would be violence and paranoia, which can be found in schizophrenia, or in manic depression.) Kallmann did not look for such potential correlations. Subsequent studies on non-institutionalized twins have found much lower concordance rates, between 10 and 50 percent. Some found no concordance at all, including in small samples of healthy, adopted-away twins.[54]

The second possibility is that homosexuality itself is a risk factor for mental illness. Either interpretation at least partially fits the observed data that mentally healthy twins have lower rates of concordance for homosexuality than do mentally ill ones and that homosexuals have higher rates of many different kinds of problems, mental illness among them.[55]

We do not know with any certainty whether overall rates of homosexuality are greater among mentally-ill individuals than among those who are mentally healthy. Indeed, the epidemiologic studies on baseline prevalence rates of mental illness even in the general population have serious, well-recognized flaws. These are the studies conducted to research the incidence of the disease in

society. Such rates for mental illness among the general population are at best considered rough estimates.

Likewise, the research conducted to determine the prevalence
of homosexuality has been seriously flawed, and has been the subject of both scientific and politicized debate. Recall that gay activists claim that 10 percent of the population is gay, while scientific
research points to but 2 percent. In the absence of solid epidemiologic data for baseline prevalence rates of either mental illness or
homosexuality, comparative rates are meaningless.

Higher Levels of Distress

Nonetheless, it is widely recognized and accepted, even within homosexual advocacy circles, that homosexuals do have a greater incidence of mental illness, particularly depression and suicide, than
do heterosexuals. Activists quickly explain that this connection
implies neither a necessary psychological nor a necessary biological link between homosexuality and depression. They argue, rather,
that suicidal depression is the unsurprising effect on otherwise
healthy individuals of living a closeted existence in an abusive and
hostile society.

Similar arguments have been made before. It has long been
obvious, for instance, that parental divorce is associated with both
severe distress and behavioral problems among children. But in
the 1970s the divorce industry argued that it was the social stigma
attached to divorce that caused children's distress, not divorce itself. If divorce were normalized, they claimed, the children could
walk away unscathed. Indeed, children would be helped by divorce,
for they would not suffer the trauma of being reared and cared for
by less-than-totally-personally-fulfilled parents.

Until recently, no scientific studies were available to "prove" what
has been painfully obvious to everyone, but science has finally caught
up with experience and common sense. Numerous studies now
confirm that divorce inflicts lifelong damage on children, far greater
than that caused by parental unhappiness. Even divorce experts
are beginning to withdraw their earlier claims.[56]

The same social-stigma theory is not only used to explain why so many homosexuals are unhappy, it is even used to explain why so many homosexuals remain unhappy about being homosexual, gay liberation notwithstanding. They label that unhappiness as itself a "symptom," or in the more politically correct literature as "internalized homophobia":

> membership of [*sic*] a stigmatized minority sexuality may exacerbate causes of sexual dysfunction. The effects of discordant lifestyle and identity, homosexual identity formation, dysphoria and internalized homophobia on sexual functioning are three examples of these factors of specific relevance to being homosexual in this culture. The effects of AIDS, difficulties arising from the mechanics of safer sex and the psychosexual effects of oppression on healthy sexual functioning all indicate how factors important to (but not caused by) minority sexual status may influence sexuality functioning.[57]

This self-serving explanation for homosexual unhappiness is undermined by what we now know about the terrible effects of childhood trauma on the emotional well-being of adults. Many studies reveal a sadly disproportionate rate of sexual abuse during the childhoods of homosexual men, at the very least suggesting that both homosexual unhappiness and homosexuality itself derive from common causes and that unhappiness is therefore an inherent accompaniment of homosexuality:

> From May 1989 through April 1990, 1,001 adult homosexual and bisexual men attending sexually transmitted disease clinics were interviewed regarding potentially abusive sexual contacts during childhood and adolescence. Thirty-seven percent of participants reported they had been encouraged or forced to have sexual contact before age 19 with an older or more powerful partner; 94 percent occurred with men. Median age of the participant at first contact was 10; median age difference between partners was 11 years. Fifty-one percent involved use of force; 33 percent involved anal sex. Black and Hispanic men were more likely than white men to report such sexual

contact. Using developmentally based criteria to define sexual abuse, 93 percent of participants reporting sexual contact with an older or more powerful partner were classified as sexually abused. Our data suggest the risk of sexual abuse may be high among some male youth and increased attention should be devoted to prevention as well as early identification and treatment.[58]

The same is true for pedophiles:

The association between perpetration of sexual abuse and the offender's own victimization as a child has been well documented in the literature. Various researchers have examined this relationship by assessing the exclusiveness of the sexual abuser's behavior, the gender of his victims and the gender of his own childhood abuser. . . . Subjects were 135 pedophiles. . . who admitted to their offenses. A total of 42 percent of pedophiles . . . reported being sexually victimized in their own childhoods. . . . [and] appear to choose their age specific victims in accordance with the age of their own experience of sexual victimization. Although the cause of child molestation remains undetermined these results support social learning and modeling theories.[59]

In spite of its superficial appeal and the activists' repeated claims, no studies support the hypothesis that the social disapproval of homosexuality is the prime cause of the high levels of internal distress evident in homosexual populations, even long before AIDS. (That social stigma would cause some distress is of course the small kernel of truth upon which the exaggeration is built.) Studies, like the one cited immediately above, do suggest that both the high levels of emotional distress and homosexuality itself have at least one common root in painful childhood experiences, as do other deviations from the sexual norm such as pedophilia. It makes as much sense to claim that the high levels of psychological abnormality and personal distress found among pedophiles are due solely to the social disapproval of pedophilia.

European advocates and researchers of homosexuality tend to

avoid twin-oriented research strategies, although these strategies figure prominently in European research on mental illness. It seems they want to avoid finding psychological, sociological, or biological explanations for homosexuality. They tend to believe that the more typically American desire to normalize homosexuality by finding a genetic basis for it actually lends itself to the interpretation that perhaps homosexuality is a true genetic illness. They argue rather that homosexuality is a choice. In an enlightened, liberal society, they would claim, it should be considered an acceptable, indeed unremarkable, choice. This difference in attitude probably reflects the much greater degree to which Europe, by contrast to America, has become a predominately atheistic society with relativized values.

If the search for a genetic cause were successful, these European advocates fear it might lead to a eugenics approach. If homosexuality is found to be caused by a gene, and if that gene can be identified prenatally, would many parents choose to abort such a child?

In fact, as early as 1980, authors began to be concerned about abortion as a means to prevent homosexuality.[60] More recently, Dorothy Nelkin, who co-authored a book on the moral dangers of behavioral genetics, worries that genetic testing "could be used to abort perfectly healthy people, and could be used by the military and by employers to discriminate' against people with the [homosexual] gene."[61] The nested ironies are apparent: The modern ethos generally supports the abortion of "perfectly healthy people" yearly by the hundreds of thousands. Why should aborting children because of their potential for undesirable (to their parents) sexual behavior be any more problematic than aborting them for an undesirable (to their parents) intelligence quotient, gender, or ability to locomote? Or simply because they are undesired?

Tellingly, the segment of the population most likely to abort children for any reason are precisely not those whose cultural and religious values would lead them to abhor not only homosexuality but abortion as well. Alas, the parents most likely to abort their "sexually challenged" children are rather the very ones who endorse both homosexuality and pragmatic abortion. The implication of this remarkably specific concern over abortion is striking: homosexual fetuses are persons, heterosexual fetuses are not.

Recent Studies on Twins

If homosexuality is anything less than 100 percent genetic, then the concordance rate for homosexuality will be less than 100 percent among monozygotic twins. That is, among identical twins there will be pairs in which one is heterosexual and the other is homosexual. In fact, the concordance rate across studies is considerably less than 100 percent, less than 50 percent, in fact, even though almost all studies to date have examined only twins that have not been adopted away after birth, but rather have been raised in the same family, as noted before. This means that some proportion of the only limited extent to which identical twins share sexual orientation must be due to uncontrolled environmental variables, such as the similarity of prenatal environment or upbringing, both being especially similar in the case of identical twins.

An article in the 1991 *Archives of General Psychiatry* summarized the findings of all the twin studies that had been conducted on homosexuality to that date. The authors examined the different concordance rates between pairs of differing degrees of genetic relatedness (that is, between pairs of identical twins, non-identical twins, siblings, and non-relatives). They then calculated the approximate contribution of non-genetic, environmental variables to homosexuality.

Their calculations depended on the actual incidence of homosexuality in the population at large. Yet this figure is itself the object of furious debate. Activists claim a much larger proportion than disinterested medical surveys reveal. Activists repeatedly cite the seriously flawed Kinsey studies, whose data, as mentioned above, was largely derived from prison populations. Furthermore, in the Kinsey studies forced homosexual behaviors among otherwise heterosexual men qualified them as homosexual. Indeed, even one homosexual act in a lifetime qualified one as homosexual.

Recently press accounts have focused on a study performed under the auspices of the Guttmacher Institute, which demonstrates a 1 to 3 percent incidence of homosexuality. This figure has been available for years through other research institutions as a more accurate alternative to the Kinsey figure long criticized by serious researchers. Perhaps these critiques are now being taken seriously because the Guttmacher researchers reproduced them. The Guttmacher Institute is the research arm of Planned Parenthood, an organization that has made common cause with the homosexual lobby.

But in the light of research on the genetic component of homosexuality, activists could take little solace should their claims of a larger proportion of homosexuals in the population prove true. For the results of the genetics study demonstrated that if 4 percent of the population is homosexual (a percentage long accepted as empirically valid by many non-activists; the true number based on more recent studies is likely to be less than 3 percent) then non-genetic factors account for at least 50 percent of the variability in sexual orientation; if 10 percent of the population is homosexual (the most common percentage cited by activists) then non-genetic factors account for considerably more of the variability in sexual orientation—at least 70 percent.[62]

This analysis confirmed what had already been demonstrated by 1991, well before the LeVay study on neuroanatomic research discussed above and well before the recent flurry of attention to the biology of homosexuality: Adult homosexual orientation can be neither entirely genetic nor entirely nongenetic, just as is the case with every other complex human behavior.

What have we learned since then? The three most important pieces of research that have emerged subsequently are not the brain anatomic studies that have aroused so much naive interest. They are, rather, three major twin studies carried out on male and then female homosexuals[63] and a comprehensive review article on all homosexuality research conducted to date.[64] One study was published in the *British Journal of Psychiatry* and three in the *American Archives of General Psychiatry*. Two of the twin studies were performed at Northwestern University by researchers who, as noted previously, explicitly acknowledged in their papers that they were motivated by social-policy considerations to demonstrate that homosexuality is predominantly genetic and to counter claims that it is largely environmental.[65] The review article was written by William Byne and Bruce Parsons, disinterested researchers at Columbia University.[66]

Although the press has taken the Northwestern articles as "proof" that homosexuality is genetic, the results of this research demonstrate no such thing. Indeed, the researchers themselves acknowledge with barely concealed disappointment that, even apart from methodological problems that tend to weaken their findings, taken at face value their work demonstrated a far smaller genetic contribution to both male and female homosexuality than they had sought.[67]

Bailey and Pillard's Study of Sexual Orientation

In this study the authors found a concordance rate for homosexuality of approximately 50 percent among identical twins who were raised together where one twin identified himself as homosexual. That is, 50 percent of the pairs of twins were both homosexual and half were composed of one homosexual and one heterosexual. If we recall that for something to be genetically determined, as opposed to merely influenced, the genetic heritability would need to approach 100 percent, this finding alone, if accurate, actually argues for the enormous importance of non-genetic factors influencing homosexuality. The concordance rate for non-identical (dizygotic) twins was only 22 percent. This finding is consistent with any of three hypotheses: that identical twins reared together share more significant environmental influences than non-identical twins reared together, that heritable factors influence some component of homosexuality, or that both factors have some degree of influence.

The finding of a potential genetic contribution to homosexuality is further weakened by the following considerations:

First, the extreme similarity of environment in which twins, especially identical twins, are raised confounds the authors' attribution of genetic factors alone influencing the finding that both twins are homosexual.

Second, the homosexual twin was recruited for study by responding to an advertisement in a homosexual magazine. The advertisement made it clear that the research would study the sexual orientation of twins and siblings. Numerous researchers have speculated independently about the bias thereby introduced into the sample. Respondents were likely to have been aware of the study's political implications and therefore over-reported a high concordance rate. Indeed, a common problem in these kinds of studies even when potential political biases seem absent is that concordant twins tend, in general, to respond to research advertisements more frequently than twins where one is a homosexual and the other a heterosexual.

Third, the sexual orientation of the non-respondent twin or other sibling was mostly assessed by report of the respondent. Here, too, many researchers have commented on not only the extraordinary imprecision of this approach, but of the obvious potential for bias to be introduced. This is especially true given the highly charged nature of the research and the well-informed and activist nature of the homosexual community.

Fourth is the problem of the so-called non-linear or non-additive dimension of genetic influence on a trait when many genes are similar. In the cases of twins all one hundred thousand genes, and all of the many millions of DNA base pairs are absolutely identical. This concept is discussed in somewhat greater detail below.

The results of Bailey and Pillard's corresponding study of female homosexuality, "Heritable Factors Influence Sexual Orientation in Women," are quite similar to those of their previous study. Again, the monozygotic twin pairs showed concordance rates of less than fifty percent: 48 percent, counting bisexual twins as homosexual.

Furthermore, in the only available study of monozygotic female twins raised apart the authors found that no female co-twins were homosexual.[68] The concordance rate for homosexuality was zero percent. Reared-apart pairs of twins are hard to find, and because the incidence of homosexuality is relatively low, the result was a sample size too small to be anything more than a suggestion. If the genetic contribution to female homosexuality is actually as much as 50 percent, the chances of zero concordance happening simply by chance would have been one in eight. Statistical significance in scientific studies generally, but arbitrarily, needs to be less than one in twenty.

King and McDonald's Study of Homosexual Twins

King and McDonald found concordance rates for homosexuality that were lower than those found by Bailey and Pillard: "Discordance for sexual orientation in the monozygotic pairs confirmed that genetic factors are insufficient explanation for the development of sexual orientation." And Byne and Parsons, the Columbia University researchers cited above, observe that "what is most intriguing about the studies of Bailey and Pillard and of King and McDonald is the large proportion of monozygotic twins who were discordant for homosexuality despite sharing not only their genes but also their prenatal and familial environments. The large proportion of discordant pairs underscores our ignorance of the factors that are involved, and the manner in which they interact, in the emergence of sexual orientation."[69]

Recognizing that the evidence pointed more strongly toward the importance of non-genetic than genetic factors, King and McDonald also sought to discover what such non-genetic factors might be. They unexpectedly found "a relatively high likelihood of sexual relations occurring with same-sex co-twins at some time, particularly in monozygotic pairs."[70]

This finding hints at a principle that turns out to be quite important in understanding the development of any embedded pattern of behavior, namely the role of early experience and of subsequent repetition. That monozygotic twins in particular tended to have sexual relations with each other at some time suggests that the experience of twinhood itself can, in its own right, contribute to the incidence of homosexuality, apart from the myriad of genes shared by both twins. (Yet another contribution to the apparent heritability is non-additivity of genetic influence as mentioned above.)

The implication of King and McDonald's finding can be easily missed. They observed that, controlling for any differences in the incidence of homosexuality between monozygotic twins and other sibling pairs, identical twins tended to have a higher rate of sexual relations with each other. Unless one were to propose a gene that specifically makes people preferentially have sex with people who look like themselves, this fact points to the environmental experience of twinship as a contributing influence on the concordance rate. Indeed, it suggests that identical male twins by virtue of their similarity, not by virtue of a gene or genes they carry, are more likely than non-twins to have homosexual experiences. Therefore they are more likely to be defined as homosexual or, by repetition, develop homosexual habits.

This suggestion implicates the psychoanalytic theory that identical twins are apt to experience an altered, heightened form of narcissism, that is of specialness, by virtue of there being two of them. So called "twin narcissism" is the heightened fascination each feels for another who is also, in effect, one's self. King and McDonald's discovery of increased homosexual experiences between identical twins is thus consistent with the idea of heightened twin-specific narcissism. Theodore Lidz, in his critique of the genetic analysis of the first Bailey and Pillard study, comments, "Because the twins grow up with mirror images of themselves that can magnify their so-called narcissism, they are apt to be raised more similarly than DZ [dizygotic] twins."[71] But Bailey and Pillard replied, "We hardly know what to make of the assertion that 'twins grow up with a mirror image of themselves that can magnify their so-called narcissism.'"

King and McDonald's study verifies what investigators had actually noted as long ago as 1981: the role of childhood incest in fostering later homosexuality. As in the case of the obviously related role of childhood trauma,[72] incest is currently being down-played or ignored as a significant determinant of homosexuality because it is a clear-cut environmental, not genetic, factor.

Critiques of Recent Research

Paul Billings and Jonathan Beckwith, cited regarding the LeVay study, criticize the quality of much of this recent genetics research as well. In *Technology Review*, they observe that "In the nineteenth century . . . 'phrenologists' claimed they could predict aspects of an individual's personality, such as sexuality, intelligence and criminal tendencies, merely by examining the skull's structure. . . . A look at recent studies seeking a genetic basis for homosexuality suggests that many of the problems of the past have recurred. We may be in for a new molecular phrenology, rather than true scientific progress and insight into behavior."[73]

Billings and Beckwith are specifically concerned about the biased conclusion Bailey and Pillard draw from their research, even if the concordance rates they reported were accepted as representative: "While the authors interpreted their findings as evidence for a genetic basis for homosexuality, we think that the data in fact provide strong evidence for the influence of the environment." More specifically, "on average, both non-identical twins and non-twin siblings share 50 percent of their genes. If homosexuality were a genetic trait, the pairs in these groups should be homosexual a similar percentage of the time. They certainly should [both] be homosexual [if one is] more often than adopted siblings. But Bailey and Pillard's data do not fit those predictions."[74]

In Bailey and Pillard's first twin study on male homosexuality the authors found a concordance rate for non-twin (but biologic) brothers of 9.2 percent. That is, roughly one out of ten male homosexuals had brothers who were also homosexual. All the other brothers were heterosexual. The concordance rate for non-identical twins ("dizygotic") was two-and-a-half-times greater than this (22 percent or roughly one in five). But non-identical twins have exactly the same degree of genetic similarity as non-twin brothers because, though they develop at the same time in the womb, they start out from two different eggs fertilized by two different sperm (i.e., from two zygotes, hence "dizygotic"), just as in the case of brothers who develop at different times. If we accept their data as meaningful at all—again, the very small sample size renders these findings quite weak—this finding point to the influence of similar environmental factors found especially between twins, even non-identical (dizygotic) twins.

The studies looked at three groups: identical twin brothers, non-identical twin brothers and non-twin brothers. There is a different concordance rate for homosexuality for pairs of brothers in all three categories. When we compare the first two groups—identical twins and non-identical twins (genetic similarity of 100 percent versus genetic similarity of 50 percent)—their concordance rates differ by a factor of 2.36 (52 percent to 22 percent). But when we compare the second two groups—non-identical twins versus non-twin brothers (genetic similarity of 50 percent for both)—their concordance rates still differ, but by an even larger factor of 2.39 (22 percent to 9 percent). This slight difference (2.36 versus 2.39) is too slight to be significant because of the sample sizes, but if anything tends to refute, and certainly does not support, the authors' claims.

This implies that either the finding that monozygotic twins are more likely to be concordant for homosexuality is less significant than environmental factors, or is of little significance altogether because of the sample size. The importance of environment is further suggested by the concordance rate in this study for biologic brothers with 50 percent genetic similarity, 9.2 percent, and non-biologic adoptive brothers with no significant genetic similarity, 11 percent—essentially identical. This result would be understandable if the genetic similarity found in biologic brothers and dizygotic twins has virtually no role in the concordance rate, but rather if environmental factors associated with twinship, especially with identical twinship, are crucial. This hypothesis is further supported by the fact that the concordance rates for homosexuality (as defined by the authors) do not differ statistically from the concordance rate one would find simply selecting individuals at random—that is, neither living together, nor related by birth or adoption, nor even acquainted with one another.

In their first study, Bailey and Pillard accounted for these puzzling findings on the basis of random sampling errors, a function of the small sample size. In their later study on female homosexuality, the authors were forced to acknowledge that the comparative concordance rates "for DZ co-twins and adoptive sisters did not differ significantly." This increases, even if it does not confirm, the possibility that the original data on male homosexuality represent a genuine, if incidental, finding whose significance is possibly greater than, and at odds with, the authors' hypothesis and title.[75]

This discrepancy between the authors' data and their conclusions was likewise noted by Byne and Parsons: "The increased concordance for homosexuality among the identical twins could be entirely accounted for by the increased similarity of their developmental experiences. In our opinion, the major finding of that study is that 48 percent of identical [female] twins who were reared together [and where at least one was homosexual] were discordant for sexual orientation."[76]

Similarly, Charles Mann, author of the lead article on genes and behavior in a special issue of *Science*, points to

> the growing understanding that the interaction of genes and environment is much more complicated than the simple "violence genes" and "intelligence genes" touted in the popular press. Indeed, renewed appreciation of environmental factors is one of the chief effects of the increased belief in genetics' effects on behavior. "Research into heritability is the best demonstration I know of the importance of the environment," says Robert Plomin, director of the Center for Developmental and Health Genetics at Pennsylvania State University. The same data that show the effects of genes also point to the enormous influence of non-genetic factors.[77]

There is yet another confounding factor in the twin study data, neither precisely genetic nor environmental, that none of these researchers have considered, the non-additivity of genetic influences caused by internal interaction of many genes. The presence of this factor is strongly suggested by the clear difference between concordance rates for homosexuality among identical twins and for non-identical twins, non-twin brothers (or sisters), and non-relatives. A high degree of genetic similarity can mimic (or exaggerate) a greater degree heritability of the trait. In other words, the influence of genes may not simply be additive, but after a certain threshold of shared genes has been crossed, may multiply the degree of apparent similarity. It is as though under these conditions 2+2, instead of making four, makes 10. In the words of one behavioral researcher,

> the standard assumption of behavioral genetics is that traits run in families and that pairs of relatives are similar *in proportion* to their genetic resemblance. Yet there is evidence of traits for which the monozygotic correlation is high, indicating a genetic basis, when the dizygotic correlation *and other first degree relatives are insignificant.* [Note that this is precisely the case in those studies where the first-degree relative concordance rates do not differ significantly from the random population rates.] When monozygotic twins are substantially more than twice as similar as dizygotic twins and other first degree relatives, a non-additive or configural determination is suggested [emphases and comment added].[78]

In the Bailey and Pillard studies of male twins, the concordance rate for monozygotic twins was 2.36 times that for dizygotic twins and 5.65 times that for monozygotic twins. These findings strongly suggest "configural determination" as part of the apparent heritability of homosexuality. The true degree of heritability would therefore be considerably less than that suggested by the nearly 50 percent concordance rate.

The reaction to Byne and Parson's criticisms provide an all-too-typical illustration of the politicization and propagandizing that surrounds and distorts this field of study. John Horgan, a senior writer for *Scientific American*, notes that two reviewers of the Byne and Parson article accused Byne of having a "right-wing agenda."

In fact, Byne has refused to address conservative groups who support the ban on homosexuals in the military because he himself is opposed to such a ban, supports "gay rights," believes that "homosexuality, whatever its cause, is not a 'choice',"[79] and at the time was preparing a major article for the activist publication *Journal of Homosexuality*.[80] But his refusal to speak to conservative groups was not sufficient for the gay activists. As Byne told the *Wall Street Journal*, "I'm told my criticism is not politically correct. . . . What they're saying therefore is that I should subjugate scientific rigor to political expediency."[81] Byne was a resident in psychiatry at Columbia at the time his paper was published.

Byne, as paraphrased by Horgan, quite correctly notes that "genetic models of behavior are just as likely to foment bigotry as to quell it." But neither Byne nor his critics seem to recognize that models depicting behavior as unchangeable, whether genetic or not, are also "as likely to foment bigotry as quell it." After all, that blacks cannot just voluntarily convert to being white has hardly eliminated racial prejudice.

Theodore Lidz, a prominent psychiatric researcher at Yale University, whose criticism of the first Bailey and Pillard study was mentioned earlier, is a long-time critic of methodological weaknesses in the various adoption studies of schizophrenia. He makes all of the above, and further, criticisms of homosexuality research. Emphasizing what we have learned about the disappointingly limited contribution of genetics to schizophrenia, Lidz observes that "there may be a genetic component to homosexuality; it is the current fashion to find a major genetic component in all behavioral conditions. I simply wish to emphasize that there is still need for more, and clearly better, studies."[82]

The difficulties presented by adoption studies can be noted in the studies of Rosenthal, Kety, and Wender,[83] carried out at great expense, all of which, despite the authors' claims, failed to show any clear-cut evidence of a notable genetic factor. These authors' erroneous claims misguided schizophrenia research for many years and still do. Tienari[84] appreciated the considerable difficulty of carrying out a properly controlled adoption study, and took stringent measures to compare the environmental milieu of the adopting in- dex and control families. It is noteworthy that the adopted-away offspring of schizophrenic biologic mothers only became schizo- phrenic when raised in seriously disturbed adoptive families.[85]

Note that the schizophrenia studies Lidz criticizes were con- siderably more numerous, detailed, and rigorous than any of the twin studies on homosexuality. These early schizophrenia studies tried to control for non-genetic familial factors that could dispro- portionately influence twins, especially identical twins. They did this by looking not at twins raised in the same family, as in the Bailey and Pillard studies, but rather at twins adopted away at birth. Yet even under these conditions, puzzling environmental factors weakened the data. By the time these factors were adequately con- trolled for, the actual genetic influence shrank to practical insignificance.[86]

The major value of identifying genes that are linked to schizo- phrenia[87] would be the possibility of informing families at risk and taking measures to prevent the conditions that would lead to the emergence of the trait. The presence of the gene, while increasing the risk, does not "cause" a person to become schizophrenic. A certain genetic background may be necessary for schizophrenia but is far from sufficient as a cause.

Note an important distinction, however. The fact that the ge- netic contribution to schizophrenia is weak does not mean that schizophrenia is psychological. It remains unequivocally a prima- rily biological condition, involving massive (not, as in the case of homosexuality, subtle and microscopic) peculiarities in brain struc- ture, function, and early development. The latest integrated hy- pothesis concerning schizophrenia unifies what has been learned from family, behavioral, psychological, and biological research. It speculates that schizophrenia consists of a prolonged, generalized neurodevelopmental abnormality, possibly caused by some environ- mental agent such as a virus that affects individuals who are ge- netically susceptible to its effects. Schizophrenia emerges in its most serious forms in the wake of prolonged psychological or other stress.[88]

Bailey and Pillard responded to the Lidz critique in a particularly interesting way, demonstrating both the weaknesses of the current genetics research on homosexuality and the fierce determination of partisan researchers to fit their results to a predetermined conclusion. After receiving Lidz's critique, they reanalyzed their data along lines not considered in their publications. They found that the non-twin brothers of a pair of twins who were both homosexual were themselves more frequently homosexual (that is, all three brothers were homosexual) than were the non-twin brothers of a pair of twins only one of whom was homosexual. They concluded that the genetic loading for homosexuality must be greater when both twins are homosexual than when only one is, and they lay down the gauntlet: "We close with an empirical challenge . . . Can this result be explained convincingly . . . by any alternative to genetic transmission?"[89]

The answer is yes. If an environmental (familial) factor makes it more likely for the identical co-twin to be homosexual (for instance, the greater likelihood of incest between the identical twins) this same factor may very well also make it more likely that a non-twin brother will be homosexual as well. Indeed, even the simple fact that both twins are homosexual might make it more likely that other, at least younger, siblings will be as well. This could be for the same reasons as noted above by King and McDonald, knowledge about the twins' sexual behavior and homosexual activity among the siblings.[90]

III

If homosexuality is not entirely genetic in origin, where does it come from? In exploring claims that homosexuality is genetic, Byne and Parsons emphasize an extremely important point. In their own model, which they describe as "a complex mosaic of biologic, psychological and social/cultural factors," "genetic factors can be conceptualized as indirectly influencing the development of sexual orientation without supposing that they either directly influence or determine sexual orientation per se. Similarly, one could imagine that prenatal hormones influence particular personality dimensions or temperamental traits, which in turn influence the emergence of sexual orientation."[91]

This last point concerning personality dimensions and traits is not an obvious one, and popular accounts of the biology of homosexuality uniformly avoid it. But the fact is that the genetic contribution to a given trait, behavioral or otherwise, need not be direct; when the trait is behavioral, the genetic contribution is usually not direct. Genes often contribute to some other phenomenon that in turn predisposes an individual to a given behavioral response.

An obvious illustration is the aptitude for basketball, mentioned earlier. No genes exist that code for becoming a basketball player. But some genes code for height and the elements of athleticism, such as quick reflexes, appropriate bone structure, height-to-weight ratio, muscle strength and refresh rate, metabolism and energy efficiency, and so on. Politically incorrect as it may seem, many such traits have obvious racial distributions, including that more men of Bantu and Nordic stock (being taller) will be found on professional basketball teams than men of Pygmy and Appenzeller Swiss stock (being shorter).

Someone born with a favorable (for basketball) combination of height and athleticism is in no way genetically programmed or forced to become a basketball player. These qualities, however, certainly facilitate that choice. As a consequence, the choice to play basketball has a clear genetic component, most evident in the very high heritability of height. (Height is also influenced by diet, mostly negatively in the sense that the maximum height is preprogrammed. Actual height, however, requires the cooperation of upbringing to be reached.) Nevertheless, the strong genetic predisposition to basketball playing does not mean that people do not choose, entirely, to play basketball.

This point was reinforced by the editors of *Science*, who devoted a recent issue almost exclusively to "Genetics and Behavior." In the opening editorial, Torsten Wiesel, president of Rockefeller

University, one of the leading international centers for genetics research, commented that

> The recent identifications of the mutations underlying Huntington's disease demonstrates that neurological disorders can also be caused by a single aberrant gene. But many other neurological diseases, such as schizophrenia and manic-depression, are likely to have polygenic roots whose interaction with environmental factors will be highly complex.
>
> It has long been known that schizophrenia clusters in families and identical twin studies have supported the belief that the susceptibility to schizophrenia has a genetic component. Yet it is also important to recognize that the genes which predispose one toward schizophrenia may not be expressed except under special environmental circumstances; for instance conditions of great stress. Indeed, understanding of how gene expression in brain cells is regulated by environmental experiences may serve as the foundation for the design of drugs or for preventive measures for better controlling gene expression patterns.
>
> The operations of the brain result from a balance between inputs from heredity and environment, nature and nurture, and this balance should also be reflected in research into the biological basis of behavior.[92]

Genetics and Behavioral Problems: Alcoholism

In the area of behavioral *problems*, the classic example of a similar phenomenon is alcoholism. It has long been thought that problem drinking has a genetic component.[93] Even after social and family influences have been taken into account, evidence remains that when a gene or set of genes are present in an individual or family there is a much higher risk for serious alcoholism. Furthermore, certain national and transnational gene pools (Irish, Scandinavian, northern European in general) seem to be predisposed to alcoholism.

Researchers have long presumed that a specific gene might code directly for alcoholism itself. Nonetheless, it always seemed strange that such an obviously counterproductive gene would exist. The

same puzzle, of course, lurks behind the proposition that homosexuality is directly genetic.

For a while it seemed that the gene in question might be somewhat like the one that makes alcohol so problematic for Native
Americans. In this particular racial pool the gene that directs the
synthesis of the enzyme responsible for breaking down alcohol commonly codes for a different form of the enzyme than is found among
Caucasians. The American Indian variant breaks down alcohol only
very slowly, and because alcohol therefore rapidly accumulates, serious intoxication can be caused by relatively small amounts of alcohol. But this theory proved to be a false lead. Irish and Nordics
metabolize alcohol rapidly and well; those who drink heavily metabolize it even more rapidly.[94]

It turns out that the genetic makeup of Northern Europeans
generally tends to code for an enhanced fight-flight response to a
given stressor. Their nervous systems are more "high strung," and
they react with relatively intense sympathetic nervous system arousal
to a perceived threat, experienced subjectively as anxiety.[95] Alcohol is the original anti-anxiety agent. It produces a response in the
brain almost identical to that of Valium or Xanax.[96] People with
this predisposition to intense anxiety responses are more likely to
find their way into greater alcohol use[97] because for them alcohol
gives a greater degree of emotional relief than it does to the more
laid-back "Mediterranean" type.[98]

Why do Northerners have this disposition in greater proportion than Southerners? The answer lies in the observation that the
most critical distinction for this aspect of human biology is not so
much "North" versus "South," or even "warm" versus "cold," as "Po-
lar" versus "Equatorial." Because 75 percent of the earth's land mass
is found in the Northern hemisphere, this translates into a distri-
bution of the various people-types corresponding mostly to the
comparison North versus South, rather than the reverse, as in the
Southern hemisphere.

At issue is not the location per se but the differing cycles of
light found close to and far from the equator. The harsher climate
and intermittently reduced intensity of light found nearer the poles

is not only associated with differences in body build and skin color but also with differences in the nervous system. This fact is less surprising than it might seem because both skin and the nervous system derive from the same precursor tissue in the developing fetus. In brief, the Northern races have adapted to the harshness of their environment by generally developing the more easily stimulated nervous systems of, say, hunter-warriors than have the equatorial races. In its pure form, this genetic type not only reacts subjectively, but also responds to stressors with intense physiologic responses such as increased heart rate and blood pressure, skin flushing, perspiring palms and soles, and so on. All these responses, subjective and physiologic, are mediated by the nervous system. Alcohol thus calms all of these by calming the underlying nerves.[99]

Thus genetics strongly predisposes individuals toward alcoholism. And yet no genes specifically code for it. This seeming contradiction can be explained by the fact that some genes do code for the anxiety (fight-flight) response and under certain circumstances an especially intense response is adaptive. Those who carry such genes may be more likely to develop alcoholism than those who do not carry them. This does not mean, however, that alcoholism is itself directly genetic, natural, a good thing, or that it is an illness in the strict sense of the word.

Of interest in comparing alcoholism to homosexuality is the fact that alcoholism is estimated to be between 50 and 60 percent heritable; homosexuality is estimated to be less than 50 percent heritable, probably considerably less. The greater risk for alcoholism nevertheless does not lead to the conclusion that alcoholics are not responsible for controlling, changing, or stopping their behavior. We should also note that early enthusiasm over alcoholism being linked to a gene that coded for the D_2 brain (dopamine) receptor proved to be as unfounded as all the other claims for behavioral genes.[100]

As we will see, this association between a directly inherited trait (intensity of flight-fight response, level of anxiety) and a genetically unrelated behavioral pattern (alcoholism) not only provides an analogy for the possible meaning of the limited contribution of genetics to homosexuality, it may also point to at least one actual explanation for at least some instances of it. For some evidence is emerging that unusually intense anxiety responses are also associated with an increased tendency toward homosexuality. We will explore this possibility in greater detail. For now, let us return to the recent research finding that homosexuality is mostly non-genetic.

NONGENETIC INFLUENCES ON HOMOSEXUALITY

The nongenetic factors that can influence the development of a behavioral pattern fall into five categories:

1. Intrauterine (prenatal) effects, such as hormonal milieu;

2. Extrauterine (postnatal) physical effects, such as trauma and viruses;

3. Extrauterine "symbolic" effects, such as familial interactions and education;

4. Extrauterine experience, such as the reinforcing effect of the repetition of behavior; and

5. Choice.

The lack of 100 percent similarity for sexual orientation of identical twins shows that the nongenetic factor or factors influencing homosexuality cannot be exclusively intrauterine. If they were, then the concordance rate for homosexuality would still be nearly 100 percent, because identical twins share the identical (or nearly identical) prenatal environment. In fact, if there are any intrauterine effects, they would contribute to the 30 to 50 percent apparently genetic effect that was described earlier.[101] Of course, once these factors were identified and segregated out, the actual remaining genetic effect would be that much smaller.

The debate over the role of non-genetic intrauterine influences on sexual orientation has had an interesting effect on feminists, who have long been sympathetic to homosexual activism. The argument that genetics can largely predetermine complex behavioral patterns, with the attending emotional, cognitive, and value orientations, cuts directly across some feminists' claims. They declare that all behavioral expression is fundamentally free for the choosing except as social pressures forcibly and illegitimately distort one's freedom. They see any statistical evidence of behavioral differences between the genders as rooted in political discrimination, not biological differences.

Masculine and Feminine Influences

Nevertheless, a vast body of research has emerged over the past decade that demonstrates how biological factors powerfully influence brain development. These factors affect cognitive, emotional, and behavioral expression. Even small differences between individuals will result in statistically significant average differences between two large populations. Perhaps unexpectedly, the most powerful effects on male versus female brain development do not occur directly from male versus female genetic differences, but indirectly by way of the maternal intrauterine hormonal milieu (environment).

Put simply, the hormonal environment in which a baby develops is a balance of androgenic (male) and estrogenic (female) hormones. A genetically male baby signals the mother to generate a more heavily androgenic environment than does a female baby. The particular hormonal balance then determines whether the baby will develop typically male or typically female genitalia, bodily characteristics, and brain structures.

Because the maternal hormonal response varies, the masculinizing or feminizing influences are different for each developing baby. The resulting degree of masculinity or femininity is therefore a "bimodal" spectrum, having two somewhat overlapping bell-shaped curves with two separate average masculine and average feminine peaks. The curve does not show a strict dimorphism, that is, two perfectly distinctly masculine or feminine spikes. This variable degree of masculine and feminine influences and results is especially so with respect to the brain. The secondary sexual characteristics (genitalia), however, take only two distinct forms, except in unusual circumstances.

Hence, in spite of the obvious general differences between men and women, a great many men have somewhat feminine physical features and a great many women have somewhat masculine features, all well within normal. Many women are actually more masculine in their behavior than many men and many men are actually more feminine than many women; yet all these, too, are well within normal. Furthermore, some women are more masculine than the average man and some men are more feminine than the average women, and these are also entirely normal. And yet it remains true that on average (which is to say, as a group), women are more feminine than men and men are more masculine than women. These differences should therefore show up in the average differences in behavior between the two groups.

To a less obvious but significant degree, these bimodal statistical differences (clustering about two somewhat separated points) extend to brain development as well. Thus the cognitive, emotional, and behavioral expressions of male and female classes as a whole are affected to various degrees by masculine and feminine influences. Again, there is much overlap, and many normal men have rather more feminine behavioral characteristics, while many normal women have rather masculine behavioral characteristics.

From time to time, for reasons that we are only just beginning to be understand, the chemical signals get crossed. The maternal hormonal milieu of, for example, a genetically male baby will then be very far to the feminine end of the spectrum. In these unfortunate cases, her genitalia, body type, brain, and behavior will develop physically as a normal-appearing female. She remains, however, genetically male and therefore infertile. We conventionally refer to such individuals according to their body type, not their genetic makeup since they will live according to the former.

In other cases, the milieu is ambiguous. Regardless of the baby's genetic structure, the baby will emerge a hermaphrodite, with variable proportions of male and female features. The parents will be obliged to choose a gender for their child to be defined surgically, which may or may not correspond to the genetic background.[102]

The Hormonal Influence on Homosexuality

Clearly an important determinant of behavioral predispositions is the hormonal environment. We know, however, that there is some genetic effect. If there were none, the concordance rate for homosexuality would probably be the same for both monozygotic and dizygotic twins, and it is not. Thus some proportion of what appears to be genetic in homosexual behavior may actually be a nongenetic intrauterine effect on the parts of the brain that influence sexual behavior. Homosexuality is not terribly rare in the population, being somewhere between 1 and 4 percent. The lower reproductive rates among homosexuals should lead to its eventual elimination from the population, unless some relatively constant non-genetic factor or factors continued to influence its reappearance.

But if homosexuality were simply caused by a greater than average, but still normal, degree of opposing-sex influence of the prenatal environment, we would expect male homosexuals, for example, to have "female" brain structures. Many of the studies to date on the biology of homosexuality have looked for such a feminization of homosexuals' brains, but nothing convincing has been found. Indeed, LeVay and other researchers point out that a certain nucleus, the "Sexually Dimorphic Nucleus" (SDN), in the brain, takes two distinct forms in men and women. This nucleus, however, is found in its typically masculine form in male homosexuals.

Nonetheless, two different sets of findings point to possible developmentally based hormonal influences on homosexuality.

First, there is some evidence that male homosexuals perform more as average females than average males on certain qualitative measures of mental functioning. This difference in performance may eventually be correlated to typical male-female brain differences. And yet it would still say nothing about the cause, as changes in the brain could be caused by repetitively reinforced behavioral differences between homosexuals and heterosexuals.

Second, studies on women have indicated a correlation between a "masculinizing" intrauterine environment and subsequent female bisexuality, homosexuality, or transsexualism. Transsexuals are individuals whose internal self-image is opposite to their biological gender. A male transsexual feels himself to be truly female, a "woman trapped in a man's body"; a female transsexual to be a "man trapped in a woman's body." Transsexuals often seek and obtain surgical alteration of their gender. Because the subjective experience and objective marks of transsexualism are so different than of homosexuality (such as male homosexuals never considering themselves other than men and female homosexuals never considering themselves other than women), studies that posit a common origin for both homosexuality and transsexualism raise more questions than they answer.

In 1991 G. Dorner, one of the major researchers of the prenatal hormonal influences on sexuality, published a review of the studies on the subject. He concluded that a prenatal deficiency of male hormones, caused by undue stress to the mother, will cause homosexual behavior:

> Sexual brain organization is dependent on sex hormone and neurotransmitter levels occurring during critical developmental periods. The higher the androgen levels during brain organization, caused by genetic and/or environmental factors, the higher is the biological predisposition to bi- and homosexuality or even transsexualism in females and the lower it is in males. Adrenal androgen excess, leading to heterotypical sexual orientation and/or gender role behavior in genetic females, can be caused by 21-hydroxylase deficiency, especially when associated with prenatal stress. . . . Testicular androgen deficiency in prenatal life, giving rise to heterotypical sexual orientation and/or gender role behavior in genetic males, may be induced by prenatal stress and/or maternal or fetal genetic alterations.[103]

Although his conclusions have been disputed, the facts of his research have not.[104] Even so, Dorner's findings have caused consternation on both sides of the current debate over homosexuality. On the one hand, if individuals are predisposed to homosexuality by intrauterine influences, even if these are not genetic, this could explain why homosexuals seem so resistant to change. Maybe, therefore, homosexuals should not be expected to change. On the other hand, if this predisposition is caused by a deficiency or trauma, perhaps homosexuality should once again be classified as a disease and a treatment developed.[105]

Other Prenatal Influences

At Harvard in 1974 the great behavioral neurologist Norman Geschwind and his colleague Ronald Galaburda first proposed the idea that homosexuality might be an intrauterine developmental abnormality, though not necessarily hormonal in nature. They had already hypothesized, and others have since confirmed, that at least one cause of left-handedness is an abnormal autoimmune effect during pregnancy: For reasons unknown, the baby's or mother's immune system responds to certain tissues in the developing brain as though they were foreign. They are attacked and destroyed. But Geschwind and Galaburda also noted, along with many other observers, that left-handedness appeared to be more common among male homosexuals than among heterosexuals. They therefore hypothesized that the same autoimmune problem might be responsible for both.[106]

In 1991 one research group concluded that although left-handedness seemed associated with autoimmune abnormalities, male homosexuality was not. Their conclusion rested on their failure to find an increased incidence of left-handedness in the population of homosexuals they studied.[107] Nevertheless, other researchers have confirmed this increased incidence in both men and women, and the possibility that homosexual disposition may at least partly be the consequence of a developmental autoimmune abnormality remains open.[108]

Another theory of intrauterine effect is the so-called maternal stress hypothesis referred to above. This theory holds that abnormal levels of stress for the pregnant mother during critical periods in fetal development alter the hormonal milieu and thereby increase the incidence of homosexuality. Although changes in the hormonal milieu have been discovered during periods of stress, they are not very great. Furthermore, direct studies on the incidence of homosexuality correlated to measures of maternal stress have not demonstrated such an effect.

One such study did confirm, however, as have the twin studies, that a strong familial link somewhat increases the likelihood that extrauterine factors common to a given family play a significant role in determining homosexual behavior. In this study 21 percent of the non-twin brothers of homosexual males were also homosexual whereas only 4 percent of the non-twin brothers of heterosexual males were homosexual.[109]

THE POSSIBLE INFLUENCE OF OVERCROWDING

The very theory that homosexuality is directly genetic contains an implicit conundrum, as a directly genetic origin would likely be associated with an early onset of "homosexual identity." We have touched on this briefly already. This conundrum arises from the observation that homosexuality is associated with far lower childbearing rates than is heterosexuality. At present, and for the past thirty years, the childbearing rate for the United States as a whole has hovered around the replacement rate of 1.05 children per adult.

This average rate, however, is a composite of the rate for heterosexuals and homosexuals. The homosexual rate is therefore considerably lower than the replacement rate. To whatever extent that homosexuality was significantly and directly genetic its presence in the population would shrink from one generation to the next. Unless it was continuously "redeveloped" by some non-heritable cause or causes, intrauterine or otherwise, it would eventually disappear: "[O]ne would expect that the role of a major gene in male homosexual orientation to be limited because of the strong selective pressures against such a gene. It is unlikely that a major gene underlying such a common trait could persist over time without an extraordinary counterbalancing mechanism."[110]

The fact that at least in recent decades the apparent incidence of homosexuality appears relatively stable, a point the activists emphasize, is thus itself an argument against its being directly genetically determined. Of course, this argument would not hold if were discovered that, for example, a relatively small dose of hypothetical homosexual genes, but not enough to produce overt homosexuality, was associated with some other trait that enhanced survival and reproduction.

Jung, however, had a different and rather interesting take on this observation about the stability of homosexuality. He contended that homosexuality was an ever present possibility in human nature that tended to manifest itself under conditions of extreme social crowding. From this perspective, homosexuality indeed serves a purpose. Namely, it reduces the rate of reproduction in a population that is reaching the limit of its supporting environment. (Jung's theory does not support the widespread, but scientifically unsubstantiated, belief that the earth as a whole or even the United States is reaching some kind of population limit. Rather his theory speculates about what might occur locally, such as on a city-wide basis.)

Jung had no direct evidence for his hypothesis. Subsequently, however, evidence has arisen that, although it does not directly address the question of homosexuality, does present some intriguing general support for his idea. Research has demonstrated that a measurable change occurs in the neuroendocrine system of females in an overcrowded population. These changes cause a lower average rate of fertility (because of relatively high rates of absolute infertility) and have been found in both experimental colonies of research animals and in human beings in crowded cities.[111] There is no reason to think that such effects are restricted to females. Conceivably a similar hormonal change might influence the incidence of homosexuality.

All of these effects, tendency to anxiety, response to stress, likelihood of alcoholism, hormonal dispositions in the mother, hormonal signals from the fetus to the mother, endocrine and stress changes in response to overcrowding, and many others besides, will have some degree of genetic background. It is not clear in any of these cases how much effect might be directly genetic and how much is indirect. Nor is it clear how many intervening levels of interaction are present between gene and behavior. Once again we need to remind ourselves that the discovery of a correlation between a gene or genes and a behavior is without significance: "It is clear that our current genetic and psychological theories are untenable. The co-twins of men and women who identify themselves as homosexual appear to have a potential for a range of sexual expression . . . more detailed exploration of the sexual relationships between twins and their later development may cast more light on the origins of sexuality than a narrow search for genetic factors."[112]

IV

The discussion in the preceding sections should help us put the most publicly trumpeted scientific research on genetics and homosexuality into its proper, limited perspective. On July 15, 1993, National Public Radio presented a lengthy piece on a new study by Dean Hamer in *Science* due to be released the next day.[113] The tenor of the report was to celebrate the so-called discovery of the gene that causes homosexuality. Near the end, the necessary caveats were quickly and quietly added, but most laypeople would have turned off the radio thinking that the question had been settled, and that homosexuality was caused by a gene. In the air was also the heated debate in Colorado over "Proposition 2," a popular measure intended by its supporters to prevent homosexuals from obtaining special rights and protections afforded minorities, vilified by its opponents as a means of fostering homophobia and institutionalized discrimination against gays.

In response to this research, the *Wall Street Journal* likewise headlined their report the next day, "Research Points Toward a Gay Gene."[114] A subheading of the *Journal* article stated, "Normal Variation," leaving the casual reader with the impression that the research somehow led to this conclusion. It did not, nor could it have. Indeed, it alludes to the researchers' own personal opinions that homosexuality "is a normal variant of human behavior." Even the

New York Times, in its more accurately titled front-page article, "Report Suggests Homosexuality is Linked to Genes" noted that researchers warned against "taking [the research] to mean anything as simplistic as that the 'gay gene' had been found."

At end of the *Wall Street Journal* article, at the bottom of the last paragraph on the last page, tucked away in the second section of the paper, a prominent geneticist observed that "the gene . . . may be involved in something other than sexual behavior. For example, it may be that the supposed gene is only 'associated' with homosexuality, rather than a 'cause' of it." This rather cryptic comment would be difficult to understand without the needed background information. Yet his comment is actually the most critical distinction in the entire article.

In the instance of this study that the media was trumpeting, the authors had performed a combined set of investigations that together form a paradigm for a new kind of behavioral genetics study now becoming widespread. This is the so-called "linkage study," in which researchers identify a behavioral trait that runs in a family and is correlated to a chromosomal variant found in the genetic material of that family.

BASIC TERMS AND PRINCIPLES IN GENETICS

In order to understand the significance, and limitations, of genetic linkage studies, we must understand certain basic principles in genetics. The first is genes. We can think of each human gene as a book that provides a complex set of instructions for the synthesis of a single protein. These proteins are then responsible for the synthesis and operation of everything else in the body.

Chromosomes

The entire collection of genes that codes for a human being (the "human genome") is vast and divided into twenty-three pairs of matched, physically distinct structures called chromosomes. We can think of them as matching libraries that contain and catalogue two copies of every required "book" (gene) in a specific order that does not vary from person to person. Chromosome libraries exist in pairs because each person actually has two instructional genes for every protein, receiving one of every gene from the mother and another from the father. The unvarying order in which the genes are catalogued allows each one of the millions and millions of genes to be matched to its proper companion during reproduction. Half the entire collection from the mother (one copy of every gene) combines with half the entire collection from the father (also one copy of every gene) to create a new, likewise doubled, set of libraries for the child.

Dominant and Recessive Genes

For some proteins only one "book" determines the trait and the other is ignored, such as with eye color. For other traits, especially the more complex ones, but sometimes simpler ones too, both genes will be used, such as with height. In the case of height, half of all the proteins responsible for the trait will follow the mother's gene's instructions and half will follow the father's. This "mosaic" of protein types will produce a child of intermediate height when all other factors are equal.

How does the body know which of the two genes to use when only one is required? The traits that will use but one gene are coded for by genes called "alleles" that come in two forms, dominant and recessive. The trait only has two forms, one associated with the dominant form of the gene and the other associated with its recessive form. Recessive genes may be passed on from generation to generation, even if they are not expressed, that is, made manifest. Dominant genes will always be expressed.

The gene for the trait "eye color" is one such gene. There are a few more complex exceptions, but in general this trait comes in two forms, brown, which is dominant, and blue, which is recessive. If people inherit either one brown gene and one blue gene, or two brown genes, their eyes will be brown. Because it is a trait linked to a recessive gene, blue eye color will only appear in those people with two blue genes, one from each parent. They may receive these blue genes, however, even if both their parents have brown eyes. In that case, both parents would have one blue and one brown gene each.

Sex-Linked Genes

One of these twenty-three library pairs, however, the so-called "sex chromosome," is unique. The library that constitutes the twenty-third chromosome comes in two forms, X and Y. In a normal female, the sex-chromosome pair consists of two Xs, usually written "XX." In a normal male, the sex-chromosome pair consists of one X and one Y, written "XY." Certain chromosomal abnormalities exist in which these may be duplicated. This gives rise, for example, to the "super male", XYY or even XYYY, long thought to be associated with abnormally high levels of aggression.

Some genetic traits and genetic illnesses are "sex-linked." The genes for these are traits are located on the X or Y chromosome. This does not mean that the traits themselves have anything to do with sexuality per se. Sex-linked traits show a specific pattern of inheritance different from traits carried on the other "autosomal" chromosomes because their manifestation depends not only on whether the trait is dominant or recessive, but also on the sex of the individual. For example, a trait carried on the Y chromosome appears only in males, for the obvious reason that only males have Y chromosomes. But the genes for many traits are carried on the X chromosome and yet are manifest only in males, even though females have two Xs.

An example of this is hemophilia. A specific gene is responsible for producing a certain protein critically necessary for the clotting of blood. When this protein is defective or absent even small bruises will not cease hemorrhaging. Because this gene is recessive, if the woman has it on one of the two X chromosomes, the trait will not be expressed. Her other X chromosome, carrying the normal variant, will produce the necessary protein.

The woman's daughters will receive one X chromosome from

her and one x chromosome from her father. On average, 50 percent of her daughters will therefore carry one defective gene. None of them, however, will suffer from hemophilia because they will receive a normal x chromosome from their father. But on average 50 percent of the woman's sons will also receive the defective x chromosome from her. Because the sons receive a y chromosome from their fathers, they receive the x chromosome only from their mother. If it is defective, they will display the recessive trait and will be "bleeders."

Frequency of Genetic Traits

The frequency of traits that do not affect the likelihood of successful reproduction, such as eye color, tends to remain quite stable, whether dominant or recessive. Those traits that carry with them reproductive advantages tend to increase over time. When recessive, this increase is likely to be slower because the trait only appears in the less common cases when a carrier has two genes for it instead of just one.

In contrast, traits that adversely affect reproduction tend to be quite rare. Hemophilia itself is such an example, affecting about one in every ten thousand individuals. Hemophilia adversely affects reproduction not because the gene affects reproductive ability directly, but because of the unfortunately greater likelihood of early death. Disadvantageous traits therefore tend to diminish in frequency over time. Recessive disadvantageous traits, however, will tend to diminish more slowly because they can be carried by individuals not affected by it, as in the case of women with one hemophilia gene.[115]

We might wonder why hemophilia has not disappeared entirely. One answer could be that the genetic mutation that causes the disease reappears spontaneously at a sufficient rate to maintain its low presence in the population. Another could be that the gene confers some other unidentified survival advantage along with its obvious disadvantage. Another could be that parents of hemophiliac children have more children to compensate for the higher rates of mortality. This would increase the number of female children, perhaps enough to maintain carriers in the population.

The same thing is true with respect to sex-linked genes. If the gene in question is on the x chromosome and is adverse and dominant, it tends to die out rapidly over time because it is expressed in both men and women. If the gene is adverse and recessive, it will die out more slowly because only the sons will demonstrate a lower reproductive rate.[116]

THE MEANING OF A "LINKAGE" TO HOMOSEXUALITY

Returning to the genetic linkage study of homosexuality, the authors of the Hamer study discovered that the maternal uncles of homosexual men, but no other relatives, were disproportionately homosexual. This finding seems to suggest that if a heritable factor contributes to male homosexuality, the x chromosome would carry it.

Mothers of male homosexuals would carry the gene on one of their x chromosomes but it would not be expressed in these mothers themselves. The lack of expression would either be caused by their having a second, normal x chromosome or because the specific trait in question would not express itself in females even if they carried two of its genes. Remember that male homosexuality and female homosexuality are not likely to be the same phenomenon.

The uncles of the homosexual men (their mothers' brothers) would also be more likely to carry and express the gene because, like their sisters, they could have received an affected x chromosome from their mothers.

After finding a family sample in which the appearance of homosexuality seemed to follow a pattern of mother-son inheritance, the authors then examined the x chromosomes of the family members. The normal, multibanded appearance of the x chromosome is well-known. What they looked for was some variation in its typical banding pattern specific to this family, and especially to its homosexual males and their mothers. Such a variation was indeed found. The chromosome consists of some one hundred genes; the variation was found on the region known as q28 (xq28, since it is the x chromosome).

To make the case that a gene or genes even influence male homosexual behavior several conditions must be met. The study must have been conducted with adequate care and its statistical assumptions must be valid. The variation in the chromosome must be present in most male homosexuals, not just in those male homosexuals whose families demonstrate a maternal-uncle pattern of male homosexuality. Or it must be present at least in other families that demonstrate such a pattern. And the inheritance pattern itself must hold when a larger family sample is examined.[117] Even if all these conditions were met, however, such studies would still not even remotely constitute evidence for the claim that "homosexuality is genetic," for all the reasons discussed previously.

As it is, the Hamer study is seriously flawed. Four months after its publication in *Science*, a critical commentary appeared in the same publication that, though it did not dispute his research methods and raw data, which met the standards for linkage studies, did take issue with the many assumptions and questionable use of statistics that underlie Hamer's conclusions. Genetics researchers from Yale, Columbia, and Louisiana State Universities noted that

> much of the discussion of the finding [by Hamer et al.] has focused on its social and political ramifications. In contrast our goal is to discuss the scientific evidence and to highlight inconsistencies that suggest that this finding should be interpreted cautiously.

> . . . .

> [The study's] results are not consistent with any genetic model. . . . Neither of these differences [between homosexuality in maternal versus paternal uncles or cousins] is statistically significant. . . . Small sample sizes make these data compatible with a range of possible genetic and environmental hypotheses.

> . . . .

The hallmark characteristic of an x-linked trait is no male-to-male transmission. Because few homosexual men tend to have children, a study of male homosexual orientation will reveal few opportunities for male-to-male transmission, giving the appearance of x-linkage. In this context, examining the rate of homosexual orientation in the fathers of homosexual men is not meaningful. In the study by Hamer et al., there were only six sons of homosexual males, clearly an inadequate number for a meaningful test. Hamer et al. also present four pedigrees [four different families] as being consistent with x-linkage. Only one homosexual male in these four pedigrees has a child (a daughter). In the context of trait-associated lack of male reproduction, such pedigrees would be relatively easy to obtain. Thus the family data presented [by Hamer et al.] present no consistent support for the subsequent linkage results.

. . . .

Such studies must be scrutinized carefully and dispassionately.[118]

Hamer responded that "We did not say that xq28 'underlies' sexuality, only that it contributes to it in some families. Nor have we said that xq28 represents a 'major' gene, only that its influence is statistically detectable in the population that we studied."[119] Nonetheless, regarding the failure of their most important "findings" to achieve even statistical significance, Hamer himself agreed, in a rather awkward circumlocution, that "the question of the appropriate significance level to apply to a non-Mendelian [that is, polygenic, multiple factors influencing expression] trait such as sexual orientation is problematic."[120]

Moreover, in a recent edition of *Science* devoted to behavioral genetics, Hamer stated to his fellow scientists that "Complex behavioral traits are the product of multiple genetic and environmental antecedents, with 'environment' meaning not only the social environment but also such factors as the 'flux of hormones during development, whether you were lying on your right or left side in the womb and a whole parade of other things'. 'The relationships among genes and environment probably have a somewhat different effect on someone in Salt Lake City than if that person were growing up in New York City.'"[121]

Nevertheless, Hamer testified as an expert witness to the Colorado court that heard a case to void the state's "Proposition 2," which would have disallowed sexual behavior as a legitimate basis for formal minority status on a par with race. On the basis of his research Hamer testified that he was "99.5 percent certain that homosexuality is genetic." The judge who heard the case ultimately struck down the law, which had been established by popular referendum.

CONCLUSIONS ON THE BIOLOGY OF HOMOSEXUALITY

What can we conclude about the biology of homosexuality? Let us turn in more detail to the most comprehensive review article, cited previously, on the subject of the biology of homosexuality, including genetics. "Human Sexual Orientation: The Biological Theories Reappraised" by Byne and Parsons was published in the same issue of *Archives of General Psychiatry* as Bailey and Pillard's study of female homosexuality, Lidz's response to their first article, and their response to Lidz.

The article reviews 135 research studies, prior reviews, academic summaries, books, and chapters of books, in essence, the entire literature, of which only a small portion is actual research. The abstract summarizes their findings concisely and is by far the best available assessment of the current status of this research:

> Recent studies postulate biologic factors [genetic, hormonal] as the primary basis for sexual orientation. However, there is no evidence at present to substantiate a biologic theory, just as there is no evidence to support any singular psychosocial explanation. While all behavior must have an ultimate biologic substrate, the appeal of current biologic explanations for sexual orientation may derive more from dissatisfaction with the current status of psychosocial explanations than from a substantiating body of experimental data. Critical review shows the evidence favoring a biologic theory to be lacking. In an alter-

native model, temperamental and personality traits interact with the familial and social milieu as the individual's sexuality emerges. Because such traits may be heritable or developmentally influenced by hormones, the model predicts an apparent non-zero heritability for homosexuality without requiring that either genes or hormones directly influence sexual orientation per se.[122]

Their analysis reveals that not only is there little convincing evidence for a biological explanation of homosexuality, but there is little high-quality, scientific research evidence for *any* explanation.

Though this fact tends to undermine all claims about homosexuality, the same can also be said about the lack of hard scientific research-based explanations for all of the more complex aspects of human behavior. The shift to a more scientific basis for explaining homosexuality appeals primarily to those who seek to undercut the vast amount of clinical experience confirming that, regardless of its origins, homosexuality is, in fact, to a large extent changeable.

We can summarize the conclusions about the biology of homosexuality in ten points.

First, the genetic contribution to homosexuality is at most a predisposition—it is not a cause. A certain genetic constitution may establish, more or less, a predisposition to homosexuality. Without that constitution it would be unlikely for an individual to choose homosexuality freely. With that constitution, it may be more likely that he or she would.

Second, even if we accept uncritically the research of the proponents of this theory, this predisposition contributes no more than 25 to 50 percent to the likelihood of an individual actually becoming homosexual. But a realistic assessment of the research shows that the genetic contribution, though not zero, is likely to turn out to be far smaller, perhaps between 10 percent and 25 percent.

Third, when the actual incidence of homosexuality in the population is higher, the influence of the possible genetic predisposition is smaller and the influence of non-genetic factors is greater. Again, this is because the arithmetic used to assess probable genetic influence in twin studies requires a baseline estimate of prevalence in the general population. The rarer the trait, the more meaning a given level of concordance will have. That is, if the trait is almost universal, two twins are just as likely to share it as two unrelated individuals. If the trait is extremely rare, the twins will likely share it only if they share some factor common to both.

Fourth, the incidence of homosexuality depends on its definition. Using definitions that activists prefer, in some cultures male homosexuality, especially between older men and adolescents, is universal. With an incidence of 100 percent, the measurable genetic contribution in a such a culture would be zero.

This huge cultural variability in incidence, from 1 to 100 percent, suggests the possibility that many strains of homosexuality could exist. At a minimum two classes exist: One homosexual class is linked indirectly to a complex genetic component of the limited sort previously discussed, such as in the relationship of height to basketball-playing; the other would be almost entirely influenced by culture. The former would tend to be present in some measure even when culturally taboo and would be associated with a very low incidence rate. The latter would predominate in cultures where the taboos against homosexuality were either nonexistent or relatively weak in their effect and would be associated with a relatively high incidence rate. In cultures such as ours where the taboo is weak (and weakening) there is likely to be a mixture of types present.

Raw statistics about incidence from a cross section in time are meaningless when the two or more types are not separated out. We cannot say that the currently presumed incidence of 1 to 3 percent for male homosexuality is necessarily the minimum, that is, the rate that would exist if the cultural type of homosexuality was eliminated. This fact renders meaningless any heritability estimates, because they all depend on meaningful general incidence rates.

Fifth, given that such cultures have existed where the incidence of homosexuality is far greater than at present, the incidence of homosexuality is clearly influenced by mores. Where people endorse and encourage homosexuality, the incidence increases; where they reject it, it decreases. These factors have nothing to do with its genetics.

Sixth, some yet-to-be determined proportion of any apparent genetic influence on homosexuality is actually a non-genetic, though innate, prenatal influence. This influence may be hormonal, autoimmune, from some undiscovered factor or factors, or a combination of all these. The proportion of this seemingly genetic, but actually intrauterine and non-genetic, influence is neither "all" nor "none." It may well be closer to the former than the latter if certain European studies on hormonal effects prove correct. This intrauterine influence may be an abnormality that could eventually prove to be correctable. Nonetheless, the practical influence of such an intrauterine predisposition can be at most no more than the maximum degree of genetic influence, that is, considerably less than 50 percent.

Seventh, of the remaining 50 to 70 percent, at minimum, of the extrauterine, non-innate causes of homosexuality, a substantial but not yet quantifiable portion represents the individual's response both to environmentally reinforced attitudes and behaviors as well as to innate predispositional pressures.

Eighth, whatever genetic contribution to homosexuality exists, it probably contributes not to homosexuality per se, but rather to some other trait that makes the homosexual "option" more readily available than to those who lack this genetic trait (as in the correlation between height and basketball). The homosexual option may be selected for personal reasons, such as a response to trauma, or social reasons, such as overcrowding or subcultural mores, or both. It is reinforced each time it is selected. Therefore it is even more likely to be reselected the next time.

Ninth, the genetic contribution to homosexuality may be sex-linked, on the x chromosome. In light of population genetics and the importance of replacement rates, the fact that homosexuality continues to exist suggests strongly that (a) genetic influences are far from sufficient to cause homosexuality, though they may increase its likelihood and (b) the genes that influence the appearance of homosexuality do not code for homosexuality per se, but rather for other traits that themselves do not adversely affect heterosexual reproduction.

And tenth, most studies to date have many flaws. Some are caused by the intrusion of political agendas into what should be objective research, and some are due to the intrinsic complexity of the subject. Our knowledge of these flaws must temper any conclusions we make. It is premature (and will almost certainly prove to be incorrect) simply to state that homosexuality "is" or "is not" genetic, innate, psychological, chosen, or social. It was extremely premature to pronounce it an illness, or not an illness, decades ago.

The Development of
a Homosexual Orientation

George Rekers

WHAT IS THE COMBINATION of conditions which make the formation of a homosexual orientation more likely? This is a very complex question for a number of reasons.[1] First, research and clinical experience indicate that there is a variety of forms of homosexuality. Alan Bell and Martin Weinberg chose the title *Homosexualities: A Study of Diversity Among Men and Women* for their 1978 book, which reported their interview research with approximately fifteen hundred individuals.[2] Not only would we expect homosexual orientation in men and women to have different origins, but even if we consider one sex only, we find a certain variety of orientations including exclusive homosexual orientation, various combinations of homosexual and heterosexual orientation, homosexual transsexualism, homosexual transvestitism, homosexual masochism, homosexual sadism, and homosexual orientation which has never been acted upon behaviorally.

Not only are there a number of variations in homosexual orientation, but there may be a certain diversity in the influences on sexual orientation. The participants at a national conference in the Washington, D.C., area on a particular date all arrived at the same conference center, but their starting points and routes to that destination varied. This is not to say that we cannot scientifically discover certain things in common among the travel patterns of the conference participants. For example, a large percentage may have come through National Airport. One subgroup may have taken the subway, while another group took a taxi from the airport to the hotel. Perhaps a minority rented cars at the airport to drive to the hotel. But then again, there were others who did not arrive through the airport, but drove from their home in an automobile. Certain common influences, perhaps a conference brochure, and certain decisions in the past contributed to behavior patterns and a narrowing of opportunities as a result of those choices, until all the participants awoke this morning with a strong predisposition to go to the conference center. It can be said, then, that a complex combination of variables led to conference-attending behavior on this particular day.

In much the same way, as we consider the issue of the formation of a homosexual orientation, the task before us is to identify the common developmental influences or pathways associated with homosexual orientation.[3] Scholars in this area have pursued three principal, interrelated research strategies: First, there have been retrospective studies of adult homosexuals, sometimes compared with data from adult heterosexuals. These studies have largely employed research interview, clinical interview or questionnaire methods. A second approach has been the prospective, longitudinal studies of the development of children with gender disturbances from adolescence or adulthood. A third strategy has been the scientific investigation of potential hormonal, genetic, and chromosomal influences on sexual orientation. Of course, various theories of personality development have guided the clinical studies and research investigations, providing hypotheses regarding which variables to study.

Adult Male Homosexuals

When Danny was eight years old, his adoptive parents brought him to my office with questions about his future development. Having recently adopted him, they wanted to provide a healthy family life

for him, in contrast to that which he had experienced during his
first seven years, when he was subjected to physical and mental abuse
and to homosexual activities initiated by his father. On the third
day that Danny had been in his new adoptive home, his adoptive
mother could tell that he had something important to say, but it
appeared to be very difficult for him to bring up what was on his
mind. So she took him aside and said, "Danny, we know that your
Daddy did some things to your body which were not good for him
or for you. Here in our home, you don't have to be afraid of that
kind of thing anymore. We just wanted you to know that we know
what happened, and we know it wasn't your fault, so it's okay." As
she told him that, a tear trickled down his cheek, and he reached
up and hugged her. He did not say a word then, but later he was
able to tell her some of what had happened to him in the past and
how he felt about it. Several weeks later, Danny was wrestling with
a neighborhood boy and his wrestling developed further into sexual
advances. His mother found him sexually involved with this other
boy, and Danny admitted that he had initiated the activity saying,
"Well, Mom, sometimes I get this in my mind. I tried to forget
what's happened to me, but when I get it in my mind, it's all I can
think about." Is Danny's childhood experience a typical route to
the destination of homosexual orientation? Or is there another
more common pathway?

Some males do not become involved in homosexual activity until
their adolescent years. A number of years ago, I received a referral
of a fifteen year old boy, Shawn, who was a foster child. He had
been removed from several foster homes because he had initiated
homosexual encounters with a number of other teenage boys. He
told me that he had never thought about homosexual activity until
he was thirteen years old and in a foster home where he shared a
bedroom with the sixteen year old biological son of his foster parents. The sixteen year old had forced Shawn into oral-genital activities at night, threatening to beat him up if he told the parents.
At first, Shawn felt disgusted and angry, but he developed a preference for homosexual activity over time as he experienced sexual

gratification through this pattern. But is Shawn's experience a common pathway to homosexual orientation?

Let's consider yet another case. Sixteen-year-old Ken was brought to my office by his mother who was concerned about his depression. After introducing Ken to me, his mother explained that Ken wanted to talk to me privately. After she left my office, he explained, "Last Friday, when nobody else was home, I took Mom's sharpest knife out of the kitchen drawer and I decided that this time I would do it. Really, there is no reason to go on living anymore. Nobody understands how frustrated and unhappy I am." Ken was a good-looking, well-developed teenager of medium athletic build, dressed in blue jeans and a t-shirt. His arm movements were only slightly effeminate.

As he stared at the carpet, he described the depth of his depression and grieving over the loss of his homosexual "lover." Over several interviews with Ken and conjoint interviews with his mother, I learned that Ken's father was emotionally distant from him throughout his preschool years and had divorced his mother when Ken was five. Ken had had very little contact with him since that time. His mother described Ken's early preoccupation with feminine toys, playing with girls, and compulsive play with her cosmetics, jewelry, and clothing. She had interpreted this as just "a passing phase" and several years later, at the age of nine, she observed a marked decrease in the frequency of effeminate movements. Ken did not have close friendships with other boys during his elementary school years and spent more of his time playing with young girls or preschool boys. Is Ken's experience the more typical pathway to a homosexual orientation? Our answer will involve a summary of some representative results of retrospective studies of male homosexuals on this question.[4]

A number of investigators have reported a family constellation for male homosexuals which included a close-binding, intimate mother and a hostile, detached father.[5] Saghir and Robins reported that the fathers of homosexual men are described by their sons as indifferent and uninvolved. Only 13 percent of the homosexuals identified with their fathers, compared to 66 percent of the heterosexual group.[6] Bene and Apperson and McAdoo reported that the fathers of homosexual sons were less affectionate than those of heterosexual sons.[7] Brown reported a study of 40 homosexual males in which there was not a single case in which the homosexual reported having had an affectionate relationship with his father.[8] In fact, several investigators including Evans, Jonas, and Terman and Miles report that homosexual males often fear and hate their fathers.[9]

Cross-Gender Behavior

Effeminate behavior in childhood is retrospectively reported by many adult male homosexuals, both in psychiatric patients and in non-patient samples. A study of non-patient homosexuals found that two-thirds of eighty-nine male homosexuals recalled "girl-like" behavior during their childhood as compared to only three percent of the heterosexual adult controls.[10]

Whitam administered questionnaires regarding non-sexual gender role behaviors in childhood to a non-patient adult group consisting of 206 male homosexuals and seventy-eight male heterosexuals. Forty-seven percent of the men with exclusive homosexual orientation reported a greater interest than other boys their age in dolls, compared to zero percent of the exclusively heterosexual men. Forty-four percent of the men with exclusive homosexual orientation reported liking to dress in women's clothing, compared to zero percent of the exclusively heterosexual men. Forty-two percent of the men with exclusive homosexual orientation reported interest in being with girls and joining in activities and games of girls more than with boys, compared to 1.5 percent of men who were exclusively heterosexual in orientation. Sixty-one percent of the men with exclusive homosexual orientation reported liking to be around older women rather than older men as a child, compared to 13 percent of men of exclusive heterosexual orientation. When asked if they were regarded as a "sissy" during childhood, 29 percent of the men with exclusive homosexual orientation answered in the affirmative, while only 1.5 percent of the exclusively heterosexual responded affirmatively. An additional 41 percent of the exclusively homosexual men reported that they were "not 'sissy' exactly, but different from other boys," compared to nine percent of the exclusively heterosexual men. Seventy-eight percent of the men with exclusive homosexual orientation reported sexual interests in other boys during their childhood, compared to 12 percent of the exclusively heterosexual men.[11]

In addition, Whitam found that the stronger one's homosexual orientation, the greater was the number of these childhood cross-gender behavior indicators. This study suggests that homosexuals and heterosexuals have "strikingly different childhoods" and that there is a relationship between adult homosexual orientation and the presence of cross-gender behaviors in childhood.[12] Whitam reported that the presence of these childhood cross-gender behaviors were not limited to adult male homosexuals who are "effeminate." "Many homosexuals who were . . . 'feminized' children are today quite masculine and 'undetectable'."[13] The smallest group of homosexuals were those who did not report displaying any childhood cross-gender behaviors, but usually reported early sexual preference for members of the same sex.

In a cross-cultural study published in 1984, Whitam and Zent replicated the findings of this earlier study, again on a non-clinical homosexual and heterosexual male sample from four societies: the United States, Guatemala, Brazil, and the Philippines.[14]

Social Relationships and Sexual Behavior

Saghir and Robins interviewed eighty-nine homosexual adult males who were not a patient sample, and though they were not demonstrably representative of the total homosexual population, the sample nevertheless avoided the selective bias of psychiatric treatment or criminal incarceration. Saghir and Robins reported that the adolescence of male homosexuals is characterized, in the majority of cases, by a lack of contact with male "buddies" and by preference for girl playmates. A great majority of them reported the onset of homosexual attachments, fantasies, and sexual stimulation prior to the age of fourteen years, with only a very small minority starting their homosexual responses after the age of nineteen years. Most began homosexual practices before the age of fifteen and typically developed a pattern of casual, "one night stands," being "rarely faithful in their relationships," to quote these investigators.[15]

Roesler and Deisher reported the results of interviews with sixty young men from age sixteen to twenty-two years who were not patients and who had at least one homosexual experience to orgasm. The mean age of first homosexual experience varied from four to twenty years of age with the median age of fourteen. In almost all cases, homosexual experience to orgasm occurred before the young man's decision to label himself as "homosexual." A majority of these young men reported prepubertal sexual experiences with other males. The median number of male sexual partners was fifty, with one eighteen-year-old reporting approximately three thousand sexual partners. Forty-eight percent had visited a psychiatrist and 31 percent had made what they considered to be a significant suicide attempt.[16]

Evaluating a Developmental Model

In 1981, Alan Bell, Martin Weinberg, and Sue Hammersmith published their book, *Sexual Preference: Its Development in Men and Women*, which reported the results of their 175-page interview schedule which they administered to 575 white homosexual males and 111 black homosexual males. For a comparison group, they interviewed 284 white heterosexual males and 53 black heterosexual males. (Their data on female subjects will be reviewed later.) Approximately two hundred of their questions pertained to the respondents' childhood and adolescence. These investigators compared developmental patterns in homosexuals and heterosexuals, using a form of data analysis called "path analysis," in order to assess a theoretical model of a complex developmental process. Following a psychoanalytic model, the senior investigator of this project formulated the following model for testing:

Stage 1: Parental traits

Stage 2: Parental relationships (dominance, amount of conflict, and affection for one another)

Stage 3: Parent-child relationships (closeness, affection, involvement vs. detachment, accepting vs. rejecting, overprotective vs. nonprotective)

Stage 4: Parental identification (desire to grow up to be like the parent of the same or opposite sex)

Stage 5: Sibling relationships (closeness, sexual aspects)

Stage 6: Sibling identifications

Stage 7: Gender conformity (masculine and feminine gender role behaviors)

Stage 8: The grade school years (friendships patterns, homosexual or heterosexual experiences, homosexual or heterosexual arousal, being called "homosexual")

Stage 9: The high school years (social relationships and sexual outlets)

The main dependent variable of their study was sexual preference as rated on the seven-point Kinsey Scale from exclusively heterosexual (a score of zero) to exclusively homosexual (a score of six).

The participants in this study were non-clinical samples specifically recruited, in the case of the homosexuals, from gay bars, gay baths, certain street locations, public parks, beaches and restrooms, and by various modes of advertisement. The heterosexuals were obtained through a stratified random sampling method using block sampling techniques. Because of prior difficulty in obtaining subjects in the Midwest, this project was conducted in the San Francisco Bay area, with the interviewing completed in 1970.[17]

Gender Conformity

Although the first six stages in the developmental model tested by Bell and his colleagues were not found to be strongly associated with sexual preference by the path analysis of their data, the seventh stage, "gender conformity," did yield a strong association. The investigators concluded that

findings tend to corroborate those of other studies that have
found pre-homosexual boys to be less stereotypically 'masculine' than pre-heterosexual boys, at least in their self-images.
Fewer of the homosexual men in our study remembered themselves as having been very masculine while growing up, and
more homosexual than heterosexual respondents recalled some
dislike for typical boys' activities and enjoyment of those they
thought were "for girls". Our path analysis shows that these
kinds of gender nonconformity are directly related to experiencing both homosexual activities and homosexual arousal
before age 19, a sense of an explicitly sexual or at least gender-
related difference from other boys, and a delay in feelings of
sexual attraction to girls, as well as an adult homosexual preference.[18]

For example, their data showed that only 11 percent of the white
homosexual males reported having enjoyed boys' activities such as
baseball and football "very much" as compared to 70 percent of the
white heterosexual males. In contrast, 46 percent of the white homosexual males reported having enjoyed stereotypical girls' activities as opposed to 11 percent of the white heterosexual males.
Thirty-seven percent of the white homosexuals reported cross-
dressing in girls' clothing and pretending to be a female compared
to 10 percent of the white heterosexuals. Only 18 percent of the
white homosexual males described themselves as "very masculine"
compared to 67 percent of the white heterosexual males.

In this study, childhood gender nonconformity not only was a
very strong predictor of adult sexual preference among the males
studied, but it also ranked first in importance among the fifteen
developmental variables studied. Gender nonconformity appeared
to influence a variety of sexually-explicit variables, including feeling sexually different from other boys, experiencing homosexual
arousal, having had some kind of homosexual genital activities in
childhood, being less likely to experience heterosexual arousal in
childhood, reporting more extensive involvement in homosexual
activities in adolescence, and increasing the probability of the boys
becoming homosexual in adulthood. Fifty-nine percent of white

homosexual males rated their sexual feelings as having been predominantly homosexual during childhood and adolescence as compared to one percent of the white heterosexual males. Ninety-five percent of the homosexual men reported having been sexually aroused by another male sometimes before they reached age nineteen, while only 20 percent of the heterosexual males reported this experience.[19] The mean age for the homosexual men for their recall of being sexually aroused by another male was 11.6 years.

Conclusions

Bell, Weinberg, and Hammersmith came to the overall conclusion that prior theories on the development of homosexuality have exaggerated the role of the parents in the development of their sons' sexual orientation. They did allow that "The notion that cold, detached fathers may predispose their children, particularly sons, toward homosexuality is somewhat more plausible in light of our findings . . .While having a cold father does have some indirect connection to sexual preference among the men in our study, it lies at the beginning of a complex chain, so that its connection is entirely dependent on the later occurrence of other factors."[20] They emphasized that their study did not provide support for other factors thought to contribute to the development of homosexuality, namely, poor peer relationships, labeling by others, atypical experience with persons of the opposite sex, or seduction by an older person of the same sex, even though they allowed for some atypical individuals (such as my cases of Danny and Shawn) having had such factors in their particular background. Identification with the parent of the same sex was found to have only a weak connection to the development of the individual's sexual orientation.

The Effect of Sexual Abuse

In contrast, a more recent study by Shrier and Johnson reported that forty male adolescents disclosed their experience of being sexually assaulted by a man before puberty. In comparison to a matched control group of forty adolescents from the same clinic, Shrier and Johnson report finding that these homosexually-assaulted males identified themselves as subsequently homosexual nearly seven times as often and bisexual nearly six times as often as the non-assaulted comparison control group. The magnitude of statistical difference for these measures between study and control groups was highly significant. A total of twenty-three (58 percent) of those adolescents who reported sexual abuse by a man prior to puberty revealed either homosexual or bisexual orientation. Of the control group, fully 90 percent reported a heterosexual orientation.[21]

An extension of the study found an additional fourteen adolescent males who, as children, were molested by men. In half of these molestations, physical force or threats were employed. The mean age at which the molestation was reported was 18.2 years, with a range of fifteen to twenty-four years. The age at molestation ranged from four to sixteen years of age, with a mean of ten years of age. Only rarely had the molestation been revealed prior to participation in the study interview. Of this group of fourteen, "one half of the victims currently identified themselves as homosexual and often linked their homosexuality to their sexual victimization experience(s)."[22] These same investigators suggested that findings of the high rate of homosexuality in the study population are a confirmation of Finkelhor's 1979 college student survey, in which nearly half of the men who reported "a childhood experience with an older man were currently involved in homosexual activity." It was Finkelhor's impression that the boy who has been molested by a man may label the experience as homosexual and misperceive himself as homosexual based on his having been found sexually attractive by an older man. Once self-labeled, the boy may place himself in situations that leave him open to homosexual activity.[23] Similarly, Cameron and Cameron found that a disproportionate number of adult homosexuals reported that they had been initiated into homosexual behavior by incestuous molestation by a homosexual parent.[24]

Recent Analysis of Older Kinsey Data

Van Wyk and Geist published a study in 1984 which reported their findings on 3,849 males in the community at large plus 294 males from gay bars and homophile organizations in Chicago.[25] They found elevated overt adult Kinsey Scale scores (that is exclusive or near exclusive homosexual behavior) in males who reported "poorer teenage relationships with their fathers, had more girl companions at age 10, fewer male companions at 10 and 16, avoided sports participation, learn[ing] of homosexuality by experience, learn[ing] to masturbate by being masturbated by another male, had intense prepubertal sexual contact with boys or men, [having] neither heterosexual contact nor petting to orgasm by age 18, [finding] thought or sight of males, but not females, arousing by age 18, [having] homosexual contact by age 18, higher Kinsey Scale scores at ages 16, and 17, and [having] higher first-year homosexual behavior frequency."[26] They concluded from their data on masturbation that "learning through experience seems to be an important pathway to later sexual preference."[27]

ADULT FEMALE HOMOSEXUALS

On her first visit to my office, Tammy confessed, "I'm coming to talk to you for my parents' sake only. Believe me, this was not my idea to come for counseling about this." Tammy was 17 years old and her mother insisted that she see a clinical psychologist after she had discovered and read Tammy's diary, which included numerous entries describing her affection for and homosexual experiences with a teenage friend, Sandy, which had begun six months earlier. Tammy had written about her sexual curiosity, which had led to some sexual experimentation with Sandy. At first Tammy had thought of Sandy as just a friend, but after several weeks of sexual involvement with Sandy, Tammy began to write of new romantic feelings towards Sandy. The diary went on to describe Tammy's crushed emotions when Sandy severed their relationship, explaining that she could not handle the guilt and the reminder of the sexual experiences when they saw each other, even as friends. Tammy wrote in the diary how she spent several weeks of night after night crying herself to sleep after the break up. After several heated conversations and confrontations over Tammy's homosexual involvement, her mother honestly confided in Tammy, "I don't understand how you turned out like this." Tammy explained, "It's not that I dislike the boys, but I wonder if I could ever feel the same intense love for a man that I felt towards Sandy."

Female homosexuals tend to seek as well as achieve more stable and faithful partnerships than do male homosexuals.[28] Schafer concluded that "Lesbian women . . . have internalized the sociosexual norms of combining love and sexuality equally as much as heterosexual women."[29] Marmor observed that the etiology of female homosexuality is no less complex than the etiology of homosexuality in the male, and he speculated that there were multiple factors involved.[30]

Cross-Gender Behavior

According to the work of Saghir and Robins who studied fifty-seven non-clinical homosexual females and forty-three heterosexual women controls, the majority of adult female homosexuals retrospectively report wishing as a child that they were a boy and having a preference for male playmates and masculine activities.[31] Adult female homosexuals typically identified with their fathers and the majority were aware of the homosexual orientation before the age of fourteen years. They reported that "a pattern emerges whereby the majority of these female (homosexuals) report being tomboys during childhood. Most of them have mainly boy playmates, are actively involved in sports, and express a dislike for dolls and domestic activity."[32] These investigators also report it is common to find a repetitive desire to belong to the opposite sex. Over two-thirds of the adult female homosexuals reported being tomboys as children, compared to 16 percent of the heterosexual control group.

But there was a distinction in the duration of the tomboy phase in that tomboyism persisted into adolescence or adulthood for approximately one-half of the homosexual females, but for none of the heterosexual females. In their 1973 study, Saghir and Robins reported that female homosexuals who were tomboys reported disliking and avoiding doll play, while female heterosexuals who were tomboys showed no such aversion. Their study found that these non-clinical homosexual females showed significantly greater overall prevalence of psychiatric disorders than single heterosexual females. Saghir and Robins reported that only 14 percent of the homosexual women reported that they primarily identified with their mothers while 76 percent stated that they either had no parental figure to identify with or identified mainly with their fathers.[33]

Kenyon reported that adult female homosexuals are significantly more likely than heterosexual controls to report having an unhappy childhood.[34] A number of studies also report that the childhood environment of female homosexuals is often marked by dysfunctional family relationships.[35] The majority of existing studies on female homosexuality indicate that the family backgrounds of most lesbians include a poor relationship with the father.[36] The fathers of female homosexuals are often described by their daughters as hostile and detached.[37] A number of studies have found that the father-daughter relationships are often distant and lacking in affection.[38] Compared to the fathers of heterosexual controls, the fathers of homosexual women are more likely to be alcoholic, physically abusive,[39] and feared by their daughters. The fathers of homosexual women tend to be puritanical, overly possessive, and inhibiting of their daughters' development as women.[40]

Rosen reported his study of twenty-six volunteer subjects from a women's homophile organization based in San Francisco. He found that in more than half of the cases (fifteen of the twenty-six) there was a hostile or fearful conception of the feminine role, and he interpreted his data as supporting the theory that lesbianism is a defense against hostility, fear, and guilt following early rejection by a mother.[41]

EVALUATING A DEVELOPMENTAL MODEL

The study in San Francisco reported by Bell, Weinberg, and Hammersmith included 229 white homosexual females, sixty-four black homosexual females, 101 white heterosexual females, and thirty-nine black heterosexual females.[42]

Gender Conformity

As was the case of the male homosexuals, childhood gender non-conformity was found to be closely associated with the development of a homosexual orientation. For example, 55 percent of the heterosexual women said they enjoyed typical girls' activities while only 13 percent of the white homosexual females reported the same thing. Seventy-one percent of the homosexual women reported enjoying typical boys' activities such as baseball and football very much as compared to 28 percent of the heterosexual controls. Forty-nine percent of the white homosexual females reported having worn boy's clothes and pretended to be a boy (excluding Halloween and school plays) as compared to only seven percent of the heterosexual controls. Sixty-two percent of the homosexual females described themselves as having been very masculine when they were growing up, compared to only 10 percent of the heterosexuals.

Blanchard and Freund studied forty-four homosexual subjects and 236 control subjects and found that homosexual females possess a greater degree of masculine gender identity than heterosexual females. Their masculine gender identity scale was useful in clinical diagnosis.[43]

Childhood and Adolescent Sexuality

With regard to childhood and adolescent sexuality, Bell and his colleagues did not find homosexual orientation related to rape, sexual molestation, parental punishments or other traumatic experiences. Homosexual women did not appear to have been more precocious sexually, but their covert sexual feelings were found to play a role in the development of homosexual orientation. Early reports of feeling sexually attracted to other females seemed to lead to an increased probability of expressing an adult homosexual orientation. Forty-four percent of the homosexual female adults reported that in childhood and adolescence they had sexual feelings that were predominantly homosexual, compared to zero percent of the heterosexual women. Seventy percent of the homosexual females recalled having been sexually aroused by another female before the age of nineteen, compared to 6 percent of the heterosexual control group. Of those who reported having been sexually aroused by a female, most reported age twelve or thirteen as the age at which it first occurred. Forty-one percent of the white homosexual females reported having masturbated or having been masturbated by another female before the age of nineteen, compared to four percent of the heterosexuals.

Recent Analysis of Older Kinsey Data

The study of Van Wyk and Geist included 3,392 females from the general population plus 134 females from sources with known homosexual bias. These investigators found that elevated overt adult Kinsey Scale or "K" scores (scores more closely associated with homosexuality) were found for females who had reported few girl companions at age ten and few male companions at age sixteen, for those who had learned to masturbate by being masturbated by a female, those who had intense prepubertal sexual contact with boys or men, those who found thought or sight of females (but not males) arousing by age eighteen, those who had homosexual contact by age eighteen, those who had higher K scores at age seventeen, and those who had higher first-year homosexual behavior frequency.[44]

MEN WITH EARLY GENDER DISTURBANCES

Retrospective studies have many methodological limitations to them, including distorted memories and inability to recall a detailed sequence of events in the early years. On the other hand, prospective studies can overcome these limitations but are quite difficult to conduct, run the risk of losing subjects at follow-up intervals, and are comparatively quite costly. Nevertheless, there have been a number of attempts at conducting prospective longitudinal studies of boys with effeminate behavior.

An Overall Analysis

In his comprehensive review of the existing research literature, Zucker summarized the psychosexual outcomes for males with gender disturbances in childhood who have been followed up over long intervals: "Of ninety-four cases, five are transsexual (5.3 percent); 43 are homosexual or bisexual (45.7 percent); one is a heterosexual transvestite (1.1 percent); 21 are heterosexual (22.3 percent); and 24 are uncertain (25.5 percent), including one child who is still prepubertal. If the uncertain cases are excluded, then 70 percent of the cases are either transsexual, homosexual or bisexual, or a transvestite and 30 percent are heterosexual."[45] Hence, the available prospective longitudinal data do indicate that effeminate behavior in boys is fairly predictive of male homosexuality.

Individual Outcomes

Of seven cases of effeminacy in boys, Bakwin found that after a nine year follow-up two were homosexual, two were probably heterosexual and three were uncertain.[46] Lebovitz studied sixteen effeminate boys, two of whom, at the time of follow-up in their young adulthood, were found to be homosexual.[47]

In one of the longest follow-up studies, Bernard Zuger followed fifty-five boys with early effeminate behavior and found that 63.6 percent were homosexual and 5.5 percent were heterosexual. In ten cases the outcome was uncertain and seven were lost to follow-up.[48] In Zuger's 1978 report, which was a twenty year prospective follow-up, 63 percent were found to be homosexual, 12 percent heterosexual, six percent transvestite and six percent transsexual. He also found that 25 percent had attempted suicide and six percent actually committed suicide.[49]

Green reported on the later sexual orientation of sixty-six boys whose behaviors were consistent with the diagnosis of gender identity disorder of childhood. He compared these to fifty-six control subjects matched for demographic variables. Forty-four of the clinically-referred boys were re-evaluated for sexual orientation upon follow-up, and it was found that thirty of the forty-four were bisexual or homosexual in orientation as compared to none of the thirty-four in the comparison group.[50]

Family Variables

In my own study of forty-six boys with gender role disturbances, I have found significantly fewer male role models in the family backgrounds of severely gender-disturbed boys. I also found male childhood gender disturbance correlated with the high incidence of psychiatric problems in both mothers and fathers and with atypical patterns of involvement with mothers and fathers. The mean age of the boys at the time of separation from their father was 3.55 years, with 80 percent of the boys being age five or under when the separation occurred. The reason for father absence was separation or divorce in 82 percent of the cases. Thirty-seven percent had no adult male role model (either biological or father substitute) present in the home, and the comparable 1977 census figures was 11.9 percent of children not living with a father figure. Seventy-five percent of the most severely gender-disturbed boys and 21 percent of the less severely gender-disturbed boys had neither biological father nor a father substitute living in the home. For the fathers present in the home, sixty percent were described as psychologically distant or remote by other family members.[51]

WOMEN WITH EARLY GENDER DISTURBANCES

There is only scanty research on girls with gender disturbances, a disorder which appears to be either quite rare or not easily detected in the general population.[52] At the present time, satisfactory prospective research studies are not available for females with gender disturbance in childhood.[53]

Adulthood Changes in Sexual Orientation

Sexual orientation may be much more fluid and subject to change than is typically reported.[54] Kirkpatrick reported the onset of stable lesbian (not bisexual) orientations and life-styles following relatively successful heterosexual marriage. Of note is the fact that such heterosexual marriages did not appear to be marriages of convenience or attempts to "prove heterosexuality," but seemed to have been characterized by a rather typical love relationship in which competing homosexual interests were conspicuously absent.[55] Kirkpatrick argues that "The presence of a durable heterosexual relationship in the life of a woman who later has a durable homosexual relationship requires us to consider that sexual orientation may not be, as we once believed, the fixed compass that directs all intrinsic and extrinsic aspects of personality formation."[56] Late lifestyle changes have been assumed to always represent a late "coming out" after a period of struggle with homosexuality. Those who recognize this evident fluidity in a change from conventional heterosexuality to homosexuality without a bisexual "transition" may be open to the contention, advanced by several "ex-gay" associations, that true conversion from homosexuality to heterosexuality is possible.[57]

Biological Factors

The "nature versus nurture" issue in human development research has been a matter of debate over the centuries, and much of the contemporary focus has been upon the interaction of hereditary and environmental causation.

Currently, a great deal of attention is being paid to so-called biological factors in the development of homosexuality.[58] However, *biological* approaches are often either reductionist models of causality or statistical inferences based upon theories that are themselves naive.

In their comprehensive review of the scientific studies on the development of sexual orientation, Byne and Parsons (1993) concluded that

> Recent studies postulate biologic factors as the primary basis for sexual orientation. However, there is no evidence at present to substantiate a biologic theory, just as there is no compelling evidence to support any singular psychosocial explanation. While all behavior must have an ultimate biologic substrate, the appeal of current biologic explanations for sexual orientation may derive more from dissatisfaction with the present status of psychosocial explanations than from a substantiating body of experimental data. Critical review shows the evidence favoring a biologic theory to be lacking. In an alternative model, temperamental and personality traits interact with the familial and social milieu as the individual's sexuality emerges. Because such traits may be heritable or developmentally influenced by hormones, the model predicts an apparent nonzero heritability for homosexuality without regarding that either genes or hormones directly influence sexual orientation per se.[59]
>
> . . . .
>
> Conspicuously absent from most theorizing on the origins of sexual orientation is an active role of the individual in constructing his or her identity . . . We propose an interactional model in which genes or hormones do not specify sexual orientation per se, but instead bias particular personality traits and thereby influence the manner in which an individual and his or her environment interact as sexual orientation and other personality characteristics unfold developmentally.

Consider the following hypothetical scenario, similar to that posed by Stoller and Herdt. Two boys had absent fathers and overly protective mothers who disparaged sports. One of these boys enthusiastically participated in baseball and developed a heterosexual erotic orientation, while the other shunned baseball and developed a homosexual orientation. This scenario (which is not intended to perpetuate cultural stereotypes) illustrates the failure of simple explanations in which parenting styles determine sexual orientation. However, would the explanation be so simple as that the prehomosexual boy had a feminized brain (i.e., small INAH3) as the result of a prenatal androgen deficiency that may have been genetically programmed?

Research into the heritability of personality variants suggests that some personality dimensions may be heritable, including novelty seeking, harm avoidance, and reward dependence. Applying these dimensions to the above scenario, one might predict that a boy who was high in novelty seeking, but low in harm avoidance and reward dependence, would be likely to disregard his mother's discouragement of baseball. On the other hand, a boy who was low in novelty seeking, but high in harm avoidance and reward dependence, would be more likely to need the rewards of maternal approval, would be less likely to seek and encounter male role models outside the family, and would be more likely to avoid baseball for fear of being hurt. In the absence of encouragement from an accepting father or alternative male role model, such a boy would be likely to feel different from his male peers and as a consequence be subject to nonerotic experiences in childhood that may contribute to the subsequent emergence of homoerotic preferences. Such experiences could include those described by Friedman (1988) as being common in pre-homosexual boys, including low masculine self-regard, isolation, scapegoating, and rejection by male peers and older males including the father. [60]

If there is a biological influence on the origin of homosexual orientation, it apparently has an indirect action which might be mediated through any number of pathways of gender differentiation: biological, psychological, social, and interactional.[61]

At the present time, we may tentatively conclude that the main source for gender and sexual behavior is found in social learning and psychological development variables,[62] although we should recognize that there remains the theoretical possibility that biological abnormalities could contribute a potential vulnerability factor in some indirect way.[63] A great deal more exacting research is needed to clarify the causes of homosexuality.

RELIGIOUS AND MORAL FACTORS

Finally, the oldest explanation for the development of sexual orientation is found in religious thought. Gallup polls have repeatedly documented, over a span of decades, that the vast majority of American parents endorse religious beliefs and values.[64] Homosexuality in particular has received attention in the predominant religions of the American people, the Judaic and Christian traditions. Both of these traditions share a view that things have gone greatly wrong with all individuals, and that the very nature of humanity has been wounded. While maintaining that homosexual behavior is wrong and to be avoided, these traditions do not classify homosexuality as a unique form of sin.[65] White, a psychiatrist and conservative Christian, argues that "*Homosexual* is a morally loaded term. It should be confined to those who engage in homosexual acts. The people we label may have neither the wish nor even the impulse to engage in such acts, and we have no right to besmirch them. On the other hand, we must grasp that homosexual behavior is not in any sense inevitable in someone who engages in it. It may be understandable. But no homosexual (certainly no Christian homosexual) has the right to say, 'I am not responsible for what I do because my homosexual nature *makes me* do it.'"[66] "Now having said all this," he continues, "let us make no mistake about what the Bible condemns. Nowhere is a man or woman condemned for having homosexual feelings. *It is the act, not the urge, that is condemned.*"[67]

Arguments about whether homosexuality is biological or inherited are secondary to arguments about whether or not it is *moral.*[68] Dallas declares that "even if it can be proven that genetic or biological influences predispose people toward homosexuality, that will never prove that homosexuality is in and of itself normal."[69] I have argued elsewhere that "it is an epistemological error to base value decisions on empirical data alone. For example, parents may reject dishonesty or homosexual behavior on moral grounds, regardless of what percentage of the population happily engages in those behaviors."[70]

The precise sequence and interaction of variables involved in the etiology of homosexual orientation are not yet completely understood,[71] but a number of plausible developmental theories have been advanced.[72]

I have published eighty academic articles and book chapters on my research on the assessment and treatment of childhood gender identity and behavior disorders. Since 1980, "gender identity disorder of childhood" has been a diagnosis in the Diagnostic and Statistical Manual of Mental Disorders of the American Psychological Association. With major research grants from the National Institute of Mental Health, I have demonstrated experimentally an effective treatment for "gender identity disorder of childhood" that appears to hold potential for preventing homosexual orientation in males, if applied extensively in the population.[73]

In the context of this review of the literature on the formation of homosexual orientation, an integration of these data[74] indicate the need for the prevention and compassionate early treatment of homosexual orientation in childhood and adolescence.[75]

3

The Origins and Therapy
of Same-Sex Attraction Disorder

Richard Fitzgibbons

For twenty years I have journeyed beside courageous men and women as they have struggled toward freedom from same-sex attraction disorder (SSAD). This disorder can enslave a person much as a powerful drug can, and the results are often fatal. Research indicates that 50 percent of men with same-sex attractions will be HIV-positive by age fifty, the majority will have more than twenty sexual partners per year, and less than 9 percent of those with same-sex attractions will have relationships that last more than three years. Unstable commitment to a partner and the concomitant lack of fulfillment leads to the rampant promiscuity and mood and substance-abuse disorders typical of the homosexual lifestyle.

Most Americans are unaware that AIDS has been granted "epidemic exceptionalism" and is rarely treated in the same manner as other, less dangerous sexually transmitted diseases. AIDS activists have fought all attempts to require the reporting of infections, tracing of contacts, and mandatory testing for high risk persons. Despite claims that extensive educational programs, coupled with widespread use of condoms, have contained the epidemic among men who have sex with men, the majority of men in the homosexual lifestyle will become HIV-positive, in part because almost 40 percent regularly engage in unsafe sexual practices. Several studies have been done recently on high risk behavior among adolescent males who have sex with men. The results are alarming because, though almost all adolescents are aware of the risk, 38 percent engage in unprotected sex. The fruits of this behavior is sadly predictable; in one study, nine percent of homosexual males between the ages of twenty and twenty-two were already HIV-positive.

Frequently, those young males in middle school or high school who have soft masculine traits as a result of a distant father relationship or lack of athletic ability are referred to homosexual support groups in their schools. Within such groups, these youngsters are usually encouraged to enter the homosexual lifestyle. They are not warned of the serious physical and emotional dangers inherent in the lifestyle, nor are they told that freedom from same-sex attractions is even possible.

In *Sexual Ecology: Aids and the Destiny of Gay Men*, Gabrielle Rotello, a well-known homosexual activist, has had the courage to present the truth about the dangers of the current homosexual lifestyle: "Each new homosexual generation is being replenished by heterosexuals whose production of gay sons is entirely unrelated to the dynamics of the epidemic. AIDS, therefore, can keep mowing down gay men and rather than dying out, phalanx after phalanx will emerge from the trenches, ready to be mowed down anew. The epidemic could literally go on forever."

Exposing the rampant sexual addiction and narcissism, as well as the return of unprotected anal sex and illegal drug usage, within the gay community, Rotello paints a grim picture of the future: "Who wants to encourage their kids to engage in a life that exposes them to a fifty percent chance of HIV infection? Who even wants to be neutral about such a possibility? If the rationale behind social tolerance of homosexuality is that it allows gay kids an equal shot at the pursuit of happiness, that rationale is hopelessly undermined by an endless epidemic that negates happiness." In other words, Rotello recognizes the possible consequences if the public learns that a teenager who is referred to a homosexual support group in high school has a 50 percent chance of becoming

HIV-positive before he is 50 years of age. Rotello understands the effect that such knowledge will have on the homosexual liberation movement because "an endless AIDS epidemic would essentially hand anti-gay forces their greatest gift: seeming proof that liberated homosexuality, inevitably, leads to disease and self-destruction." Rotello's conclusion is accurate: Involvement in a homosexual lifestyles starts many young men down a clear path of self-destruction.

HEALING SSAD

For a number of years, my area of expertise has been in the nature and treatment of excessive anger. Through my work, it became clear to me that the most important relationship in which men and women deny their anger is the father relationship. Since anger at rejecting peers or a distant father is extremely common among men who experience same-sex attractions, many men who struggle with SSAD have come to my practice.[1]

My goal with these patients was not necessarily to change their sexual orientation, but to try to help them understand and overcome their emotional pain, which most often was the result of childhood and adolescent conflicts. In using the healing approach that I will describe, I found that many clients could resolve the emotional hurts which led to same-sex attractions and, as a result, over an extended period of time, that they were able to resolve their homosexual attractions and behaviors. The first stage of the healing process is to understand the operative emotional conflicts. There are several different origins of same-sex attraction, and in addition, there is a marked distinction between the origins of homosexual attractions in males and in females.

SSAD IN MEN

The three most important risk factors for the development of SSAD in men are weak masculine identity, mistrust of women, and narcissism.

Weak Masculine Identity

Weak masculine identity is easily identified and, in my clinical experience, is the major cause of SSAD in men. Surprisingly, it can be an outgrowth of weak eye-hand coordination which results in an inability to play sports well. This condition is usually accompanied by severe peer rejection. In a sports oriented culture such as our own, if a young boy is unable to throw, catch, or kick a ball, he is likely to be excluded, isolated, and ridiculed. Continued rejection can be a major source of conflict for a child and teenager. In an attempt to overcome feelings of loneliness and inadequacy, he may spend more time on academic studies or fostering comfortable friendships with girls. The "sports wound" will negatively affect the boy's image of himself, his relationships with peers, his gender identity, and his body image. His negative view of his masculinity and his loneliness can lead him to crave the masculinity of his male peers.

The second and crucial conflict in the development of a weak masculine identity is a poor emotional relationship with the father. A number of therapists characterize the childhood experiences of the homosexual adult as a form of defensive detachment from a disappointing father. As children and adolescents, these men yearned for acceptance, praise, and physical affection from their fathers, but their needs were never met. The profound inner void that develops from a lack of physical affection and father love can lead a man to promiscuous behavior in a misguided attempt to fill an emotional emptiness.

Another reason that some men have a weak masculine identity is poor body image. I have found that many active homosexual men are totally obsessed with other men's bodies. They often express hatred for their own bodies and desire the bodies of other men. A final reason can be a history of sexual abuse by older, more powerful children or by adults. Such abuse over a prolonged period of time may have made the child believe that he must be a homosexual.

Mistrust of Women

The second most common cause of SSAD among males is a mistrust of women's love. Feelings of mistrust may develop as a result of a difficult mother relationship or from experiences of betrayal by women. Male children in fatherless homes often feel overly responsible for their mothers. As they enter their adolescence, they may come to view female love as draining and exhausting. They want a relationship that is lighthearted and enjoyable and, by default, turn to male love. Feelings of mistrust may also arise from having a mother who was chemically addicted, overly controlling, possessive, or emotionally distant. A very small percentage of homosexual men have experienced such devastating female betrayal in personal or professional relationships that they fear and avoid female love. Subsequently, they only feel safe making themselves vulnerable to a person of the same sex.

Narcissism and Sexual Addiction

Narcissism is defined in the DSM-IV as "a pervasive pattern of grandiosity, need for admiration, and a lack of empathy." The narcissistic person is preoccupied with fantasies of unlimited success, power, brilliance, beauty, or ideal love. For the homosexual narcissist, the goal is the pursuit of pleasure. A certain segment of the homosexual community expresses narcissism by promoting total and absolute sexual freedom. They advocate the pleasures of anonymous sex and insist that the freedom to engage in the most extreme behaviors is an essential part of homosexual liberation. Most homosexual persons with narcissistic personalities are not interested in any healing. Narcissism may also explain an extreme irresponsibility in sexual practices.

In 1994, one study found that a newly diagnosed AIDS patient had an average of sixty sexual partners in the previous year. Other reports are even more frightening and lend credence to the speculation that many male homosexuals suffer from an addictive disorder. The first men diagnosed with AIDS reported an average of one thousand partners during their lives. Those who have researched the HIV-AIDS epidemic have noted that some homosexual males actually have five to ten sexual encounters in a single night.

Other causes of Same-Sex Attraction Disorder are loneliness, rebellion for its own sake (or against Judeo-Christian values), and even the desire to punish a parent. Some people develop an excessive sense of responsibility and attempt to find relief in homosexual behaviors. Gerard Van den Aardweg, a Dutch psychologist, believes self-pity is an important factor in homosexual attractions. Finally, increasing numbers of young people become involved in sexual experimentation and develop an addiction to same-sex activity.

SSAD IN WOMEN

The major conflicts that lead to SSAD in women are, in my opinion, a mistrust of men's love, a weak feminine identity, or intense loneliness.

Mistrust of Men

A number of women who become involved in same-sex relationships had fathers who were emotionally insensitive, alcoholic, or abusive. Such women, as a result of painful childhood and teenage experiences, have good reason to fear being vulnerable to men.

Women who have been betrayed by a man after a long-term relationship often fear trusting other men and seek relief from their loneliness through involvement in homosexual relationships. Women who have been sexually abused or raped as children or adolescents may find it difficult or almost impossible to trust men. They may, therefore, turn to a woman for affection and to fulfill their sexual desires.

Weak Feminine Identity

The second most common cause of SSAD in women is a weak femi-

With admiration and gratitude
for those who have courageously struggled
with the affliction of same-sex attraction,
and for those who have dedicated their lives
to helping them.

nine identity. Three basic areas of conflict lead to such difficulty: mother conflicts, peer rejection, and poor body image. In those cases that involve maternal conflict, the woman usually had a mother who was emotionally distant and who had difficulty in affirming her child's femininity. Such negligence can lead to an inner sadness and emptiness which no amount of adult love can overcome. This condition is far more rare than weak masculine identity, and this is why, in my view, male homosexuality is much more common then female homosexuality. The female role model, the mother, is much more likely to be affirming, to be giving, to be nurturing to her daughter than the father to his son.

Loneliness

Finally for some women, loneliness is also a major factor in the development of homosexual attractions. A number of women in their late twenties or early thirties have spent considerable time in a disappointing search for the right male relationship. The resultant loneliness and disillusionment about men may lead them into a sexual relationship with a woman.

PREVENTION

As I noted, many of the emotional conflicts that lead to SSAD begin very early, and this may explain why some homosexuals feel they were born that way. Early identification of possible conflicts offers hope that prevention is possible. Boys with poor hand-eye coordination and poor father relationships can be easily identified. If the fathers or surrogate fathers become extremely active in these boy's lives and talk to them about masculine identity and what it means to be a man, it can make a difference. It is important for these boys to know that it is possible to be a good, strong man without playing sports.

Prevention of the father wound would involve making sure that every little boy receives physical affection from his father. In this regard, I agree with Jeffrey Satinover and a number of others who have emphasized the need for warmth between father and son. Because in our culture almost 40 percent of children will spend some time in a home without a father, where their needs are not met, I predict that there will be a notable increase in the incidence of SSAD.

Overview of the Healing Process

The boy who has been betrayed either by his peers or by his father does not simply accept the hurts that were inflicted—he often reacts to them with sadness, anger, and feelings of insecurity. The work of therapy is, in part, to understand and resolve the betrayal pain. Betrayal anger is one of the major reasons a notable element of sado-masochism is found in homosexual practices. When the extreme sado-masochistic behaviors engaged in by homosexual men are reported, most people are shocked. They do not stop to consider the possibility that people who abuse others or allow themselves to be abused in violent, dangerous, and unhealthy practices may be driven by unresolved betrayal anger and feelings of inadequacy or other psychological forces. If the same type of behaviors took place among heterosexuals, the identical acts would be considered forms of abuse and evidence of a disorder, yet they are considered "normal" among homosexual men.

It has been my clinical experience that the degree of emotional pain in our culture can be so profound that there is no mental health technique that can totally resolve this pain without a spiritual component. My approach is very similar to one used in the field of addictive disorders. Those involved in the treatment of alcoholism and addiction to drugs find that significant healing rarely occurs unless some form of spirituality is brought into the healing process by turning the emotional pain and compulsive behaviors over to a higher power.

In summary, it is necessary to identify the emotional conflicts, uncover and treat the anger, attempt to resolve the sadness, overcome profound feelings of inadequacy, and build trust.

Therapy

The individuals in the groups described are quite different. Not only are the causes of their emotional struggles quite diverse, but the behaviors and level of desire to seek treatment may also be part of the equation. Men and women who suffer from a weak masculine or feminine identity or a mistrust of the opposite sex are generally more open to therapy than those who fall into other categories. Frequently, young men come into treatment because of a fear of AIDS, an inability to establish healthy committed relationships, and the fear of an early death. They are tired of the lack of commitment they have found in the homosexual lifestyle, and they do not want to continue to be used any longer as sexual objects.

The treatment I have described involves the identification of the causes of SSAD. For many people there is considerable resistance, particularly in the examination of their relationship with their father. The therapist can lead the client to recognize that though many men have not had a particularly close father relationship, most do not have same-sex attractions. Most men who did not have close father relationships had their masculinity affirmed through involvement in team sports and in other activities with their male peers. They bonded with other males through sports, affirming their masculinity over a period of time.

In addressing a lack of involvement by the father in the life of a son, the approach that seems to be successful is to help the client face the pain, resolve the betrayal anger by working at understanding and forgiving his father, and be healed of the craving for father love. The latter is accomplished through spiritual reflection on God as a loving father.

A common pattern of reaction to emotional pain can be observed and identified. When a person is hurt in a relationship a series of reactions occur. First sadness develops, then anger accompanied by low self esteem, and finally a loss of trust. It is essential to resolve the anger associated with all these types of betrayal pain. The majority of therapists have recognized two methods of dealing with anger—the denial of the anger or the expression of it.

The expression of anger is important, but has limitations as a means of coping with anger. The adult expression of anger does not resolve the anger which began in childhood and adolescence. The only way anger can be completely removed is through a process of forgiveness during which the offended person becomes willing to look at the people who caused his suffering, attempt to understand them, and then make a decision to give up his anger. The person imagines himself as a boy or teenager, expresses disappointment and anger at those who hurt him—for example, rejecting peers or a distant father—and then tries to reflect upon forgiving the offender so that he can be freed from the pain of the past.

Giving up the anger through forgiveness can be done on three levels: intellectual, emotional, and spiritual. In order to forgive intellectually, a man who has same-sex attractions can reflect on his experience with his father: "Did my father really love me as much as he was able to love me? Perhaps my father communicated his love as he experienced it from his own father. He didn't deliberately mean to hurt me." As he comes to understand his father's family history, he usually finds it easier to let go of the anger. It is possible that forgiveness may stay at the intellectual level for an extended period, but with perseverance emotional forgiveness will follow. It can be identified easily, for it happens when the person truly feels like forgiving the offender. The third level is spiritual forgiveness. It occurs when the person is unable to forgive intellectually or emotionally. This type of forgiveness is used by those who were regularly rejected or ridiculed by their peers because of their inability to play sports or who were severely traumatized by a parent or loved one.

Most of the males who were scapegoated when they were younger, simply because they were not good at sports, can experience tremendous repressed anger later in life. Many were ridiculed, beaten, and called "queer" or "faggot" by peers, and even by adults, and they harbor violent impulses as a result. When the therapist asks them to imagine releasing their anger against those who ridiculed them, many are surprised to discover that they feel as if they would like to physically hurt their tormentors. Spiritual forgiveness for the men I described involves a process borrowed from the twelve steps of Alcoholics Anonymous. The angry person is encouraged to think: "I am powerless and want to turn this resentment over to God," or "revenge belongs to God."

In the process of resolving a client's betrayal anger at peers, parents, or others, the therapist may lead the client back and forth on the three levels of forgiveness. It is not unusual that the injured person may feel like forgiving one day, and the very next day feel only hatred for the people who hurt him. Tremendous patience is needed by both the therapist and client during this part of the struggle for freedom from the pain of the past.

When the betrayal anger is resolved significantly, the individual is left with an inner emptiness and a sadness resulting from the lack of acceptance by peers. The person has often attempted to fill the emptiness experienced in childhood or adolescence with numerous sexual encounters but it is an emptiness that is never satisfied sexually. The experience of this void is the fundamental emotional dynamic that fuels the promiscuous behavior in those with homosexual attractions. Nothing seems to fill the sadness or make up for what that little child or that teenager failed to receive from his peers or from his father or mother.

It is possible for a therapist to praise and affirm his clients, but such a technique reaches only the adult, not the child and teenager within. Some therapists use strategies that involve going back and suggesting that the adult love the little boy or little girl within. Since the adult still wants to be loved at the stage where the deprivation took place, such strategies are of limited value. It is helpful, therefore, to have clients reflect on earlier stages of their lives and, using practices learned as part of a Judeo-Christian heritage, meditate on being loved when they did not feel loved. If they did not have a father to love them as a child, they can work on their sense of God as a loving Father. Christians who were regularly ridiculed and belittled as youngsters are encouraged to meditate on the Lord with them as a friend and a brother loving them on sports or athletic fields. For those who are Catholic, meditating upon Mary as a loving and joyful mother with them as children and teenagers can be very consoling and comforting.[2]

Experience has taught me that healing is a difficult process, but through the mutual efforts of the therapist and the client, serious emotional wounds can be healed over a period of time. For example, for those with sports wounds, it is necessary to work to strengthen their masculine identity. The individual should spend time daily being thankful for his God-given male gifts and masculinity in childhood, adolescence, and adult life. As his identity is strengthened, homosexual attractions usually diminish and usually, over time, they are extinguished. Then these individuals may develop heterosexual attractions or, in the case of clergy, have a stronger desire to be faithful to their vows. Peter Rudegeair, an associate of mine, has group therapy sessions for those with sports wounds who need to strengthen their masculine identity. With the father wound, as George Rekers has said, if the person is younger, every effort should be made to get the father more involved in his life. Frequently, however, the father is no longer available and so the therapist can affirm the person's unique identity and strengthen his ability to form non-sexual masculine relationships.

Unfortunately, rather than encourage young men and women to take this path to facing and resolving emotional pain, many mental health professionals, even those who claim to espouse Judeo-Christian values, tell these young men and women that God has made them this way, that this is who they are meant to be. But this is not who they are meant to be. They are the way they are because they were wounded deeply in the past. Healing and freedom from emotional woundedness is possible.

Sexual addiction may likewise be a major problem with many in the homosexual lifestyle. Considering the number of sexual partners, dangerous behaviors, and other negative aspects typical of the homosexual lifestyle, it is difficult to understand how people can claim that there is no disorder present. Sexual addiction with extreme narcissism causes serious illnesses and early deaths in many young men and we must take some steps to change a very dangerous trend. In dealing with sexual addiction, Prozac or other anti-depressants can help to a degree. They will cut down sexually compulsive behaviors, but they will not resolve the emotional pain leading to the attractions.

Sexual trauma in childhood predisposes people toward homosexual behavior and can be extremely difficult to treat. One can work at trying to help the client understand and resolve the anger against the abuser, if for no other reason than to alleviate the abuser's negative influence. We need to help those who have been abused before they become sexually addicted or involved in sado-masochistic practices. Only when, through forgiveness, they are free from their anger and from this dark side of abuse will they be able to develop a healthy identity.

Our schools need to take a proactive stance in this time of crisis. The practice of turning at-risk children and adolescents over to groups which usher them into a homosexual lifestyle can be fatal. Homosexual tendencies can be recognized early and treatment is available.

It is a time of real crisis, but we are not without hope. While the mental health field is a new field, we know how to identify the origins of same-sex attractions and behaviors. We have treatment for weak masculine and feminine identity, for mistrust of those of the opposite sex, for betrayal anger, for sexual addiction and for the other conflicts associated with same-sex attraction disorder. As a therapist I deal with the psychological. Yet I must admit there is little meaningful healing without the use of spirituality. If we combine spirituality and good psychotherapy, as in the treatment of alcoholism, we can expect resolution and healing for those who struggle with same-sex attractions and behaviors.

4

The Gay Deception

Joseph Nicolosi

I WOULD LIKE TO PROPOSE a socio-analytic view of the formation of "gay" identity. This view is based upon the perspective I have gained from the clinical treatment of over four hundred homosexually-oriented men during eighteen years as a practicing psychologist.

"Gay" is, I believe, a self-deceptive identity. It has been brilliantly marketed and bought without question by the most influential institutions—professional psychology and psychiatry, churches, educators, and the media—of American society.

"Homosexual" Is Not "Gay"

We begin with the understanding that I will *not* discuss the person who struggles with same-sex attraction, but rather the gay-*identified* person—a person who is personally identified with the idea that homosexual behavior is as normal and natural as heterosexual behavior. A man who recognizes that he has a homosexual problem and struggles to overcome it is not "gay." He is, simply, "homosexual."

Second, I wish to make clear my belief that there is no such thing as a gay person. Gay is a *fictitious identity* seized upon by an individual to resolve painful emotional challenges. To consider that the concept of a gay identity is valid, a person must necessarily deny significant aspects of human nature. The foundation for the gay identity is typically laid during early childhood.

I propose a three-step, psycho-social model for the development of a gay identity—first, we see the gender distortion of the prehomosexual child; second, his eventual assimilation into the gay counterculture, reinforcing those same distortions; and finally, we see the expansion of the gay community's successful *self*-deception into the further deception of a large portion of society.

EARLY GENDER IDENTITY

At a critical developmental period called the gender-identity phase, the child discovers that the world is divided between male and female. Which one is he going to be? He is personally challenged to assume maleness or femaleness—"Am I a boy? Or am I a girl?" (I will discuss primarily boys, because there are some variations for the lesbian.)

Confronted with the reality of a gendered world, male and female, and forced to make a choice, the child may first resort to an avoidance strategy—regressing into an androgynous phase: "I need not relinquish the benefits of either sex. I can be both male and female." In psychoanalytic terms, he can have a penis and make babies. However, reality pushes in and language now enters, and he hears "he" and "she," and "his" and "hers."

Both boys and girls are first identified with the mother—the "first love object"—but the boy has the additional developmental task of disidentifying from the mother and identifying with the father. We must make no mistake about this: Masculinity, as Robert Stoller said, is an achievement. The child—especially the boy—has to work not only for the acquisition of identity, but for the acquisition of gender. Every culture that has ever survived understands this matter of the "achievement" of gender, and will support and assist the boy through rites of passage and male initiation.

Increasingly we are abandoning support of our boys' formation of masculine identity, particularly the support needed from parents. For the boy, the father is most important in the identification process. If the father is warm and receptive and inviting, the boy will disidentify with his mother and bond with his father to fulfill his natural masculine strivings. If the father is cold, detached, harsh, or even simply disinterested, the boy may reach out, but eventually will feel hurt and discouraged and will surrender his natural masculine inclinations, returning to his mother.

There is no convincing scientific evidence of a "gay gene," but certain boys do seem especially vulnerable to homosexual development. Clinical experience indicates that a boy who is sensitive, passive, gentle, and aesthetically oriented may be more easily discouraged from the developmental challenge to gender-identify with his father. A tougher, bolder, thicker-skinned son may well succeed in surmounting an emotional barrier, but a sensitive son thinks, "I can't be male, but I'm not completely female either; so I will remain in my own little androgynous world, my secret place of fantasy." This androgynous fantasy is a fundamental feature of gay culture and implies not only the narcissistic refusal to identify with a gendered culture, but the refusal to identify with the *human biological reality* upon which our gendered society is based. In fact, gender—a core feature of personal identity—is central to the way we relate to ourselves and others. It is also a central pathway through which we grow to maturity.

A host of studies confirm the correlation between childhood gender nonconformity, which is suggestive of gender-identity confusion, and later homosexuality. Not all homosexuality develops this way, but this is a common developmental pathway. We hear echoes of this theme over and over in gay literature—the repeated story of the prehomosexual boy who is isolated and "on the outs" with male friends, who feels different, insecure in his maleness, lonely, and detached from his father, and retreats back to mother.

Because gender, for many who identify themselves as gay, was such a source of pain in childhood, the annihilation of gender differences is—not surprisingly—a central theme of gay culture. Gays often call their attitude "an indifference to gender." One well-

known theorist, himself a gay man, spoke recently of his own uto-
pian society as a "non-gender-polarizing culture" in which everyone would potentially be anyone else's lover.

DETACHMENT FROM SELF AND OTHERS

The person who accepts the gay label in adulthood, then, has typically spent much of his childhood emotionally disconnected from
people, particularly his male peers and his father. He also has likely
assumed a false, rigid, "good little boy" role within the family.

The emotionally disconnected reveal themselves in their view
of their family life: "I was a non-entity. I didn't have a place to
feel"; "I always acted out other people's scripts for me. I was an
actor in other people's plays"; "My parents watched me grow up"; "I
watched myself grow up." The quality of detachment from self is
unmistakable—"I *watched myself* grow up." No wonder the pre-
homosexual boy is often interested in theatre and acting. Life is
theatre. We are all actors. Reality is what we wish it to be. In the
absence of an authentic identity, it is easy to self-reinvent. Oscar
Wilde (who probably was the first person to give a face to "gay")
asserted that "Naturalness is just another pose." Without domestic
emotional bonds to ground him in organic identity, the gay man is
plastic. He is the transformist, a Victor-Victoria, or the character
from *La Cage Aux Folles*. He is pretender, jokester—what French
psychoanalyst Chasseguet-Smirgel calls "the imposter."

Freud claimed that "The father is the reality principle." The
father represents the transition from the blissful mother-child sym-
biosis to harsh reality. But the prehomosexual boy says to himself,
"If my father makes me unimportant, I make *him* unimportant. If
he rejects me, I reject *him* and all that he represents." Here we see
the infantile power of "no"—"My father has nothing to teach me.
His power to procreate and affect the world are nothing compared
to my fantasy world. What he accomplishes, I can dream. Dream
and reality are the same." Rather than striving to discover his own
masculine, procreative power, he chooses, instead, to stay in the
dreamy, good-little-boy role. Detached, not only from father and

other boys, but from maleness and his own male body—including the first symbol of masculinity, his own penis—he will later try to find healing through another man's penis. That is what homosexual behavior is: the search for the lost masculine self.

Since anatomically-grounded gender is a core feature of individual identity, the homosexual has not so much a sexual problem as an identity problem. He has a sense of not being a part of other people's lives. It follows that narcissism and preoccupation with self are commonly observed in male homosexuals. In his early teenage years, unconscious drives to fill this emotional vacuum—to want to connect with his maleness—are felt as homoerotic desires. The next stage will be entry into the gay world.

Then, for the first time in his life, this lonely, alienated young man meets (through gay romance novels from the library, television personalities, or internet chat rooms) people who share the same feelings. But he gets more than empathy. Along with the empathy comes an entire package of new ideas and concepts about sex, gender, human relationships, anatomical relationships, and personal destiny.

Next, he experiences that heady, euphoric, pseudo-rite-of-passage called "coming out of the closet." It is just one more constructed role to distract him from the deeper, more painful issue of self-identity. Gay identity is not "discovered" as if it existed *a priori* as a natural trait. Rather, it is a culturally approved process of *self-reinvention* by a group of people in order to mask their collective emotional hurts. This false claim to have finally found one's authentic identity through gayness is perhaps the most dangerous of all the false roles attempted by the young person seeking identity and belonging. At this point, he has gone from compliant, "good little boy" of childhood, to sexual outlaw. One of the benefits of membership in the gay subculture is the support and reinforcement he receives for reverting to fantasy as a method of problem solving.

THE FANTASY OPTION

He is now able to do collectively what he did alone as a child. When reality is painful, he chooses the fantasy option: "I have merely to redefine myself and redefine the world. If others won't play my game, I'll charm and manipulate them. If that doesn't work, I'll have a temper tantrum."

The lonely child receives awesome benefits of membership by assuming the gay self-label. He receives unlimited sex and unlimited power by turning reality on its head. He enjoys vindication of early childhood hurts. Plus as an added bonus, he gets to reject his rejecting father and similarly, the Judeo-Christian Father-God who separated good from bad, right from wrong, truth from deception. Oscar Wilde said, "morality is simply an attitude we adopt toward people whom we personally dislike."

How has this group of hurt boys and girls—now known in adulthood as the gay community—managed to promote their make-believe liberation to the larger culture, as well as to legislators, public policy makers, universities, and churches? Three such avenues stand out for mention.

The first is the civil-rights movement, probably the single most influential force in forming the collective consciousness of American society in this century. Gay apologists have exploited *authentic* rights issues to promote their redefinition of human sexuality and, essentially, human nature. And one powerful tool that has been used time and time again is the Coming Out Story. It is that same generic story that has been repeated almost verbatim for thirty years now—from the committee rooms of the American Psychiatric Association in 1973, to the Oprah Winfrey Show. I have seen religious clergy warmly applauding coming-out stories. And why not? Because "finding oneself" and "being who one *really is*" are popular late-twentieth-century themes which have a heroic and attractive ring to them. Certainly, the person telling the story is sincere. He means what he says, but the audience rarely looks beyond his words to understand his coming-out in the larger context.

Second is the crisis in sexuality itself, prompting fundamental changes in our definition of family, community, procreation, marriage, and gender. All these changes have been brought about in the interest of the individual right to pursue sexual pleasure. But historically, although the gay rights movement followed along on the coattails of the civil-rights movement, it continues to draw its ideological power from the sexual liberation movement.

Moreover, ours is a consumer-oriented society, and consumer products shape our views of ourselves. Marketing strategists are all-too-ready to target consumer groups. Gay couples are called "DINKS"—dual income, no kids—and that means they have expendable income. Merchants have always been ready to cater to a gay clientele, and merchant-solicitors have given the gay community the face of legitimacy. Today, nearly every major corporation offers services specially tailored for homosexuals. Alcohol and cigarettes are popular gay items. We see gay resorts, gay cruises, gay theatre, gay film festivals. Gay magazines, movies, and fiction give face and theme to individuals whose essential problem is identity and belonging. Luxury items—jewelry, fashions, furnishings, and cosmetics—are ready to soothe, flatter, and gratify a hurting minority. But beyond material reassurance, these luxury items equate gay identity with economic success—the gay life is the good life.

We suffer, at this time, a cultural vulnerability to the rhetoric of gay liberation. Chasseguet-Smirgel claims that the "pervert" (in the traditional psychoanalytic sense of the term) confuses two essential human realities: the distinction between the generations and the distinction between the sexes. In gay ideology, we see just this sort of obliteration of differences. Midge Decter observes, for example, that we treat our children like adults (we have only to look at sex education in elementary school), at the same time that adults are acting like children. A number of contemporary movements, including the animal rights movement (with its idea that man is no higher than animals), also exemplify the confusion. As animal liberationist and founder of PETA Ingrid Newkirk says, "a rat . . . is a pig . . . is a dog . . . is a boy." There are movements to break down the barriers between generations: Witness the recent change in the definition of pedophilia and the publishing of the double *Journal of Homosexuality* issue, "Male Intergenerational Love" (an apologia for pedophilia). Thus we see animal confused with human, sacred confused with profane, adult confused with child, male confused with female, and life confused with death—all of these, *tradition-ally the most profound of distinctions and separations*, are now under siege.

We cannot escape these confusions even in children's films. In the recent animated Disney film, *The Lion King*, we see the age-old generational link in the proud and loving relationship between the father, Mufasa, king of the lions, and his little son, Simba, the future king. They live in the balanced, ordered world of the lion kingdom. But Scar, the brooding, resentful brother of the king, lives his life on the margins of society and is full of envy and anger. It has been argued that Scar is a gay figure.

In the film, Scar ruptures the link between the generations by killing the Lion King and aligning himself with a scavenger pack of hyenas. Thus Scar turns the ordered lion kingdom into chaos and ruin. Before all this occurs, however, we hear a brief, light-hearted exchange between the young male cub, Simba, and his uncle, Scar. Laughingly, Simba says, "Uncle Scar, you're weird." Meaningfully, Scar replies, "You have no idea."

A Collective Illusion

"Gay" is a counter-identity, a negative. By that I mean it gets its psychic energy by *"what I am not,"* and is an infantile refusal to accept reality. It is a compromise identity seized upon by an individual, and increasingly supported by our society, to resolve emotional conflicts. It is a collective illusion; truly, I believe, "the gay deception."

5

THE AIDS PANDEMIC

Patrick Derr

THIS PAPER OFFERS A SKETCH of the global HIV pandemic, with special attention to the ways in which the politics of homosexuality in the United States has distorted both our perception of and our national response to that pandemic.

Readers unfamiliar with epidemiological data will need brief defiinitions of key terms: *Incidence* is a measure of *new* cases; *Prevalence* is a measure of *existing* cases; *Cumulative cases* is a measure of the *total* number of cases, whether new, existing, or deceased, since the beginning of the pandemic. Hence, HIV incidence in a given region in a given year is a measure of the new infections occurring in that region in that year, while HIV prevalence is a measure of total number of infected persons alive in that region in that year. Incidence and prevalence are typically reported as rates per one hundred thousand population per year.

HIV (*H*uman *I*mmunodeficiency *V*irus) is the virus which causes AIDS; it is a bloodborne virus, and, like most bloodborne viruses, is generally transmitted by blood, sexual contact, or mother-child contact during pregnancy or lactation. AIDS (*A*cquired *I*mmune *D*eficiency *S*yndrome) is the result of long-term HIV infection. In order to understand the epidemiological data below, it is critical to remember that the average time required for initial HIV infection to progress to AIDS (the so-called *latency period*) is more than ten years. Data on AIDS incidence, thus, is properly understood as a *ten year old* report on HIV incidence: to know that the AIDS *incidence* in Washington D.C. was 232 per one hundred thousand in 1996, is to know, roughly, that in 1986—when the epidemic was much younger and smaller—HIV incidence (the new HIV infection rate) in Washington D.C. was 232 per one hundred thousand.

The account which follows draws on more than two hundred sources, most of which will be almost two years old as this book goes to press.* In some, and perhaps most, developing countries, actual HIV prevalence may, by late 1998, be as much as double the levels reported here. Moreover, the surveys, reports, estimates and projections assembled here—although drawn from the best sources, national and international, public and private—are collectively incomplete and often mutually inconsistent. This account must not be considered definitive. At best, it is a prudent and well-informed approximation. The sad but utterly uncontroversial truth is that no one knows the exact size, shape, or trajectory of the global HIV pandemic. In some areas, such as China, it is possible that the best reports err by whole orders of magnitude.

Finally, beneath all the numbing epidemiological data lies a human tragedy of unprecedented scope and intensity, a global catastrophe which will soon claim more lives than all the wars that mankind has fought. Dismissed as alarmist only five years ago, expert projections of more than five hundred million AIDS deaths by 2050 are now common and sadly credible. It is for us, the educated adults of the world's industrial democracies, to confirm or refute Adolph Eichmann's claim that a few deaths are a tragedy, but a million are just a statistic.

THE DEVELOPING WORLD

In mid-July 1996, an estimated 21.8 million adults and children worldwide were living with HIV-AIDS, of whom 20.4 million (94

---

* An annotated bibliographic note on the pandemic appears on p. 283.

percent) were in the developing world. Nineteen million of these adults and children (86 percent of the world total) were living with HIV/AIDS in sub-Saharan Africa or in South and Southeast Asia. Of the adults, 12.2 million (58 percent) were male and 8.8 million (42 percent) were female.

Worldwide during 1995, there were 2.7 million new adult HIV infections (roughly 7,400 new infections per day); about 1 million of these (nearly three thousand per day) occurred in Southeast Asia, and 1.4 million (roughly four thousand per day) in sub-Saharan Africa. The entire industrialized world—including Western Europe, Japan, and the U. S.—accounted for only about fifty-five thousand new HIV infections (2 percent of the global total) in 1995.

Also in 1995, approximately five hundred thousand children were born with HIV infection. Of these children, 67 percent were in sub-Saharan Africa, 30 percent in South and Southeast Asia, and 2 to 3 percent in Latin America and the Caribbean. Only a small fraction of 1 percent were born in Western Europe, Japan, and the U.S.

From the beginning of the pandemic until mid-1996, an estimated 27.9 million people worldwide have been infected with HIV, including nineteen million (68 percent of the global total) in sub-Saharan Africa and five million (18 percent of the global total) in South and Southeast Asia. Since the beginning of the pandemic, 93 percent of all HIV infections—twenty-six million—have occurred in the developing world. Worldwide, the cumulative number of HIV infections among adults more than doubled between 1990 (about 10 million) and mid-1996 (25.5 million).

As of July 1996, more than 7.6 million persons had progressed from HIV infection to AIDS, and 75 percent (4.5 million adults and 1.3 million children) had already died. Of the six million adults, 4.5 million (75 percent) were in sub-Saharan Africa, four hundred thousand (7 percent) were in Latin America and the Caribbean, 0.75 million (12 percent) were in North America, Western Europe and Japan. In South and Southeast Asia, where the pandemic has only recently gained intensity, 0.33 million adults have already progressed to AIDS. Of the 1.6 million children, 1.4 million (85 percent) were in sub-Saharan Africa.[1]

According to the World Health Organization, the number of AIDS orphans in developing countries may reach ten million by the year 2000. Also by the year 2000, forty to fifty million men, women, and children will be infected with HIV, nearly all in developing countries.

By the end of 1995, the AIDS pandemic had already deeply undermined national development in many sub-Saharan nations. On the UNDP Human Development Index (HDI), Zambia had lost more than ten development years, Tanzania eight years, Rwanda seven years and the Central African Republic more than six years. Burundi, Kenya, Malawi, Uganda and Zimbabwe had lost between three and five years. Hard-won gains in child survival, life expectancy, and economic development are rapidly being eroded.

These aggregated statistics give some indication of the scope of the global HIV pandemic and of its profoundly disproportionate impact on the peoples of the developing world. The global pandemic, however, is composed of dozens of distinct national and regional epidemics, each with its own features and force. The following sections of this report will survey some of these distinct regional and national epidemics.

ASIA

HIV is spreading rapidly in Asia, which contains sixty percent of the world's adult population and had barely been touched by HIV ten years ago. An estimated three to six million people in India and 0.8 to one million people in Thailand are now infected with HIV. Cambodia, Malaysia, Myanmar, Vietnam, and China all have rapidly growing epidemics. The World Health Organization (WHO) projects ten to twelve million HIV cases in Asia by the end of 1999. India alone is expected to have at least five million cases. Especially dramatic is the spread of HIV among young adults, adolescents, and children. In many Asian countries, the number of infected women now roughly equals that of men. WHO projects that sometime in 1998 or 1999, HIV incidence in Asia will equal and then surpass HIV incidence in Africa. By the year 2000, 42 percent of the world's projected forty to fifty million HIV-infected persons are expected to live in Asia.

Burma/Myanmar

The heroin trade in Southeast Asia's "Golden Triangle" is fueling an exploding HIV epidemic in Myanmar and three northeastern Indian states. In August 1996, HIV infections in Myanmar were estimated to total 350,000 to 500,000 persons.

The United Nations (UN) reports that 60 to 70 percent of injection drug users (IDUs) in Myanmar are HIV-positive. WHO estimates that there are five hundred thousand IDUs in Myanmar (1 percent of the national population); some Asian non-governmental organizations (NGOs) estimate that IDUs may number one to two million, or up to 4 percent of the Myanmar population. In Hpa Kant in Kachin State, about 50 percent of the youth are thought to be IDUs. Over the Indian border in Manipur, HIV prevalence among IDUs jumped from zero in 1988 to nearly 70 percent in 1992, according to U. S. Census Bureau research.

Cambodia

Cambodia had virtually no AIDS cases in 1991. By 1996, it had the highest HIV prevalence rate in Asia. Health officials estimate that between 100,000 and 150,000 of Cambodia's 10.5 million people, including 2.5 percent of pregnant women, were infected with HIV by the end of 1996. Of these, only about two thousand had yet progressed to AIDS.

In 1991, 0.08 percent of blood donors in Phnom Penh tested positive for HIV. In 1992, the figure was 0.8 percent. In 1994, 4.3 percent. By early 1995 the rate 6.1 percent. And by the end of 1995, 8.6 percent—*a one-hundred-fold increase in just four years.* In 1995, 8 percent of Cambodian police tested were HIV infected compared to zero percent in 1992. Also in 1995, 8 percent of Cambodian tuberculosis patients, over 8 percent of Cambodian government soldiers, and 33 percent of prostitutes tested HIV positive. By mid 1996, infection among prostitutes had risen to 41 percent.

Cambodian authorities expect the HIV epidemic to severely retard their country's economic and social development. Dr. Hor Bun Leng, Director of the National AIDS Program, said Cambodia's HIV epidemic is the most severe in southeast Asia and will begin to claim large numbers of lives in 1998: "We are looking at a tragedy in 1998 or 1999—we cannot avoid it." By the year 2000—in just the ninth year of its epidemic—the Cambodian Ministry of Health and WHO expect forty thousand AIDS deaths and 250,000 to 500,000 persons infected. In sum, HIV is spreading faster in Cambodia than in any other Asian nation, except Burma and India.

China

By August 1996, Chinese authorities had reported 4,305 HIV-positive cases. The actual number of HIV-positive people in China could be ten or even a hundred times higher; official estimates range from fifty to two hundred thousand. All but two of China's provinces, regions and municipalities have reported HIV-AIDS cases. The Ministry of Health estimates that ten thousand people are infected with HIV, but the Chinese Academy of Preventive Medicine estimated that there were 100,000 HIV-infected persons in China as of the end of 1995, and that HIV prevalence was doubling annually. If the Academy is correct, HIV prevalence could reach eight hundred thousand by 1999. By 1997, some Chinese health officials warned that an uncontrolled AIDS epidemic might be unavoidable.

India

According to the United Nations AIDS program, India now has more HIV-infected persons than any other country. At the end of 1994, WHO estimated that India had 1.75 million HIV infections. By mid-1996, 3 million infections had been diagnosed. By late 1996, five million persons may have been infected.

In Bombay, HIV prevalence in STD clinics was 36 percent in 1994. HIV prevalence among prostitutes rose from 1 percent to 51 percent between 1987 and 1993. Antenatal clinic patients tested positive at a 2.5 percent rate in 1994. In Vellore, HIV prevalence at STD clinics was 15 percent in 1995. In Manipur, HIV prevalence among IDUS was 60 percent in 1992, and 1 percent of women attending antenatal clinics were infected with HIV. In India generally, annual incidences (new HIV infections) in sex workers as high as 25 percent and in clients of almost 10 percent have been documented. Surveys found 5 to 10 percent of truck drivers in the country infected with HIV by 1995.

Indonesia

The Indonesian government officially reported 449 HIV cases in late 1996. Independent experts estimate that the actual number was between ninety-five and two hundred thousand persons. Both groups project up to 2.5 million Indonesians infected by the year 2000.

Japan

The Japanese Ministry of Health and Welfare, AIDS Surveillance Committee, reported 112 new HIV cases in 1997. If this figure is correct, Japan would have the lowest documented HIV prevalence in Asia.

Malaysia

In Malaysia, HIV prevalence among IDUS reached 20 percent in 1994. Among prostitutes, prevalence reached 10 percent in 1994. The Malaysian government reported 16,963 HIV infections in 1996; Asian and international NGOS estimate that the actual figure was thirty-five to seventy-five thousand.

Nepal

In 1996, WHO estimated that ten thousand persons in Nepal were HIV infected. No other credible data seems to be available.

Pakistan

Seroprevalence surveys performed between in mid-1995 in Lahore and Peshawar found 3.7 percent of STD clinic patients HIV infected. The rate at the Quetta tuberculosis clinic was 2.8 percent. Among Lahore IDUS, HIV prevalence was 11.5 percent.

Taiwan

Serum antibody testing of male homosexuals in southern Taiwan found that 9.5 percent were HIV infected in late 1995.

Thailand

In August, 1996, HIV infections in Thailand were estimated to total 750,000 to 800,000 persons. By 2000, more than one million persons will be infected, three hundred thousand will have died, and almost 50,000 children will be orphaned by AIDS.

By mid-1996, HIV prevalence among IDUS was between 29 and 35 percent; with incidence estimated to exceed 10 percent per year, prevalence among IDUS will likely pass 50 percent in 1998. HIV prevalence among prostitutes was 33 percent in 1994. HIV prevalence among women attending antenatal clinics reached 2.3 percent in 1995—the highest antenatal rate in all of Asia according to the Thai Health Ministry. AIDS could quash Thailand's economic growth. Direct and indirect costs of the epidemic will probably exceed ten billion dollars by the year 2000.

Among Burmese girls rescued from Thai brothels, 74 percent (fourteen of nineteen) were HIV infected. Other studies of Thai sex workers have yielded HIV prevalences between 50 percent and

100 percent. Fear of AIDS in Thailand and other countries has increased the demand for child virgins in the commercial sex industry, and numerous NGOs report that brothel agents have intensified the kidnapping of very young girls from remote villages.

There is also good news in Thailand. Among young men drafted into the Royal Thai Army, HIV prevalence rose from 10.4 percent in 1991 to 12.5 percent 1993, but dropped to 6.7 percent in 1995. The percentage of draftees who had sex with a prostitute in the previous year decreased from 57 percent in 1991 to 24 percent in 1995.

Vietnam

One percent of Vietnam's population was HIV infected at the end of 1996. HIV prevalence among IDUs was 32 percent in 1995. Prevalence among prostitutes was 38 percent in 1994-95. The National AIDS committee of Vietnam projects three hundred thousand cumulative infections by the year 2000, including twenty thousand persons with AIDS and more than fifteen thousand dead.

SUB-SAHARAN AFRICA

Sub-Saharan Africa, the original epicenter of the global HIV pandemic, accounted for 68 percent of the world's new HIV infections in 1995. By 1996, life expectancy had fallen from almost seventy to below forty in some countries. The Southern Africa Development Community calculates that AIDS will reduce regional life expectancy to forty years. In some large cities, 40 percent of pregnant women are HIV infected and 25 percent of those who die from AIDS are children. Regional prevalence was estimated to be 5 percent in 1995, and is expected to reach 20 percent in 1998. In 1996, new infections exceeded three million and deaths exceeded 1.5 million.

A French study of Central African armies in 1996 found that in seven of the armies surveyed, more than 50 percent of the troops tested were HIV-infected.

AIDS has orphaned hundreds of thousands of African chil-

dren. Many will be forced into prostitution. Many will die of star-
vation or other causes and not be counted as AIDS casualties. UN-
AIDS projects that 9 million children will be orphaned in Africa by
the year 2000.

Côte d'Ivoire

HIV prevalence among adults was estimated to be between 15 percent and 20 percent in 1996. HIV prevalence among pregnant
women was 14.8 percent in 1992. The UN projects that life expectancy will fall below thirty-five years by the year 2000.

Kenya

In early 1996, Kenya reported that 1.2 million people were infected
with HIV and that over two hundred thousand people had died of
AIDS in both 1994 and 1995. Assistant Minister for Health Basil
Criticos said that AIDS deaths in 1996 would probably reach 240,000,
and that 1.7 million Kenyans would be living with HIV infection by
early 1997. By the year 2010, average life expectancy is expected to
fall from sixty-eight to forty. Provincial Medical Officers report
that the casualties include Kenya's most productive workers. The
consequences for national development may be catastrophic.

Malawi

AIDS has claimed two hundred thousand lives in Malawi since the
first case was reported in 1985. According to WHO, the Malawian
National AIDS Control Program, and the World Bank, about 10 percent million of Malawi's eleven million people were HIV-infected
at the end of 1996. By the year 2000, two million will be infected
and 350,000 children will have lost both parents to the disease. In
1996, HIV prevalence among pregnant women was over 33 percent,
and among prostitutes was nearly 98 percent. The average life span
in Malawi is expected to decrease from fifty-seven to thirty-three.

Namibia

NGOs estimate that two hundred thousand persons (12.5 percent of the national population) was HIV-infected by mid-1996. Namibia's Health and Social Services Ministry estimates that two hundred thousand more will be infected each year. HIV prevalence could reach 30 percent in 1998 or 1999.

Nigeria

According Nigeria's Federal Ministry of Health, at least 1 million of Nigeria's 118 million people were HIV infected in 1996; independent experts believe that the figure may be two to three times higher. Some studies of young educated urban adults have found prevalence rates as high as 70 percent. More than seven million Nigerians are expected to be infected with HIV by the year 2000.

Republic of South Africa

Between 1.8 million and 2.4 million South Africans (7.8 percent to 10.4 percent of all adults) were infected with HIV by 1997. Between 0.6 million and 1.4 million new infections were expected in 1997. In late 1996, nearly 20 percent of the population aged thirty to forty-five was HIV infected. HIV infection in the work force is expected to reach 25 percent before 2000. By 2010, HIV prevalence among thirty- to forty-five-year-old adults is expected to reach 40 percent, and 22 percent of persons 35-44 years old are expected be dying of AIDS.

Surveys conducted by the South African Department of Health at antenatal clinics found that 7.6 percent of pregnant women in the country were infected with HIV at the end of 1994. By November 1995, more than 10 percent were infected, including more than 13 percent of women aged twenty to twenty-four. In kwaZulu/Natal, 20 percent of women attending antenatal clinics in 1995 were HIV infected, and government experts expect the figure to reach 35 percent soon. Five hundred thousand AIDS orphans are expected in kwaZulu/Natal alone by the year 2000.

Despite these grim figures, South Africa's exploding HIV epidemic is still so young that only approximately fifty thousand South Africans had died of AIDS by early 1996.

Sudan

Sudan reported more than one hundred thousand people infected with HIV at the end of 1996. According to the Sudanese Health Ministry, fourteen thousand children were AIDS orphans in 1995, and the number will reach ninety thousand in 1998.

Tanzania

According to WHO, 1.5 million of Tanzania's 27 million people were HIV infected in 1996; 2.7 million will be infected by the year 2000; four hundred thousand have already progressed to AIDS.

Uganda

Ugandan authorities estimate that roughly two million people (10 percent of its population) were HIV infected by 1997. Seroprevalence studies in 1991 found prevalence rates in some urban areas as high as 35 percent, and in semiurban areas as high as 23 percent. Since 1995, AIDS has caused the loss of more total years of productive life than all other causes added together. By the year 2010, average Ugandan life expectancy is expected to fall from fifty-nine to thirty-one, with catastrophic consequences for national development.

Against this grim background, Uganda—which has dealt more openly with its HIV epidemic than many other African governments—has recently been able to report some modest progress: Between 1992 and 1995, for example, HIV prevalence among pregnant women at two surveillance sites decreased from 24 percent to 15 percent.

Zambia

By 1995, the HIV epidemic had reduced average life expectancy in Zambia from sixty-two to fifty-one. Average Zambian life expectancy is expected to reach forty-five by 2002, and thirty-three by 2010.

Zimbabwe

An estimated one million of Zimbabwe's 10.5 million residents, including up to 30 percent of Zimbabwe's working adults, were HIV infected in mid-1996. More than one hundred thousand persons died from AIDS in 1997, most of them aged fifteen to forty-five. Infant mortality is expected to increase 500 percent by the year 2005, and the total national population is expected to begin dropping by about 1.5 percent a year. One hundred and fifty thousand AIDS orphans are expected in the country by the year 2000. By the year 2010, AIDS will have lowered the average life expectancy from seventy to forty years.

THE U. S. EPIDEMIC

From the first reports of AIDS in 1981 through December 31, 1996, 581,429 persons with AIDS have been reported to the Center for Disease Control (CDC) by state and local health departments in the U. S. Of these, 84 percent were men, 15 percent were women, and 1 percent were children less than 13 years old. Among these cumulative cases, the proportion accounted for by men who have sex with men declined to 50 percent in 1996. Among women, heterosexual contact and injection drug use account for the vast majority of cases. AIDS incidence rates in 1996 declined or leveled for whites, men who have sex with men, IDUs, and children under 13 years old; rates increased for blacks, women, and persons infected through heterosexual contact.

The number of Americans living with AIDS in mid-1996 was estimated to be at least 223,000. The total number of people who have died from AIDS in the U.S. since the beginning of the epidemic is roughly 360,000. The number of persons currently estimated to be HIV infected is between 0.8 and 1 million, or a little less than 0.5 percent of the population.

Putting all these data together, and using 900,000 as our estimate of current HIV prevalence, we get this picture: From the beginning of the American epidemic to January 1, 1997, approximately 1.3 million persons were infected with HIV. Of these, about 360,000 had died, at least 223,000 were living with AIDS, and about seven hundred thousand were HIV infected but had not progressed to AIDS. Of these seven hundred thousand many, perhaps the majority, did not know that they were infected.

Variation in AIDS incidence by location is enormous. AIDS incidence rates (per one hundred thousand) for major cities in 1996 ranged from 8.3 in Pittsburgh to 95 in San Francisco, 120 in New York and 232 in Washington, D.C. Rates for states ranged from 1.5 in Wyoming to 68.1 in New York. For the entire United States, the rate was 25.6.

With each passing year, men who have sex with men account for a smaller and smaller percentage of new AIDS cases in the U.S. In 1995, they accounted for 43 percent of new cases; in 1996, 40 percent of new cases. But with an average interval between infection and AIDS of roughly ten years, what these data really mean is this: *Between 1985 and 1986—in the very early years of the U. S. epidemic—the percentage of new HIV infections accounted for by men who have sex with men was already far below 50 percent and dropping rapidly.*

As reported by the CDC, AIDS incidence rates for 1996 divide very sharply on racial lines: 178 for black men, 89 for Hispanic men, 30 for white-not-Hispanic men. Among women, the differences are even more dramatic: 62 for black women, 23 for Hispanic women, and only 3.5 for white-not-Hispanic women.

Annual U.S. deaths from AIDS appear to have peaked in 1994 at forty-seven thousand, but reporting delays and the life-prolonging effects of new (but unfortunately not curative) multi-drug anti-HIV treatments make this datum difficult to interpret.[2]

VIRAL SUBTYPES AND HIV TRANSMISSION

There are two major genetic branches of HIV, called HIV-1 and HIV-2. HIV-2 is almost entirely confined to west Africa and appears to be less pathogenic than HIV-1. HIV-1 is found in eastern and southern Africa, Europe, Asia, and the Americas. Within the HIV-1 branch, there are nine viral subtypes (A, B, C, D, E, F, G, H, and O). The HIV epidemic in the United States has been almost exclusively fueled by subtype HIV-1/B. In most of Africa and Asia, subtypes HIV-1/A, HIV-1/C and HIV-1/E are dominant.

The process by which a virus infects a human cell is often explained by analogy to the process by which a space vehicle docks with an orbiting space station. An Apollo vehicle fitted to dock with Skylab 1, for example, could not dock with MIR: The hatches and other connections simply did not fit. The Shuttle Atlantis, on the other hand, although unable to dock with Skylab, is perfectly fitted to dock with MIR. HIV infects human cell through a "docking" process called membrane fusion. As with space vehicle docking, successful infection depends on exquisite 'fit' between the virus and the target cell. In the case of HIV, this fit requires both an exact molecular match between the gp160 glycoprotein on the surface of the virus—the main part of the virus' "docking mechanism"—and the CD4 receptor on the surface of the human cell, and the presence on the human cell of a particular chemokine receptor which facilitates membrane fusion. Because very few human cell types have CD4 receptors (T4 helper lymphocytes, T1 inducer lymphocytes, macrophages, and microglial brain cells are the most important), only those very few human cell types can be infected by HIV.

Different populations of CD-4 bearing human cells have different chemokine receptors. In addition, the precise molecular structure of the CD-4 receptor (the "docking bay" in terms of our aeronautical analogy) will vary between populations of the same type of human cell at different locations in the body. Thus, epithelial langerhans cells in rectal mucosa have a slightly different CD-4 receptor and present a slightly different docking problem for HIV than do the same cells in the oral or vaginal mucosa.

The precise structure of the gp160 molecule is determined by HIV's *env* gene, an eighteen hundred nucleotide segment of HIV's complete 9,749 nucleotide genome. The *env* gene varies significantly between different subtypes of HIV-1, and, as a result, different subtypes of HIV-1 are better or worse fitted to infect CD-4 bearing cells in different parts of the body.

Research since 1995 has shown that subtypes C and E (the dominant strains in India, sub-Saharan Africa, and Thailand) are better adapted to infect oral and genital mucosa than is subtype B (the dominant strain in the United States and Europe). Subtype B, on the other hand, is better adapted to infect rectal mucosa. In other words, subtypes C and E (the dominant strains in India, sub-Saharan Africa, and Thailand) are better adapted to heterosexual transmission during vaginal intercourse than is subtype B.[3]

These new findings suggest that the low incidence of heterosexual HIV transmission in the United States and Europe during the early years of their epidemics was due, at least in part, to biological rather than social factors: HIV-1/B, the strain present in the U.S., is simply not very efficient at infecting vaginal mucosa during heterosexual intercourse. Subtypes A, C, or E would—as Soto-Ramirez and colleagues have warned—pose a significantly greater threat to heterosexuals in the West than has so far been presented by subtype B. Authorities such as Dr. Max Essex, chairman of the Harvard AIDS Institute, warn that the United States may soon face a second AIDS epidemic involving the non-B subtypes, especially C and E, that are common in Asia and Africa. If (or more properly, *when*) these non-B strains gain a foothold in the U.S., they may launch a second and significantly larger "heterosexual" epidemic.

Most experts believe that it is only a matter of time before subtypes C and E become established in America and Western Europe, joining the more familiar subtype B. Indeed, in late 1996, seventy-three cases of subtype E infection were diagnosed in Britain. Given the realities of international travel, and the presence of Western tourists and military personnel in many of the world's developing countries, the appearance of subtypes C and E in America and Western Europe seems inevitable.

HOMOSEXUALITY AND HIV IN THE U. S.

Most prudent public health authorities argue that HIV-related disease ought not to be treated differently from other similar infectious diseases. "AIDS Exceptionalism" is a very poor basis for sound public health policy. Yet, from the very beginning, AIDS exceptionalism has profoundly distorted America's response to its own HIV epidemic. Worse, by perpetuating the view that AIDS is largely or only a "homosexual" issue, AIDS exceptionalism has crippled America's response to the vastly more devastating pandemic now far advanced in the world's developing countries.

No one can deny that support and sympathy for a set of political and moral values which are commonly (but misleadingly) subsumed under the label of "gay rights" have had destructive effects on the U. S. response to the HIV epidemic. Indeed, these effects have been exquisitely catalogued by such gay writers as Randy Shilts and Larry Kramer. But neither can any one deny that support and sympathy for a set of political and moral values which are commonly (but also misleadingly) subsumed under the label of "homophobia" have also had a destructive effect on the U. S. response to the HIV epidemic. Four brief examples may serve to illustrate the institutional effects of AIDS exceptionalism.

If the *New York Times* and other mass media had given the first *thousand* AIDS victims even a fraction of the coverage given to the *seven* victims of poisoned Tylenol capsules, millons of Americans would have learned of the new disease much earlier, and tens or hundreds of thousands of Americans who are now dead might be living. Instead, the *Times* published fifty-four stories on the Tylenol affair (several on the front page) and a total of three stories on AIDS— none of which appeared on the front page, and none of which used the words "sex" or "homosexual."

If the U. S. Public Health Service had given Dr. James Curran's Kaposi's Sarcoma and Opportunistic Infections (KSOI) Task Force at CDC *any* financial support, stalled lab research and field cluster studies could have been completed years earlier—proving that the virus was bloodborne and sexually transmissible and accelerating development of an antibody test—and tens or hundreds of thousands of Americans who are now dead might be living. Instead, the same federal agencies which had assigned more than one *thousand* lab and field employees to work the Tylenol affair refused to fund even *one* part time secretary for the KSOI task force.

If the Mayor of New York, Ed Koch, had not for eighteen months refused all requests to meet with New York's gay health experts, his Public Health Department might have acted on early reports of vertical transmission (from mother to child) in New York hospitals, and hundreds or thousands of American children who are now dead might be living. Instead, apparently fearful that rumors regarding his own sexual orientation might be reinforced, he agreed to such a meeting only in April of 1983, when he was politically cornered by the combined efforts of Larry Kramer, noted gay playwright, Dr. Kevin Cahill, prominent Irish Catholic physician, and His Eminence Terence Cardinal Cooke.

If the American blood products industry had accepted the conclusions of CDC experts showing that HIV was a blood-borne disease, tens or hundreds of thousands of Americans who are now dead might be alive. Instead, for almost two years—hammered on the one side by gay activists arguing that screening would be discriminatory and on the other by concern for profit margins—the Red Cross and other institutions resisted pleas to institute donor screening, killing thousands of transfusion recipients and nearly every American hemophiliac who received even a single dose of clotting factor between 1980 and 1985.

Honest scholars can disagree about precisely *how* attitudes toward homosexuality have distorted the American response to HIV. They can also disagree about whether the greatest damage was wrought by the "gay-rights" or by the "homophobic" variety of AIDS exceptionalism. But to rest of the world, and to the overwhelming majority of the tens of millions of human victims of the global HIV pandemic, this disagreement is unimportant. In different ways, *both* varieties of AIDS exceptionalism have perpetuated the uniquely

American belief that the AIDS epidemic is a homosexual issue, and thereby helped to stifle any effective U. S. response to the threat that the global HIV pandemic poses.

PUBLIC POLICY CHALLENGES

Vaccine Development

A vaccine that blocks HIV infection is urgently needed to stem the tide of HIV in developing nations. New multi-drug therapies promise better treatment for HIV disease in the developed world, but at fifteen to thirty thousand dollars per person per year, these treatment regimens will never be available to citizens of developing countries with yearly national health expenditures of less than two dollars per person. Despite the international importance of developing an HIV vaccine, and despite direct pleas by international authorities, including the head of the UN-AIDS program, less than 1 percent of all U. S. HIV research dollars has been spent on vaccine development. And even this 1 percent has been spent in ways which systematically disadvantage the developing world: The vaccine now being tested in Uganda, for example, is designed to protect against HIV subtype B—not the subtypes A and D which predominate there.

Such shortsighted policies might have a certain attractiveness to American citizens who believe that American tax dollars should be spent on American problems. But infectious diseases neither understand nor respect national boundaries. Failure to control the global HIV pandemic will inevitably result in new U. S. epidemics of the HIV subtypes now epidemic elsewhere.

Sexual Exploitation of Children

The global HIV pandemic has exacerbated the already terrible problem of the sexual exploitation of children, often by tourists visiting from the developed world. First, by killing adults, the pandemic has left millions of children without parents and without nurture or protection. The World Health Organization has estimated that ten million children under ten years of age will be orphaned by 2000 as a result of AIDS. Fear of AIDS also fuels demand for child sexual partners. Some estimates put the number of under-age prostitutes in Thailand at four hundred thousand; in the Philippines, at about sixty thousand; in India, at about 400,000; in Taiwan, between forty and sixty thousand. A child can be bought for as little as $1.40 in Delhi. A virgin or a child under age six can cost 140 dollars. In Malaysia, the price of a child virgin is two thousand dollars, in Singapore, five hundred dollars. Once de-flowered, the young girl's price drops to ten dollars, and after a week's use, to five dollars. If she survives a year, sex may cost only $3; but by then, she will be HIV infected. Despite this terrible situation, specialized "tour services" in the U. S. and Europe continue openly to organize and advertise "sex adventure" tours to these developing countries.

Population Policy

No competent demographer who is familiar with the HIV pandemic believes that Sub-Saharan Africa now faces an overpopulation problem. On the contrary, Sub-Saharan Africa faces a potentially disastrous depopulation problem. Nevertheless, in its first year in office, the Clinton administration ordered the U. S. Agency for International Development to treat "population control", and not HIV control, as its first U. S. priority in Africa. Vocal African critics of U. S. policy can be forgiven for wondering aloud whether current U. S. policy aims at the depopulation of their continent.

CONCLUSION

The global HIV pandemic is not a "gay plague." It is not a "homosexual issue." It is a human tragedy of unprecedented magnitude. To the extent that Americans continue to view the HIV pandemic through a lens of sexual politics—whether that lens is homosexual or heterosexual, conservative or liberal—America will fail to respond to the greatest public health threat that mankind has faced since the beginning. We can do better. We must.

PART II

Moral Norms

6

Thomas Aquinas
on Homosexuality

Janet E. Smith

PERHAPS NO THINKER is as closely associated with natural law theory as Thomas Aquinas. It should come as no surprise, then, that his thought is, at the very least, a point of departure for those who appeal to the natural law tradition in arguing against the liceity of a homosexual "lifestyle". Likewise, we would expect those who wish to undermine the natural-law understanding of homosexuality to attack or attempt to reinterpret Aquinas. For if Aquinas's understanding of homosexuality should turn out to be groundless or incoherent, the natural-law approach to this question could well be vitiated. Thus John Boswell in his *Christianity, Social Tolerance, and Homosexuality* observes: "It is difficult to see how Aquinas's attitudes towards homosexual behavior could even be made consonant with his general moral principles, much less understood as the outgrowth of them."[1] And after reviewing Aquinas's statements about homosexuality, Boswell concludes that "[i]n the end Aquinas admits more or less frankly that his categorization of homosexual acts as 'unnatural' is a concession to popular sentiment and parlance."[2]

Not surprisingly, there is reason to challenge these statements of Boswell's. Indeed, several scholars have found them completely discordant with a proper interpretation of Aquinas's teaching on homosexuality.[3] Thus, Boswell's work provides a good foil for an exposition of that teaching.

It must be kept in mind that Aquinas does not provide a thorough or systematic treatment of homosexuality. He treats the topic largely as an adjunct to other points under consideration. We must also note that Aquinas was not providing a pastoral treatment of homosexuality; he was not endeavoring to choose the most sensitive rhetoric or terminology to present his views. His treatment is philosophical, partial, and expressed in a terminology that is no longer current, easily misunderstood, and therefore occasionally offensive to some.

THE MEANING OF "NATURE"

Boswell, like many others, fails to understand Aquinas's teaching on nature and its role in Aquinas's evaluation of ethics. Admittedly, Aquinas's use of the term "nature" is diverse, but sufficient attention to the larger context of Aquinas's understanding of the cosmos should permit us to see that his teaching on homosexual acts does grow naturally out of his general moral principles and that his categorization of homosexual acts as "unnatural" is not a "concession to popular sentiment and parlance."

There are several fundamental principles that one must keep in mind when interpreting Aquinas's natural law teachings: 1. Aquinas understands God to be the author of nature and thus what is natural is good; 2. The primary meaning of the word "nature" for Aquinas is not physical or biological but ontological. "Nature" most precisely refers to the essence of a substance, in the case of man, to a substance that is a unity of spirit and body[4]; 3. Natural law ethics and virtue ethics are integrally related, for virtues are a perfection of man's nature. All sins are a violation of some virtue; and 4. Since the Fall, man's physical nature and intellectual nature are flawed and can mislead him in his actions. Natural law ethics also involves various epistemological claims, but such elements are not of great relevance here.

THE NATURALISTIC FALLACY

Likewise, here is not the place to do a full exposition and defense of Aquinas's natural law theory, but perhaps one crucial point must be made. Aquinas and Aquinas's interpreters are often accused of committing the naturalistic fallacy—that is, of moving from what "is" the case to what "ought" to be the case.[5] Certainly Aquinas uses what "is" the case as a guide to what "ought" to be the case, but in a sense that it seems most everyone does quite spontaneously. For instance, it "is" the case that it is natural for human beings to have two eyes; therefore, human beings "ought" to have two eyes. Aquinas would not leave it at that, of course; he would inquire into human nature and attempt to discover why it is fitting that humans have two eyes. What is the case is a guide to what is fitting, but ultimately it is what is fitting that is the determinative principle. What is fitting is what is ordered to the good and the good is the perfection of one's nature. And what is fitting involves an "ought." The move to a moral ought is also common and spontaneous; for example, since it is a fact that children need food and that parents are responsible for their children, it is good and fitting that parents ensure that their children are fed; in other words, parents ought to feed their children.

KEY TEXTS

Now let us turn to Aquinas's position on homosexual acts.[6] The most extensive discussion of this question is found in his *Summa contra gentiles*. The key text deserves quotation at length:

> We have said that God exercises care over every person on the basis of what is good for him. Now, it is good for each person to attain his end, whereas it is bad for him to swerve away from his proper end. Now, this should be considered applicable to the parts, just as to the whole being; for instance, each and every one of his acts, should attain the proper end. Now, though the male semen is superfluous in regard to the preservation of the individual, it is nevertheless necessary in regard

to the propagation of the species. Other superfluous things, such as excrement, urine, sweat, and such things, are not at all necessary; hence, their emission contributes to man's good. Now, this is not what is sought in the case of semen, but, rather, to emit it for the purpose of generation, to which purpose the sexual act is directed. But man's generative process would be frustrated unless it were followed by proper nutrition, because the offspring would not survive if proper nutrition were withheld. Therefore, the emission of semen ought to be so ordered that it will result in both the production of the proper offspring and in the upbringing of this offspring.[7]

Not much further on, we also read that "[i]t is evident . . . that every emission of semen, in such a way that generation cannot follow, is contrary to the good for man. And if this be done deliberately, it must be a sin. Now, I am speaking of a way from which, *in itself*, generation could not result: Such would be any emission of semen apart from the natural union of male and female. For which reason, sins of this type are called *contrary to nature*."[8] This kind of objection to homosexuality strikes many as being absurd for they argue that one can certainly use bodily parts for purposes other than their "natural" one; one could, for instance, use discarded hair to stuff pillows or ear wax to stick things together. Aquinas himself considers such a counter-argument when he states some might argue that it is not immoral to walk on one's hands or to do something with one's feet that one usually does with the hands. Aquinas responds that he believes such actions are not "unnatural" because "man's good is not much opposed by such inordinate use." One supposes that he is thinking of instances where such use is not necessary—for example, he is not thinking of instances where one uses one's feet instead of one's hands because one is without hands, but rather when one does so when one's hands would serve one better. To use instrumental goods which are parts of a whole—hands and feet, hair and earwax—for purposes beyond their most immediately natural one is permissible since the immediate natural purposes are subordinate to the purpose of the whole and they exist to serve the good of the whole. Hence, one could use parts for other than their immediate natural purpose, if doing so aided the whole, and even if it did not, the offense would be small, since man's good would not be much affected.

The good of some parts, however, is so distinguished that it would be seriously wrong to misuse those parts, for in doing so one would violate the good towards which it is directed. Aquinas maintains that the good towards which semen is directed is such that to use it for something other than its purpose is to violate the very good of human life towards which it is directed. (We must, of course, realize that Aquinas's analysis applies not just to semen but to any organs or secretions essential to the reproductive process.)

THE GOOD OF HUMAN LIFE

It is very important to recognize the full status of the good towards which semen is directed, in order to understand Aquinas's insistence that it cannot be used for any other purpose. Semen, of course, is reproductive material, and the good to which it is directed is inherently connected with the good of sexuality and the good of new human life. Aquinas holds that God created two sexes for the very purpose of bringing forth new human life—if God had not intended humans to share in the procreation of new human life he would not have created humans of two sexes.[9] Although Aquinas speaks of the good of sexuality as being "the propagation of the species," the propagation of the human species should not be understood in the same way as the propagation of all other species, since humans have immortal souls and are destined not just to contribute to the longevity of the species. Rather, each individual has an intrinsic value in his own right and humans in generating offspring are not just preserving the species; they are "multiplying individuals," that is, they are helping to populate heaven (not just earth).[10]

Boswell's discussion suggests he misunderstands Aquinas on this point. He claims that Aquinas's advocacy on behalf of the preservation of the species was based on the ethical premise "that the physical increase of the human species constitutes a major moral good."[11] This certainly is not Aquinas's view: He makes it very clear that the mere physical increase of the species is not a good; parents should bring forth children to raise them to share eternity with God—not to populate the earth.[12] Humans not only reproduce; more properly they procreate; that is, they participate in the coming to be of a new human soul. God is the Creator of each and every human soul but he requires the provision of matter by human beings in order to effect the coming to be of a new human being. Human beings provide the matter whereas God provides the soul for the creation of each and every new human being.[13] Semen (and the ovum), then, is part of the matter into which God infuses the human soul. To deliberately misuse semen, that is, to use it in a way that prevents it from providing the matter for new human life, is, then, to violate a great good—the good of potential new human life.[14]

HOMOSEXUAL ACTS AS CONTRARY TO NATURE

Aquinas speaks of acts of homosexual sexual intercourse as acts that are "contrary to nature."[15] Now, it is certainly true that Aquinas speaks of all immoral acts as being contrary to nature since all immoral acts violate human nature; they are not in accord with human nature, which is rational. In short, they are unnatural because they are not in accord with reason; yet some immoral actions retain some degree of naturalness. For instance, acts of fornication are unnatural because they violate reason; they do so because provision for offspring has not been made. Yet, since acts of fornication can fulfill the purpose of sexual intercourse in generating offspring, they are still natural insofar as they allow the semen and ovum to partially fulfill their natures. Homosexual acts of sexual intercourse do not achieve even this level of naturalness.

Again, some might think that Aquinas has given an absurdly high value to semen; after all there is an abundance of it and much is "wasted" in many ways. But, again, we should not isolate his view of semen apart from the value of the whole human person and the value of the heterosexual relation that completes the human person both physically and psychologically, the fitting context in which to bring forth new human life. Aquinas's understanding of the value of semen is part and parcel of his understanding of the reason for the differentiation of the sexes and of the love of God for new human souls.

Seeing that Aquinas's evaluation of homosexual acts is set within the broader context of human destiny might help us better understand Aquinas's view that the deliberate misuse of semen is a very grave sin: "Hence, after the sin of homicide whereby a human nature already in existence is destroyed, this type of sin appears to take next place, for by it the generation of human nature is precluded."[16] Homosexuality, like masturbation and contraception, are immoral because they involve wasting the matter that should be directed towards the creation of new life. None are morally equivalent to homicide, of course, but all are like it in being sins against life.

The Unitive Purpose of Sexual Acts

In discussing the unnaturalness of homosexual sexual acts, Aquinas does not make reference to the unitive purpose of the sexual act and the incompatibility of homosexual acts with the unitive meaning. A suggestion that he shares the understanding that homosexual acts are not truly unitive can be found in his description of them as sins against the sixth commandment, the commandment against adultery. All sins that involve a misuse of sexual faculties are considered to be sins of unfaithfulness—one is using one's sexual powers outside of the marital relationship or not in accord with the goods of the marital relationship. In other words, one is not sharing one's sexuality with one's spouse, or one is not sharing one's sexuality with one's spouse properly (as in contracepted sexual intercourse). In Aquinas's view there is a sense in which one's sexual powers belong to one's spouse, for they exist to strengthen the spousal relationship and to create a family. Homosexual sexual intercourse bestows one's sexual favors on someone other than a spouse.

A complete treatment of the evil of homosexual acts would

involve addressing the psychological complementarity of male and female and the ways in which sexual intercourse fosters the intimacy that permits spouses to achieve the union proper to marriage. Nonetheless, Aquinas would likely understand the psychological differences distinguishing male and female to be related to their different roles in the business of parenting; even the unitive meaning of the sexual act cannot be explained without reference to its procreative meaning. God made man male and female so they could be one and so they could give new life. The sexual faculties are directed towards these purposes. To use them otherwise is to misuse them. Aquinas, then, judges homosexual acts of sexual intercourse to be objectively disordered because they are not ordered to the goods naturally embedded in sexual intercourse.

Animal Behavior

Because Aquinas regularly refers to the behavior of animals in his discussion of human sexuality, some, like Boswell, believe he evaluates human sexual behavior according to animal sexual behavior. Boswell makes the claim that Aquinas "resorted again and again to animal behavior as the final arbiter in matters of human sexuality."[17] Yet his own reading of Aquinas implicitly contradicts that claim, because he maintains that Aquinas does not accept animal sexual behavior as totally determinative of human sexual behavior. As Boswell notes, Aquinas occasionally speaks of sexual behavior, engaged in by humans, as animal sexual behavior and not in accord with the proper norms for human beings. In his discussion of monogamy, Aquinas argues that humans should not imitate the many species of animals that are promiscuous. He finds that birds too must unite in their raising of offspring and notes that birds are monogamous. Since humans and birds are similar in needing the care of both parents to thrive, Aquinas concludes that humans, like birds, should be monogamous.

Boswell asserts that "[i]t is difficult to believe . . . that animal behavior actually suggested this position to Saint Thomas."[18] He is right that the simple discovery of monogamy among animals is not what leads Aquinas to posit monogamy as fitting for humans. Aquinas does not simply see what animals do and conclude that such is what humans either ought to do or ought not to do. He looks to animals to see what they do and why; if humans share a certain good with some animal, it is likely that behavior which is conducive to that good would be beneficial for humans also. Boswell laments that "Aquinas does not explain the principle by which he determines which aspects of animal sexuality should be avoided by humans (for instance, the position they adopt in coitus) and which imitated (for instance, ornithological monogamy)."[19] Yet Aquinas's principle is quite clear. He uses behavior in the animal kingdom to help him discover what about certain animals would make certain behavior deleterious or beneficial. If humans are like those animals in a certain respect (such as needing parents of both sexes), he would use that information to help him determine what is appropriate behavior for humans.

Boswell also makes the claim that two parents are not necessary for the successful rearing of children and claims that Aquinas is "devious or mistaken" when he makes appeal to what is "commonly" the case to support the claim that two parents are necessary (and it is only because I live in the 1990s that I feel I must say, a male and female parent).[20] Boswell accuses Aquinas of "ignoring the intent" of those who may raise children as single parents for good reasons and of addressing himself "only to statistical probabilities and physical consequences." In Boswell's view, some may have good reason for bearing children outside of wedlock; that most bear children within marriage and that such children thrive is in his mind only a statistical probability. Aquinas is most certainly not using statistical probability as his norm for nature; again, he uses what is fitting. Boswell himself acknowledges that Aquinas thinks that males and females bring something distinct to parenting and hence both are necessary for successful parenting. Aquinas does not make this claim on the basis of statistical probabilities or physical consequences, but on the nature of males and females.

THE HOMOSEXUAL CONDITION

To this point we have been considering Aquinas's evaluation of homosexual acts. He also makes some remarks that indicate his views about the source of the homosexual condition. Let us first note that, while Aquinas speaks of homosexual acts as being particularly objectionable, he does not make that claim about the homosexual condition. And we must also note that when he speaks of homosexual acts as being particularly objectionable, he is comparing them to other sins of intemperance. Sins of intemperance are not the most serious sins; sins of pride and sins against charity are much worse. As for all human action, Aquinas maintains that one cannot judge the moral value of an action apart from a consideration of the state, character, and intention of the agent. There is ample evidence that Aquinas shared the modern understanding that the homosexual condition may not be one that an individual has chosen; he allows that it may be the result of a bodily temperament, of a psychological disease, or of bad conditioning.[21]

In an article entitled "Whether Any Pleasure is Not Natural?", Aquinas quotes Aristotle in maintaining that "some things are pleasant not from nature but from some corruption of man's nature." He speaks of "some pleasures that are not natural speaking absolutely, and yet connatural in some respect." Those with corrupt natures find what is unpleasant to humans as a species to be pleasant to them as individuals—Aquinas speaks of corruptions of both the body and the soul. As an example of a corruption of the body that would distort natural pleasures he gives a man with a fever to whom sweet things seem bitter. As a examples of a corruption of the soul, he speaks of a man who through custom takes some pleasure in unnatural intercourse, bestiality, or cannibalism.[22]

Now Boswell argues that this reasoning should lead Aquinas to see that homosexuality is natural in some individuals, since Aquinas holds that some individuals take a connatural delight in pleasures that are not pleasant to humans as a species.[23] But Aquinas finds the origin of the "connaturality" to be some corruption, and hence would not understand the condition to be natural.

Boswell also argues that although Aquinas speaks of homosexuality coming about through some defect, Aquinas may not necessarily mean some moral defect. And Boswell is certainly correct in this observation.[24] The text upon which Aquinas draws here is from Aristotle, in which Aristotle uses the desire for one's own sex as an example of a perverse desire that may have been fostered by childhood sexual abuse.[25] Certainly, if such was the source of one's homosexual desires, one would not be morally culpable for possessing the desires, though one most likely has some moral culpability for acting upon these desires, unless they could be considered truly uncontrollable obsessions.[26] And certainly some may be morally responsible for having homosexual desires; they may recklessly "experiment" with homosexual actions and they may expose themselves to homosexual erotica and arouse desires in themselves that otherwise may not have been activated. But however the homosexual condition comes to be, whether one is morally culpable for acquiring the condition or not, Aquinas would still consider the condition a disordered condition—even if one's homosexuality were genetically determined. According to Aquinas's principles those who are made lame by others, those who make themselves lame because of bad choices, and those who are born lame, are all suffering some defect, some disorder in their being.

Boswell observes that some conditions that come about through defects are not in themselves defects. For example, although Aquinas thought that females came to be because of some defect in the semen or because of the presence of a moist south wind, Aquinas did not think females, for that reason, were without a natural purpose. Boswell reasons that "[s]ince both homosexuality and femaleness occur 'naturally' in some individuals, neither can be said to be inherently bad, and both must be said to have an end."[27] He observes that the "*Summa [theologiae]* does not speculate on what the 'end' of homosexuality might be, but this is hardly surprising in light of the prejudices of the day." But he does some fancy distorting of texts to come to this conclusion. Boswell fails, for instance, to note that there are many kinds of imperfection, one being something that is not a perfect instance of something (as a child is an imperfect adult), or something that is a privation of a good (such as blindness). Women may be "naturally" inferior to males because, for instance, they are the passive as opposed to the active principle in procreation, but both maleness and femaleness are ordered to some good. In Aquinas's view, homosexuality would be like blindness; it is an absence of a good and not ordered to any good.

Moderns are unlikely to understand and accept Aquinas's analysis because few share his view of man's ontological dependence on God. Few share his view that God wills each soul into existence and wants to share an eternity with every human being. Few share his view that sexuality has a purpose designed by God and that we must live in accord with that purpose. Nor do many share his view that all of us must carry some portion of the cross. Original sin alone makes every human being disordered; many of us have acquired more specific disorders through our genetic heritage, our upbringing, our choices. Many of these make it difficult for us to avoid disordered and sinful actions. For Aquinas, homosexuality is simply one more of those disordered conditions; he would assure us that God's grace is available to assist us in being healed and in avoiding sinful behavior.

7

"Same-Sex Marriage" and "Moral Neutrality"

Robert P. George

FREQUENTLY I HEAR STUDENTS (AND OTHERS) SAY, "I believe that marriage is a union of one man and one woman. But I think that it is wrong for the state to base its law of marriage on a controversial moral judgment, even if I happen to believe that judgment to be true. Therefore, I support proposals to revise our law to authorize same-sex 'marriages.'" The thought here is that the state ought to be neutral regarding competing understandings of the nature and value of marriage.

Of course, the claim that the law ought to be morally neutral about marriage or anything else is itself a moral claim. As such, *it* is not morally neutral, nor can it rest on an appeal to moral neutrality. People who believe that the law of marriage (or other areas of the law) ought to be morally neutral do not assert, nor does their position presuppose, that the law ought to be neutral regarding the view that the law ought to be neutral and competing moral views. It is obvious that neutrality between neutrality and unneutrality is logically impossible. Sophisticated proponents of moral neutrality therefore acknowledge that theirs is a controversial moral position whose truth, soundness, correctness, or, at least, reasonableness, they are prepared to defend against competing moral positions. They assert, in other words, that the best understanding of political morality, at least for societies such as ours, is one that includes a requirement that the law be morally neutral with respect to marriage. Alternative understandings of political morality, insofar as they fail to recognize the principle of moral neutrality, are, they say, mistaken and ought, as such, to be rejected.

Now, to recognize that any justification offered for the requirement of moral neutrality cannot itself be morally neutral is by no means to establish the falsity of the alleged requirement of moral neutrality. My purpose in calling attention to it is not to propose a retorsive argument purporting to identify self-referential inconsistency in arguments for moral neutrality. Although I shall argue that the moral neutrality of marriage law is neither desirable nor, strictly speaking, possible, I do not propose to show that there is a logical or performative inconsistency in saying that "the law (of marriage) ought to be neutral regarding competing moral ideas." It is not like saying "No statement is true." Nor is it like singing "I am not singing." At the same time, the putative requirement of moral neutrality is neither self-evident nor self-justifying. If it is to be vindicated as a principle of political morality, it needs to be shown to be true by a valid argument.

It is certainly the case that implicit in our matrimonial law is a (now controversial) moral judgment, namely, the judgment that marriage is inherently heterosexual—a union of one man and one woman. (In a moment, I will discuss the deeper grounds of that judgment.) Of course, this is not the only possible moral judgment. In some cultures, polygyny or (far less frequently) polyandry is legally sanctioned. Some historians claim that "marriages" (or their equivalent) between two men or two women have been recognized by certain cultures in the past.[1] However that may be, influential voices in our own culture today demand the revision of matrimonial law to authorize such "marriages." Indeed, the Supreme Court of the State of Hawaii has for some time been on the verge of requiring officials of that State to issue marriage licenses to otherwise qualified same-sex couples under the Equal Rights Amendment to the Hawaii Constitution. Unless the people of Hawaii are able to amend their state constitution to prevent the imposition of "same-sex marriage," it will then fall to the federal courts, and, ultimately, to the Supreme Court of the United States, to decide whether the "full faith and credit" clause of the Constitution of the United States requires every state in the Union to recognize such "marriages" contracted in Hawaii.

Anticipating the Hawaii Supreme Court's action, Congress passed the Defense of Marriage Act, which guarantees the right of states to refuse to recognize same-sex "marriages." The Act went to the President to sign or veto in the course of the 1996 presidential campaign. After denouncing the Act as both mean-spirited and unnecessary, Clinton quietly signed it into law, literally in the middle of the night. Of course, a second opportunity for a veto effectively rests with any five justices of the Supreme Court of the United States. Although it is impossible to say with confidence how the Supreme Court will ultimately rule on the inevitable constitutional challenge to the Defense of Marriage Act, the stated ground of the Court's decision in the 1996 case of *Romer v. Evans* (the so-called Colorado Amendment 2 Case) will surely inspire hope among those whom Clinton disappointed by failing to veto the Act. In *Romer*, the Court invalidated an amendment to the Constitution of the State of Colorado by which the people of that State sought to prevent its municipalities from enacting ordinances granting protected status or preferences based on homosexual or bisexual orientation. Six justices joined in an opinion written by Associate Justice Anthony Kennedy holding that Amendment 2 could only have been motivated by constitutionally impermissible "animus" against a politically vulnerable minority group.

There are two ways to argue for the proposition that it is unjust for government to refuse to authorize same-sex (and, for that matter, polygamous) "marriages." The first is to deny the reasonableness, soundness, or truth of the moral judgment implicit in the proposition that marriage is a union of one man and one woman. The second is to argue that this moral judgment cannot justly serve as the basis for the public law of matrimony, notwithstanding its reasonableness, soundness, or even its truth.

I maintain that the moral neutrality to which this way of arguing appeals is, and cannot but be, illusory. To that end, it will be necessary for me to explain the philosophical grounds of the moral judgment that marriage is a union of one man and one woman and to discuss the arguments advanced by certain critics of traditional matrimonial law in their efforts to undermine this judgment.

TWO IN ONE FLESH

Here is the core of the traditional understanding: Marriage is a two-in-one-flesh communion of persons that is consummated and actualized by acts which are reproductive *in type*, whether or not they are reproductive *in effect* (or are motivated, even in part, by a desire to reproduce). Reproductive-type acts have unique meaning, value, and significance because they belong to the class of acts by which children come into being. More precisely, these acts have their unique meaning, value, and significance because they belong to the *only* class of acts by which children can come into being, not as "products" which their parents choose to "make," but, rather, as perfective participants in the organic community (that is, the family) that is established by their parents' marriage. The bodily union of spouses in marital acts is the biological matrix of their marriage as a multi-level relationship that unites them at the bodily, emotional, dispositional, and spiritual levels of their being.

Marriage, precisely as such a relationship, is naturally ordered to the good of procreation (and to the nurturing and education of children), as well as to the good of spousal unity, and these goods are tightly bound together. The distinctive unity of spouses is possible *because* men and women, in reproductive-type acts, become a single reproductive principle. Although reproduction is a single act, in humans the reproductive act is performed not by individual members of the species, but by a mated pair as an organic unit. The point has been explained by Germain Grisez: "Though a male and a female are complete individuals with respect to other functions—for example, nutrition, sensation, and locomotion—with respect to reproduction they are only potential parts of a mated pair, which is the complete organism capable of reproducing sexually. Even if the mated pair is sterile, intercourse, provided it is the reproductive behavior characteristic of the species, makes the copulating male and female one organism."[2]

Although not all reproductive-type acts are marital,[3] there can be no marital act that is not reproductive in type. Masturbatory, sodomitical, or other sexual acts which are not reproductive in type cannot unite persons organically, that is, as a single reproductive principle.[4] Therefore, such acts cannot be intelligibly engaged in for the sake of marital unity as such: They cannot be marital acts. Rather, persons who perform such acts must be doing so for the sake of ends or goals which are *extrinsic* to themselves as bodily persons: Sexual satisfaction, or (perhaps) mutual sexual satisfaction, is sought as a means of releasing tension, or obtaining or sharing pleasure, either as an end in itself, or as a means to some other end, such as expressing affection. In any case, where one-flesh union cannot (or cannot rightly) be sought as an end in itself, sexual activity necessarily involves the instrumentalization of the bodies of those participating in such activity to extrinsic ends.

In marital acts, by contrast, the bodies of persons who unite biologically are not reduced to the status of mere instruments. Rather, the end, goal, and intelligible point of sexual union is the good of marriage itself. On this understanding, such union is not merely an instrumental good, that is, a reason for action whose intelligibility as a reason depends on other ends to which it is a means, but is, rather, an intrinsic good, that is, a reason for action whose intelligibility as a reason depends on no such other end. The central and justifying point of sex is not pleasure, or even the sharing of pleasure, *per se*, however much sexual pleasure is rightly sought as an aspect of the perfection of marital union. The point of sex, rather, is *marriage itself*, considered as a bodily union of persons consummated and actualized by acts which are reproductive in type. Because in marital acts sex is not instrumentalized,[5] such acts are free of the self-alienating and dis-integrating qualities of masturbatory and sodomitical sex. Unlike these and other nonmarital sex acts, marital acts establish no practical dualism which volitionally and, thus, existentially (though, of course, not metaphysically) separates the body from the conscious and desiring aspect of the self, understood as the "true" self that uses the body as its instrument.[6] As John Finnis has observed, marital acts are truly unitive, and in no way self-alienating, because the bodily or biological aspect of human beings is "part of, and not merely an instrument of, their *personal* reality."[7]

But, one may ask, what about procreation? On the traditional view, isn't the sexual union of spouses instrumentalized to the goal of having children? It is true that St. Augustine was an influential proponent of such a view. The strict Augustinian position was rejected, however, by the mainstream of philosophy and theology from the late Middle Ages forward, and the understanding of sex and marriage that came to be embodied in both the canon law of the Church and the civil law of matrimony does not treat marriage as a merely instrumental good. Matrimonial law has traditionally understood marriage to be consummated by, and only by, the reproductive-type acts of spouses. The sterility of spouses—so long as they are capable of consummating their marriage by a reproductive-type act (and, thus, of achieving bodily, organic unity)—has never been treated as an impediment to marriage, even where sterility is certain, and even certain to be permanent (as in the case of the marriage of a woman who has been through menopause or has undergone a hysterectomy).[8]

According to the traditional understanding of marriage, then, it is the nature of marital acts as reproductive in type that makes it possible for such acts to be unitive in the distinctively marital way. And this type of unity has intrinsic, and not merely instrumental value. Thus, the unitive good of marriage provides a noninstrumental (and sufficient) reason for spouses to perform sexual acts of a type which consummates and actualizes their marriage. In performing marital acts, the spouses do not reduce themselves as bodily persons (or their marriage) to the status of means or instruments.

At the same time, where marriage is understood as a one-flesh union of persons, children who may be conceived in marital acts are understood, not as ends which are extrinsic to marriage (either in the Augustinian sense, or the modern liberal one), but rather as gifts which supervene on acts whose central justifying point is precisely the marital unity of the spouses.[9] It is thus that children are properly understood and treated—even in their conception—not as means to their parents' ends, but as ends-in-themselves; not as *objects* of the desire[10] or will of their parents, but as *subjects* of justice (and inviolable human rights); not as *property*, but as *persons*. It goes without saying that not all cultures have fully grasped these truths about the moral status of children. What is less frequently noticed is that our culture's grasp of these truths is connected to a basic understanding of sex and marriage that is not only fast eroding, but is now under severe assault from people who have no conscious desire to reduce children to the status of mere means, or objects, or property.

LIBERAL DUALISM

It is sometimes thought that defenders of traditional marriage law deny the possibility of something whose possibility critics of the law affirm. "Love," these critics say, "makes a family." And it is committed love that justifies homosexual sex as much as it justifies heterosexual sex. If marriage is the proper, or best, context for sexual love, the argument goes, then marriage should be made available as well to loving, committed same-sex partners on terms of strict equality. To think otherwise is to suppose that same-sex partners cannot really love each other, or love each other in a committed way, or that the orgasmic "sexual expression" of their love is somehow inferior to the orgasmic "sexual expression" of couples who "arrange the plumbing differently."

In fact, however, at the bottom of the debate is a possibility that defenders of traditional marriage law affirm and its critics deny, namely, the possibility of marriage as a one-flesh communion of persons. The denial of this possibility is central to any argument designed to show that the moral judgment at the heart of the traditional understanding of marriage as inherently heterosexual is unreasonable, unsound, or untrue. If reproductive-type acts in fact unite spouses interpersonally, as traditional sexual morality and marriage law suppose, then such acts differ fundamentally in meaning, value, and significance from the only types of sexual acts which can be performed by same-sex partners.

Liberal sexual morality that denies that marriage is inherently heterosexual necessarily supposes that the value of sex must be instrumental *either* to procreation *or* to pleasure. Proponents of the liberal view suppose that homosexual sex acts are indistinguishable from heterosexual acts whenever the motivation for such acts is something other than procreation. The sexual acts of homosexual partners, that is to say, are indistinguishable in motivation, meaning, value, and significance from the marital acts of spouses who know that at least one spouse is temporarily or permanently infertile. Therefore, the argument goes, traditional matrimonial law is guilty of unfairness in treating sterile heterosexuals as capable of marrying while treating homosexual partners as ineligible to marry.

Stephen Macedo has accused the traditional view and its defenders of precisely this apparent "double standard." He asks, "What is the point of sex in an infertile marriage? Not procreation: the partners (let us assume) know that they are infertile. If they have sex, it is for pleasure and to express their love, or friendship, or some other shared good. It will be for precisely the same reason that committed, loving gay couples have sex."[11]

But Macedo's criticism fails to tell against the traditional view because it presupposes as true precisely what the traditional view denies, namely, that the value (and, thus, the point) of sex in marriage can only be instrumental. On the contrary, it is a central tenet of the traditional view that the value (and point) of sex is the *intrinsic* good of marriage itself which is actualized in sexual acts which unite spouses biologically and, thus, interpersonally. The traditional view rejects the instrumentalization of sex (and, thus, of the bodies of sexual partners) to any extrinsic end. This does not mean that procreation and pleasure are not rightly sought in marital acts; it means merely that they are rightly sought when they are integrated with the basic good and justifying point of marital sex, namely, the one-flesh union of marriage itself.

It is necessary, therefore, for critics of traditional matrimonial law to argue that the apparent one-flesh unity that distinguishes marital acts from sodomitical acts is illusory, and, thus, that the apparent bodily communion of spouses in reproductive-type acts is not really possible. And so Macedo claims that "the 'one-flesh communion' of sterile couples would appear . . . to be more a matter of appearance than reality." Because of their sterility such couples cannot really unite biologically: "[T]heir bodies, like those of homosexuals, can form no 'single reproductive principle,' no real unity."[12] Indeed, Macedo goes so far as to argue that even fertile couples who conceive children in acts of sexual intercourse do not truly unite biologically, because, he asserts, "penises and vaginas do not unite biologically, sperm and eggs do."[13]

John Finnis has aptly replied that "in this reductivist, word-legislating mood, one might declare that sperm and egg unite only physically and only their pronuclei are biologically united. But it would be more realistic to acknowledge that the whole process of copulation, involving as it does the brains of the man and woman, their nerves, blood, vaginal and other secretions, and coordinated activity is biological through and through."[14]

Moreover, as Finnis points out, the organic unity which is instantiated in an act of the reproductive kind is not, as Macedo "reductively imagine[s], the unity of penis and vagina. It is the unity of the persons in the intentional, consensual *act* of seminal emission/reception in the woman's reproductive tract."[15]

The unity to which Finnis refers—unity of body, sense, emotion, reason, and will—is, in my view, central to our understanding of humanness itself. Yet it is a unity of which Macedo and others who deny the possibility of true marital communion can give no account. For their denial presupposes a dualism of "person" (as conscious and desiring self), on the one hand, and "body" (as instrument of the conscious and desiring self), on the other, which is flatly incompatible with this unity. Dualism is implicit in the idea, central to Macedo's denial of the possibility of one-flesh marital union, that sodomitical acts differ from what I have described as acts of the reproductive type only as a matter of the arrangement of the "plumbing." According to this idea, the genital organs of an infertile woman (and, of course, all women are infertile most of the time) or of an infertile man are not really "reproductive organs"—any more than, say, mouths, rectums, tongues, or fingers are reproductive organs. Therefore, the intercourse of a man and a women where at least one partner is temporarily or permanently sterile cannot really be an act of the reproductive type.

But the plain fact is that the genitals of men and woman are reproductive organs all of the time—even during periods of sterility. And acts which fulfill the behavioral conditions of reproduction are acts of the reproductive type even where the nonbehavioral conditions of reproduction do not happen to obtain. Insofar as the object of sexual intercourse is marital union, the partners achieve the desired unity (become "two-in-one-flesh") precisely insofar as they mate, that is, fulfill the behavioral conditions of reproduction, or, if you will, perform the type of act—the only type of act—upon which the gift of a child may supervene.[16]

The dualistic presuppositions of the liberal position are fully on display in the frequent references of Macedo and its other proponents to sexual organs as "equipment." Neither sperm nor eggs, neither penises nor vaginas, are properly conceived in such impersonal terms. Nor are they "used" by persons considered as somehow standing over and apart from these and other aspects of their biological reality. The biological reality of persons is, rather, part of their personal reality. Hence, where a person treats his body as a subpersonal object, the practical dualism he thereby effects brings with it a certain self-alienation, a damaging of the intrinsic good of personal self-integration. In any event, the biological union of persons—which is effected in reproductive type acts but not in sodomitical ones—really is an interpersonal ("one-flesh") communion.

THE LAW AS TEACHER

Now, Macedo considers the possibility that defenders of the traditional understanding are right about all this: that marriage truly is a "one-flesh union" consummated and actualized by marital acts; that sodomitical and other intrinsically nonmarital sexual acts really are self-alienating and, as such, immoral; that the true conception of marriage is one according to which it is an intrinsically heterosexual (and, one might here add, monogamous) relationship. But even if the traditional understanding of marriage is the morally correct one—even if it is true—he argues, the state cannot justly recognize it as such. For, if disagreements about the nature of marriage "lie in . . . difficult philosophical quarrels, about which reasonable people have long disagreed, then our differences lie in precisely the territory that John Rawls rightly marks off as inappropriate to the fashioning of our basic rights and liberties."[17] And from this it follows that government must remain neutral as between conceptions of marriage as intrinsically heterosexual (and monogamous) and conceptions according to which "marriages" may be contracted not only between a man and a woman, but also between two men, two women (and, presumably, a man or a woman and multiple male or female "spouses"). Otherwise, according to Macedo, the state would "inappropriately" be "deny[ing] people fundamental aspects of equality based on reasons and arguments whose force can only be appreciated by those who accept difficult to assess [metaphysical and moral] claims."[18]

It seems to me, however, that something very much like the contrary is true. The true meaning, value, and significance of marriage are fairly easily grasped, even if people sometimes have difficulty living up to its moral demands, when a culture—including, critically, a legal culture—promotes and supports a sound understanding of marriage, both formally and informally. Ideologies and practices which are hostile to a sound understanding and practice of marriage in a culture tend to undermine the institution of marriage, making it difficult for people to grasp the true meaning, value, and significance of marriage. It is, therefore, extremely important that government eschew attempts to be "neutral" with regard to competing conceptions of marriage and try hard to embody in its law and policy the soundest, most nearly correct conception. Moreover, any effort to achieve neutrality will inevitably prove to be self-defeating. For the law is a teacher: It will teach *either* that marriage is a reality that people can choose to participate in, but whose contours people cannot make and remake at will *or* the law will teach that marriage is a mere convention which is malleable in such a way that individuals, couples, or, indeed, groups, can choose to make of it whatever suits them. The result, given the biases of human sexual psychology, will be the development of practices and ideologies which truly do tend to undermine the sound understanding and practice of marriage, together with the pathologies that tend to reinforce the very practices and ideologies that cause them.

Joseph Raz, though himself a liberal who does not share my views on homosexuality or sexual morality generally, is rightly critical of forms of liberalism, including Rawlsianism, which suppose that law and government can and should be neutral with respect to competing conceptions of morality. In this regard, he has noted that "monogamy, assuming that it is the only valuable form of marriage, cannot be practised by an individual. It requires a culture which recognizes and supports it through the force of public opinion and its own formal institutions."[19]

Now, Raz does not suppose that in a culture whose law and public morality do not support monogamy a man who happens to believe in it will somehow be unable to restrict himself to having one wife or will be required to take additional wives. His point, rather, is that even if monogamy is a key element of a sound understanding of marriage, large numbers of people will fail to understand it or why it is the case—and will therefore fail to grasp the value of monogamy and the intelligible point of practicing it—unless they are assisted by a culture which supports, formally and informally, monogamous marriage. And what is true of monogamy is equally true of the other marks or aspects of a morally sound understanding of marriage. In other words, marriage is the type of good which can be participated in, or fully participated in, only by people who properly understand it and choose it with a proper understanding in mind; yet people's ability properly to understand it, and thus to choose it, depends upon institutions and cultural understandings that transcend individual choice.

But what about Macedo's claim that when matrimonial law deviates from neutrality by embodying the moral judgment that marriage is inherently heterosexual, it denies same-sex partners who wish to marry "fundamental aspects of equality?" Does a due regard for equality require moral neutrality? I think that the appeal to neutrality actually does no work here. If the moral judgment that marriage is between a man and a woman is false, then the reason for recognizing same-sex marriages is that such unions are as a matter of moral fact indistinguishable from marriages of the traditional type. If, however, the moral judgment that marriage is between a man and a woman is true, then Macedo's claim that the recognition of this truth by government "denies fundamental aspects of equality" simply cannot be sustained. If, in other words, the marital acts of spouses consummate and actualize marriage as a one-flesh communion, and serve thereby as the biological matrix of the relationship of marriage at all its levels, then the embodiment in law and policy of an understanding of marriage as inherently heterosexual denies no one fundamental aspects of equality. True, many persons who are homosexually oriented lack a psychological prerequisite to enter into marital relationships. But this is no fault of the law. Indeed, the law would embody a lie (and a damaging one insofar as it truly would contribute to the undermining of the sound understanding and practice of marriage in a culture) if it were to pretend that a marital relationship could be formed on the basis of, and integrated around, sodomitical or other intrinsically nonmarital (and, as such, self-alienating) sex acts.

It is certainly unjust arbitrarily to deny legal marriage to persons who are capable of performing marital acts and entering into the marital relationship. So, for example, laws forbidding interracial marriages truly were violations of equality. Contrary to the claims of Andrew Koppelman, Andrew Sullivan, and others, however, laws which embody the judgment that marriage is intrinsically heterosexual are in no way analogous to laws against miscegenation. Laws forbidding whites to marry blacks were unjust, not because they embodied a *particular* moral view and thus violated the alleged requirement of moral neutrality; rather, they were unjust because they embodied an *unsound* (indeed a grotesquely false) moral view—one that was racist and, as such, immoral.

PART III

LAW

8

HOMOSEXUALITY
AND THE LAW

Hadley Arkes

THIS PROBLEM OF HOMOSEXUALITY—or the new thing among us, the public controversy over homosexuality—has involved for most of us the test, and the strain, of friendship. There is the matter, always delicate, of speaking frankly on this question while preserving our relations with friends who confide that they are gay. But at the core of the problem itself, homosexuality may involve the mistaking or misplacing of friendship, or the specious use of friendship to cover something else. During the debate last year over the Defense of Marriage Act, I had the occasion several times to point out that the most genuine love may subsist between parents and children, grandparents and grandchildren, brothers and sisters, and in the nature of things—*in the nature of things*—nothing in those loves could possibly be diminished as love because they are not attended by penetration or expressed in marriage.[1] None of the love that male friends have for one another could possibly be impaired as loves because there is no orgasmic ingredient in that relation. It reveals a false notion of friendship to suggest that love is placed on a deeper plane when it is attended by forms of copulation that we are even embarrassed to mention.

But at the same time, it is a false definition of sexuality itself to suggest that these relations are sexual because they involve penetration and orgasm. This matter has been obscured to us because we have been reluctant, for quite proper reasons of delicacy, to make these topics the subject of our public conversation. And one of the things we have sought to protect with that delicacy and reticence has been our friends who regard themselves as gay.

I happened to note, several years ago, at a meeting in Washington, the settlement that seemed to be worked out, with a kind of Henry Jamesian subtlety, among many conservatives and their gay, conservative friends: We try to shelter our friends from wounding words and gay-bashing, and they, on their own part, seek to extract from us no global endorsement for their way of life. The gays who are politically conservative have paid a certain price for standing with their friends who are conservative, and one of the prices for them has been a discreet silence, or reticence, on this matter. But as I remarked at that meeting in Washington, at war or at dinner, those conservative gays may be the most reliable allies, the most engaging companions. And then I recall putting the question to the audience: "Honestly, folks, whom would you rather spend a whole evening with: Noel Coward or Al Gore?"

Many of us have held back, in our own reticence, out of our concern for our friends, and the result has been a pattern of tolerance—of leaving people to their private lives and their private judgments without offering lectures and reproaches. But that tolerance seems to have begotten that sequence of moves we remarked upon, just a few years ago, in the statement of the Ramsey Colloquium.[2] We recalled there the lines of Alexander Pope: that as vice becomes familiar, or our sympathy becomes engaged, "we first endure, then pity, then embrace." And so the sequence, we said, unfolded in that way: "To endure (tolerance), to pity (compassion) to embrace (affirmation)."[3] We move then from tolerance to a certain receding from judgment, or a position of neutrality—the sense that there is nothing really to be condemned, nothing that merits reproach—and from there we have moved to the position of positive approval. As the cycle completes itself, people arrive at the posture of judgment once again, but now they conclude that the only thing we can cast judgments upon are the people who cast judgments on the sexuality of others. Homosexuality does not apparently lend itself to judgment, but the people who would even question its rightness are now picked out for the sternest censure, without qualification or shading. And when it becomes a matter of casting protections on the homosexual life, then in the most curious way, the ancient connection between morality and law is suddenly discovered anew and asserted quite vigorously again. If it is thought "wrong" to cast judgments on people for their sexual orientation, or their style of sexuality, there is a renewed willingness to mark that sense of a wrong with the powers of law—to bring down punishments of all kinds (fines, citations, compulsory counseling) on those who would be so retrograde as to cast a moral judgment on someone else's sexual tastes.

INEXORABLE LOGIC

But this is not the only place in which the movement for gay rights reveals its understanding of the logic that connects morality and law. In fact, the movement for gay rights depends, at many points, on the same logic of morals that has persisted from the Bible and from Aristotle, and the connection produces this lasting irony: The movement cannot purge even from itself the kinds of moral understandings that eventually call into question the defense of homosexuality. Those understandings run rather deep, and at times they can be called forth only in the most disarming ways, when the guard is down and people may not realize that the argument is even being engaged.

My friends know, in that vein, the argument I have made for many years that comedians are really in the same business as philosophers, that they make their livings by playing off the shadings of logic tucked away in our language. In one notable case, my favorite epistemologist, Lou Costello, remarked on an idea that sprang from his partner, Bud Abbott. "That's an excellent thought," said Costello, "I was just going to think of it myself." The laugh is the quick, decisive measure of the fact that the point has been understood; for if people don't "get it," there is no joke. In fact it turns out at times that people will concede, unguardedly, with the laugh, what they will resist if it were put to them explicitly in the form of an argument.

And so I have suggested that the argument against homosexuality could be unfolded from the laugh that people cannot seem to hold back in response to that line of Rodney Dangerfield's: "I was afraid the first time I had sex. I was afraid . . . because I was all alone." The line never fails to elicit a laugh, and the laugh is the telling sign that the audience "gets it." There would be no laugh if Dangerfield could not count on this understanding on the part of the audience: that this sex *di solo* was not really sex. It is genital stimulation, but not—as we instantly understand—*really* sex. But in that event, the act would not suddenly become "sex" if two people simply replicated, in tandem, the masturbation implicit in the joke.[4]

The confusion involved here affects the core of the argument over gay sex and was reflected in a piece by Andrew Sullivan warning of the provocative nature of "queer politics." That aggressive style, he thought, "broke off dialogue with the heterosexual families whose cooperation is needed in every generation, if gay children are to be accorded a modicum of dignity and hope."[5]

The delicacy barely concealed that "cooperation is needed in every generation" precisely because "homosexual families" cannot produce "gay children." Gay children must come into being through the only kind of family that nature knows. What is obscured here is that we are not dealing with two different styles of family, standing on the same plane, any more than we are dealing with two different styles of sexuality. In the strictest sense, there is only one form of sexuality, the sexuality that is simply marked in the ineffaceable fact of gender. As the Congregation for the Doctrine of Faith once observed, there may not always be nations—there may not always be an Italy or Hungary—but there must always be men and women. The very existence of gender, as an ineffaceable fact, discloses its own teleology, its own purpose, grounded in nature. It also marks the meaning of sexuality in the strictest sense, or as John Paul II puts it, the sexuality imprinted in our natures.

The common sense of the matter is conceded, tacitly at least, even by the proponents of gay rights. Every act of genital stimulation simply cannot count as a "sexual" act. Obviously, gay activists do not consider sex with animals to be real sex, and they are quick to back away from any attempt to defend those committed, vocal members of the Man-Boy Love Association. And yet, just as plainly, they are not willing to cross this critical threshold: They are not willing to concede, in public, that there are moral grounds on which we may judge certain "sexual orientations" to be wrong or illegitimate. For any "orientation" that could be judged in that way would amply justify adverse inferences; it would supply then a justified ground of discrimination. If we knew, for example, that a man had a sexual orientation to boys, we may indeed have grounds on which to wonder about the maturity of his judgment and his qualification to serve as an adoptive parent. There would be no justification then for those laws, spreading through the country now, that ban in a sweeping way all discrimination based on sexual orientation. In a word, that concession, frankly made, would remove the ground of virtually all the laws on "gay rights."

As for myself, I would lean toward a regime of tolerance. I would wish mainly to leave people alone, rather than making their orgasmic relations part of a public conversation. I would prefer to hold back from saying that there is a "wrong" here that ought to be condemned in the law and made the object of prosecutions. I would have the law, rather, withhold its endorsement and scrupulously refrain from promoting and encouraging. And with that understanding, the law may refuse to confer certain claims, like a "right" of adoption, on people who identify themselves by their "sexual orientation," as gays and lesbians. That, as I say, is what I would prefer to do. But there is a serious question of whether I could preserve a policy in that cast, or whether the logic of the moral problem would finally move me out of that position of detachment, and nudge me in one direction or the other. Of that, I will have more to say in a while.

But for moment, let us say that I would hold back from pronouncing these homosexual acts to be "wrongs" that the law ought to condemn. I may plausibly say instead that there is something merely "disordered" about the willingness to take this aspect of human beings and raise it to a level that seems to define them in the first instance in their juridical standing, in their moral definitions, and in the things that constitute them as persons. We can only wonder at the state of mind that would ever think it illuminating, or even especially apt, to describe people, on any occasion, by the way in which they seek their orgasms. It would be taken, I think, as the sign of a sensibility out of order if we heard an announcement for a meeting of "The Missionary Position Subdivision of the Heterosexual Alumni of the University of Chicago." And what would we think of a school that divides its alumni by an interest, say, in Anal or Oral sex?

The Law of Toleration

The law may avoid these awkward situations through the expedient of mainly avoiding the subject: The law may hold back from prosecuting, but then it may hold back, quite as well, from any temptation to promote and endorse homosexuality. That seemed to be the sense of the matter held by the voters of Colorado when they passed Amendment 2, the constitutional amendment that was struck down by the Court in *Romer v. Evans*. The legislature of Colorado had already repealed the laws on sodomy in that State, and Amendment 2 did not seek to license a regime of prosecutions directed at gays and lesbians. What the movers of that Amendment were seeking to avert instead was the kind of use they had encountered with ordinances on gay rights in Denver and Boulder, where religious people were being compelled to undergo counseling if they suggested, say, to an employee, that he might get help in dealing with his homosexuality.

The people of Colorado responded with an amendment that simply sought to remove, from the hands of legislatures, the power to pass sweeping measures to ban discriminations based on "sexual orientation." The aim of the Amendment, in my reading, was simply to preserve for people, in their private settings, the freedom to honor their own judgments about the morality of homosexuality.

Still, there was a kind of awkwardness that would show itself later in a move that sought to deal with this problem while trying at the same time to preserve a posture of tolerance. The framers of the legislation drafted the law in this way: they would try to bar the tendency to treat the gay, lesbian, or bisexual orientation as the mark of a victimized class, standing on the same plane as the groups that have suffered discriminations based on race, gender, and religion. The drafters would try to accomplish that end by stipulating that a homosexual orientation or relation should not be the basis of a "claim [to] any minority status, quota preferences, protected status or claim of discrimination."

Justice Scalia would later remark in *Romer v. Evans* that the Supreme Court did not call back, or revise, its decision in *Bowers v. Hardwick*, the case in 1986 in which the Court refused to overturn the laws on sodomy in the separate States. It was within the constitutional authority of the State then to make homosexual practice a criminal offense. But if that is the case, Scalia asked, how could it be unconstitutional simply to say that homosexuality may not be picked out for special favoritism in the law?[6] As Scalia also pointed out, the protections of the law were not to be withdrawn for gays. The laws on assault barred the bashing of anyone; there was no reason to think that those laws would now fail to cover assaults that might be directed toward gays.[7]

But the Supreme Court did strike down that Amendment in Colorado in *Romer v. Evans*, and brought us to the threshold of establishing in the law quite a radical premise. For my own surmise here is that the judges will be inclined to read *Romer v. Evans* in the most expansive way, and they are likely to draw from that case this lesson: that a State may not plant, anywhere in its laws or public policy, an adverse judgment on homosexuality or refuse to treat homosexuality with the anything less than the legitimacy that attaches to the sexuality imprinted in our natures. With that decision, the Court has also created a powerful new device for purging, from executive suites in corporate offices, in the law firms, and in the academy, people who are serious Christians and Jews.[8] In his opinion for the majority in *Romer*, Justice Kennedy remarked that

the Amendment "seems inexplicable by anything but animus toward the class that it affects; it lacks a rational relationship to legitimate state interests."[9] Justice Kennedy professes to be a Catholic,
and the teaching of his Church, on homosexuality, has been shaped
and settled over two thousand years. Yet he is willing to dismiss a
carefully drawn and sustained teaching, in a gesture of summary
contempt, as a blind "animus" with no rational purpose, no rea-
soned ground of justification.

As Justice Scalia aptly observed, Kennedy and his colleagues in
the majority had been willing to disparage as "bigotry" an adher-
ence to the traditional teaching of Christianity and Judaism.[10] And
in that way, Kennedy and the Court have provided the predicate
for further litigation. For the teaching of the Court will now be
incorporated, even more fully, in the regulations of professional
associations. Scalia noted, in his opinion in *Romer*, that the Association of American Law Schools requires its members to extract,
from the firms interviewing their students, an "assurance of the
employer's willingness" to hire homosexuals. If an interviewer har-
bors traditional moral views on homosexuality, his firm could be in
violation of the rule established by the Assocation of Law Schools.
We can expect, or course, that rules of this kind will quickly make
their way into the bar associations, as well as other groups of professionals.

In that vein, an account was recently offered to me by a friend
who is a senior partner in quite an established law firm in New
York. My friend, who happens to be a serious Catholic, had expressed publicly his reservations about the new crop of laws and
regulations dealing with discriminations based on "sexual orientation." His critical remarks on this head had been published, in
fact, in a newspaper devoted to the legal profession. As the issue
seemed to heat up in the politics of the law schools, my friend was
discreetly dropped from the recruitment committee of his firm, the
committee that would be sent out to conduct interviews at schools
like Harvard. The implication, and the reasoning, seemed quite
transparent: Could it not be claimed now that the process of re-
cruiting had been biased at the outset by the presence of a senior

partner with known moral objections to homosexuality and the most serious reservations about "gay rights"? But the problem would not end with his removal from the committee on recruitment. For did the firm not house a senior partner with these views, in a position to vote on the hiring, firing, and promotion of young associates? In sum, the very presence of my friend in this firm would constitute the immediate ground for a grievance, or for litigation. Law firms are nothing if not sensitive to cues and incentives, and there would spring up here the clearest incentive to forestall the problem at the threshold by simply avoiding, in the future, the hiring of people who are "overly religious."

This tendency would be amplified by the passage in Congress of the proposed ENDA, a bill that would bar discrimination against gays and lesbians in private businesses. The bill should be called, more aptly, the "Christian and Jewish Removal Act," for it promises to purge serious Christians and Jews from the executive suites of corporations, universities, and law firms. That bill has been supported by both Senators from New York, Senators Daniel Patrick Moynihan and Alfonse d'Amato, both professing Catholics. It would seem to me highly fitting then, and quite urgent, for Cardinal O'Connor to request a meeting with the Senators from New York and earnestly inquire just what they have done to assure that this bill will not become the Christian and Jewish Removal Act.

BILLS OF ATTAINDER

I had been consulting with the Solicitor General of Colorado in the work on *Romer v. Evans,* and I had done some work with the law firm representing the City of Cincinnati during the defense of the comparable measure, Issue 3, in Cincinnati. The oral argument was held before the Supreme Court in October 1995, and there were signs, quite plain then, that the decision would come out against us. I was giving a talk to the Federalist Society in Boston in April of last year, just before we sprung the Defense of Marriage Act, and I was explaining that the case for the act seemed all the more urgent because we were expecting that *Romer v. Evans* would indeed turn out badly. And I remarked at the time on something I was reluctant to discuss in public: I mentioned my own hunch that the Court would invoke the notion of a bill of attainder in striking down the amendment in Colorado. I did not think that that argument would be apt or justified, but that the judges and their clerks would look for anything even remotely plausible—something good enough to cast up a haze and get them through the day.

But in the aftermath of that case, Professor Akhil Amar of the law school at Yale wrote a piece in the law review at Michigan, in which he sought to interpret Justice Kennedy's opinion as an opinion cast in terms of bills of attainder even though Kennedy had not summoned the genius to make that argument explicitly himself. Professor Amar has suggested that Justice Kennedy had written even better than he knew, and he now sought to make the case more fully.[11] I would raise that argument now for those with a serious interest in law and philosophy, because it is a thoughtful argument, which invites further reflection, and a response. My own judgment is that the argument over the bill of attainder does not finally work, but it does raise questions that lead us back into the center of the problem. Indeed, it tests the question in an even sharper way as to how we may ever legislate on this subject, especially if we do not seek to use the criminal laws against gays and lesbians. As we work through the issue, I think we would eventually find ourselves at the oldest and most familiar ground, now rendered unfamiliar to us: We may be separated from Professor Amar by the confusions that have arisen and divided people over the meaning of a "sexual orientation." That term has cast a benign fog over the subject, which allows people to talk about homosexuality in a rather abstract way, or even an approving way, while receding from judgment. And one of the critical things obscured in this fog of sentiment is the obdurate fact that there really are, in the end, no rival sexualities; that the only sexuality, in the strictest sense, is that "sexuality imprinted in our natures."

When I take up the question of bills of attainder with my own students, I usually take this angle into the problem: I recall the routine that Johnny Carson used to do of The Great Karnak. The

Great Karnak would announce first the answer to the question, and then he would open up the envelope, supplying the question. (And so the answer might be, "El Paso," and the question would be: "What do you try after you try El Runno and El Kicko?") For this problem, however, I did a slight variant: I would supply the answers in the form of names, and the question is whether you can describe the category, or the class, that the names would represent. And so the names were: Frank Sinatra and Alexander Hamilton. The category was: Born or died in Hoboken. Another: Joe DiMaggio, Ted Williams, Willie Mays. Answers: Outfielders whose careers were interrupted by military service.

I might have taken an easy one and said: Joe DiMaggio and Arthur Miller (and the answer would have been: married to Marilyn Monroe). But then, if I added one more name to the list, I would have produced an entirely different category: Joe DiMaggio, Arthur Miller, and John F. Kennedy. But as I suggested in the other examples, the categories may be quite refined and far less than obvious, and even people tuned into the world may find it hard to see the list and understand at once the class, or the principle, of which the names are supposed to stand as instances or examples. And so now imagine that Congress passes a law saying that no appropriations from the Treasury shall be used to pay any part of the salary or compensation of Mr. Robert Morris Lovett, Mr. Goodwin B. Watson, and Mr. William E. Dodd, Jr.[12] The fact that they are named does not reveal to us the category, or the principle, of which they are offered as examples. As it happened, Lovett and his colleagues were suspected of disloyalty, but if Congress had made explicit the ground of its judgment, it would have exposed to legal challenge everything that was problematic in the ground on which it was acting. If Congress says that we may inflict penalties on people who are *suspected* of disloyalty, the legislation is quickly open to the challenge that no wrongdoing has been proved; that no charges have been made; that no evidence has been presented and tested in a court.

If Congress were stipulating criminal penalties, these kinds of defects would be telling—and damning. But they would still be serious, and still satisfy the definition of bills of attainder (or bills of "pains and penalties") even if there were no criminal charges involved. It seems to be widely forgotten that the landmark cases on Bills of Attainder in our own law did not involve criminal penalties: They involved, for example, a priest who was barred from serving in his vocation (in *Cummings v. Missouri*[13]), or a lawyer who would have been barred from arguing before the Supreme Court of the United States (*Ex parte Garland*[14]). These cases involved a deprivation of livelihood, but also the sting of a reproach or condemnation, a calumny pronounced by the law. And that is what made it all the more curious when the civil libertarians acquiesced in the move to deprive one former president of the United States of control of his personal papers and tapes, and do that *by name*. Richard Nixon was affected in that way by a dispossession that was not applied to the papers of any president who had preceded him, nor of any president who would succeed him. Of course, the suggestion was made at the time that Mr. Nixon was in "a class by himself." Still, the Congress would have encountered real awkwardness if it had undertaken the discipline of explaining the class of which Mr. Nixon was taken as the sole example.[15]

But all of this is meant to point up again the critical difference between mentioning names and defining, in *impersonal* terms, the class of wrongdoers. Defining the class is virtually the same as defining the nature of the wrong. As Felix Frankfurter remarked, the decision was made in America to get legislatures eventually out of the business of acting in the style of courts. A legislature should act as a legislature, and it does that by accepting the discipline of defining, in impersonal terms, the character of the wrong and the wrongdoers. The logic of the separation of powers may act as a further incentive for legislators to hold closely to this discipline of legislating, for it makes a profound difference if one knows, in advance, that the legislation one shapes will be put in the hands of others to enforce, and those others may happen to be adversaries rather than friends. In that sense, we are reminded, that the separation of powers reflects the logic of what the philosophers call the "universalizability" principle, or what Kant called the "categorical imperative," or what others have recognized as the Golden Rule: Do unto others as you would have them do unto you. Act only on that maxim that one would will as a universal law. Act, then, only on the kind of measure, so impersonally just, that you would have it applied to yourself as well as to others. Locke caught, rather precisely, the sense of this connection between the separation of powers and the logic of a moral principle, when he wrote, in the *Second Treatise* that "[in] well-ordered commonwealths, where the good of the whole is so considered as it ought, the legislative power is put into the hands of divers persons who, duly assembled, have by themselves, or jointly with others, a power to make laws, which when they have done, being separated again, they are themselves subject to the laws they have made; which is a new and near tie upon them to take care that they make them for the public good."[16]

When we begin to sketch in this way the ingredients, or the concerns in principle, that mark for us the problem of bills of attainder, it would have appeared on the face that Amendment 2 in Colorado, in *Romer v. Evans*, would not come close. There was no mention of any names; there was simply an attempt to describe a class in the terms that have currency in our language: homosexuals, lesbians, bisexuals. And there was a decisive difference between a class defined in these terms and a class defined in terms of race or gender. To note the race or the gender of any person is not to reveal anything that tells us whether we are dealing with people who are good or bad, who have done anything that merits punishments or rewards. And so, as we say, it is quite different to create disabilities for people on the basis of race, as opposed to creating disabilities for people because they fall into a class called "arsonists." Arsonists may be picked out for punishment as a class because they are identified as a class through the commission of the same, defining acts.

Now if the question were posed as a matter of comparison, "homosexuality" would not be like race or gender in that respect; it would name a category of people who are identified by their conduct. None of this would seem to fit, then, the notion of a bill of attainder, because the Amendment in Colorado marked off a class, defined in impersonal terms—no mention of names—and a class defined by its conduct. Yet, as I told the Federalist Society in Boston, those ingredients would not be enough to repel the argument over bills of attainder, since the Supreme Court has now expanded the concept to include even groups defined in impersonal terms. And so, in one notable case, the Court struck down an act of Congress that sought to bar, from positions in labor unions, members of the Communist party.[17]

I happen to think, myself, that this move by the Court rather missed the logic that attends the bill of attainder—and missed, at the same time, the compelling reasons that may justify the Congress in barring members of the Communist party from offices in labor unions. Of course, Congress might have cast its legislation more broadly, to encompass all totalitarian parties aimed at subversion, and extended the ban to other parts of the economy. And yet, there might have been a good reason for picking out the Communist party in the 1950s as a special object of concern, and treating, with a heightened concern, the capacity of the Communists to gain access to a foothold that would give them a certain leverage in disrupting American industries. Still, the Court might have had a point that is not entirely implausible: What if a Congress of the Left banned from federal employment all men who held memberships in private clubs that refused to accept women? We may be coming close to that state of affairs today in regard to federal judges. A private involvement, which is legitimate in the eyes of the law, may be taken as a ground of disability. That state of affairs might well inspire arguments about a bill of attainder—but it may also be close to the kinds of disabilities we think it quite legitimate, in other instances, to establish.

LEGAL RETICENCE

In any event, the Court has broken past the old boundaries in defining bills of attainder, and that makes it possible for Professor Amar to make one fairly plausible argument here. The libertarians among us are acutely aware that every use of political power, every attempt to make binding laws, will have the effect of delivering benefits to some groups and imposing costs on others. The exercise of political power virtually invites what the libertarians call "rent-seeking," the efforts of various groups to seek benefits for themselves, at the expense of others, by using the monopoly powers of the law. That danger is simply endemic in politics, and it is the classic form of corruption identified by Aristotle: that the power over the whole will be used to serve the self-interest of a part, the private interests of the rulers and their friends. Now, what if the legislature addressed the universe of potential rent-seekers and passed a law saying that "plumbers should never claim any special privilege or protected status, or become the beneficiary of any quota"? We could not quarrel about the rightness of barring special treatment or unequal privilege. But would it not be rather curious that we pick out, for particular mention, this one class of people, as though they were particularly worse, or that they were more egregious examples of the vice we were trying to resist? Would it not seem odd that we pick them out, mainly by themselves, in a public containing a vast number of groups quite anxious to seek special privileges or favored treatment for themselves? The singling out of this group, under these conditions, may begin to strike us as invidious, even though, as I say, we could hardly fault the interest in denying, to particular groups, a privileged standing.

To that extent, Akhil Amar may have a plausible point—unless it turns out that, for the people of Colorado, there was no practicable alternative to the measure they had devised: To foreclose simply a special privilege or standing was the only thing they could do, *unless* they wished to drop their policy of tolerance and restore the laws on sodomy. For it may be that Scalia's argument, cast in a form *a leniori*, curiously marked a point of vulnerability in the argument for the Amendment on homosexuality: As Scalia said, the State could have made homosexuality criminal, and if it could have done that, surely it should have been able to enact the weaker measure, which merely disfavors homosexuality. (If the stronger, then certainly the weaker—*a leniori*.) But this argument plays precisely into the argument over the bill of attainder: The State declares that there is nothing here that it would condemn in the law, and yet it picks out a certain class of the public, who have not done anything wrong, and imposes on them disabilities it is not imposing on any other group. But on the other hand, if homosexuality *had been* proscribed in the law, then there would have been no oddity in a law that held back special protection from an activity that was condemned outright in the law.

And so Amar was in a position then to notice what suddenly stands out as an asymmetry in the law. The Amendment meant to overturn or cancel out the laws, in different cities, that forbade discriminations based on "sexual orientation." But in the reading offered by Kennedy and Amar, the Amendment would not in fact have done that: The Amendment would merely have prevented gays and lesbians from using the law to seek any protection for the assaults and discriminations that are visited *on them*. But in Amar's construal—and Kennedy's—those laws on "sexual orientation" remain on the books, and what they now forbid are the acts of discrimination that may be directed at "straights" or people who are not gay. Hence, there would be a breach of the Equal Protection of the Laws: Discriminations against heterosexuals may be litigated and prosecuted, but discriminations against gays, lesbians, and "bisexuals" will go unpunished, and unreproached by the law.[18]

Amar argues that, in *Bowers v. Hardwick*, the Court never considered an argument cast in terms of Equal Protection; and seen through that prism, as he says, we would notice that the law would punish oral sex between men or between women, but not oral sex between a man and a woman.[19] This is but one disparity that marks, for Amar, a state of mind, and a state of law, that finally cannot be defensible. For that law would depend thoroughly on discriminations that cannot be rationally explained, and indeed, distinctions that can hardly even be discussed in public.

But I would suggest that this reticence is indeed a key. The same understanding that condemns men lying down with other men, or with animals, is not likely to express itself in regulations that fill out, in precise detail, the things that men should not do in these encounters, or the devices they ought not use. If members of the public remain innocent of these things—if they know nothing, of "fisting" or the inventive use of shunts—there are good reasons why they should not be made wise to these unseemly ways of the world by imprinting, in our statutes, a permanent manual or guide to these practices. It would be a profoundly mistaken account of the law to characterize this reticence as the sign of an intention to conceal— and to regard the thing concealed as the unequal treatment of different sexual styles. We can be rather certain that our ancestors never intended to cover over the treatment of different sexualities or sexual styles, for the simple reason that they had not the least awareness of different "sexualites." An older generation could not have read the statutes in *Romer v. Evans* in the way that Justice Kennedy read them or found what Kennedy—and Amar—saw in the record. Kennedy assumed that the various statutes on sexual orientation, would still be in play, but they would be used now to combat discriminations against heterosexuals, while the law would be barred from dealing with any comparable discriminations against homosexuals.

REASONABLE DISTINCTIONS

But in this assumption, I think Justice Kennedy and Professor Amar make a profound mistake, in seeing the problem from a false angle. The rejoinder may have to come then from a slightly different angle, and so the point might be conveyed in this way: If someone asked my late father what his "sexual orientation" was, he would not have had the faintest notion as to what he was being asked—and by that I do not mean simply that the vocabulary would have been unfamiliar to him. It may be rather like the problem of asking a pious Jew whether he thought that the world came about randomly or whether a decision had been made by a Creator that there shall be something rather than nothing. Or it may be like asking a conductor on a train whether he has made up his mind yet about the law of contradiction, and whether there is a real difference between the purchasers of tickets and the non-purchasers, or the people getting off and the people getting on. It would have been incomprehensible to my father that the question would arise, just as it would be incomprehensible to the pious Jew that he and the world might have come from nothing. My father knew that he was a man grown from a boy, that there were men and women, and that is what sex was about. He knew that there were effeminate men, that some of them were homosexuals, but the fact that they had their own ways did not reveal anything problematic about the arrangement of the world into male and female. I can tell you, from a direct engagement with the people in Colorado and Cincinnati, that no one I knew in this project thought that the laws on "sexual orientation" would remain, in a residual form, to protect heterosexuals. And it must have some bearing on the problem that no one involved in the litigating of the case actually thought, in this way, that a success in the case would provide a powerful new device for launching prosecutions against gays. The lead attorney on the case in Cincinnati was my friend and colleague, Michael Carvin; and as Carvin explained, the people who were pressing the amendment in Cincinnati assumed that gays could have gay bars, that no one would have a lever in the law for accusing them of discrimination and inflicting penalties.

The activists who brought forth these measures assumed that they were removing altogether, from the hands of authority, the power to declare, in a sweeping away, the wrongness of all discriminations made on the basis of sex or what some people were pleased to call "sexual orientation." But at the same time, that move would preserve the possibility of making reasonable distinctions, both in public and in private, in the cases in which it would indeed be justified to make discriminations based on sex or sexual conduct. And so, for example, a couple in Rhode Island held group sex parties in their home, and that became a condition for removing for a while the custody of their children. Even a court composed of men and women quite averse to casting judgments may not be able to put out of view the faults that are expressed in sexual conduct. And for that reason the judges could not work practically under a rule that forbids them from making any discriminations based on the "sexual orientations" that may be revealed in the pattern of that conduct. In another example, the question had been posed in New York about counselors in the public schools of New York who also happened to be members of the North American Man-Boy Love Association. Since these people respected their own "sexual orientation," they had a rather hard time seeing just why they should not be free to commend that orientation to the teenage males who came under their counseling. Nor did they see that their orientation should be the ground of disabilities in barring them from this vocation of counseling boys. My own reading is that those who passed the Colorado legislation would have found it legitimate to make this kind of discrimination and to bar, from the counseling of children, people who professed their orientation to "pedophilia."

Professor Amar suggested that Amendment 2 in Colorado might have avoided the faults of a bill of attainder, or the test of Equal Protection, if it had simply moved in an even-handed way to bar legislatures from pronouncing upon the wrongness of any discrimination based on sexual orientation. But with that construction, as I have suggested, the State could not bar pedophiles or members of the Man-Boy Love Association from the position of counseling children in the public schools. Nor could the State have refused to accord, to homosexual couples, the standing of couples eligible to adopt children. Nor could it have made a host of other judgments, where the sexual conduct of the parties may become quite relevant. In point of fact, then, a policy of that kind is hardly the neutral or even-handed policy that Amar would suggest. Under the facade of even-handedness this arrangement would simply import once again the assumption that we are dealing with different or rival forms of sexuality. And from there it would seem to move on to the assumption that the Constitution incorporates this ethic of detachment, that the Constitution itself would require us to be utterly neutral, utterly wanting in judgment, in distinguishing among these varieties of sexuality—as though what Amar calls "straights" were simply one among a variety of styles, equally legitimate. To put it gently, we would find here in the end what we used to call a begging of the question: Even without intending it, Amar would simply install the premises that deliver his conclusion. He would treat as a settled, moral fact what the moral tradition, and the American Founders, understood to be entirely implausible and illegitimate. In his reasoning about the Constitution, he would in fact incorporate all of the essential assumptions of gay rights, even though those assumptions would be utterly at odds with the understanding of nature held by the Founders. And yet, without that understanding held by the Founders, there would be no way of giving a coherent account of a regime, or a Constitution, that was framed for the purpose of protecting rights that exist *by nature*, in beings who are by nature fitted to live in a polis and be the bearers of rights.

Professor Harry Jaffa once remarked on the controversy over slavery that, whether the black man was, or was not, a human being, could not be a "value judgment." It was not a question to be delegated to the legislators, for that is a question that had to be answered before we could even have legislators. Who, after all, would be fit to serve as a legislator or vote to constitute a legislature? Could horses and cattle vote? Could they serve if elected? Or did the whole enterprise not begin where Aristotle began it, with a recognition of the kind of being who was suited by *nature* to live in a polis?

But in the same way, we could suggest that, in the understanding of the American Founders, it simply was not open to us, through the positive law, to redefine the nature of a human being. No more is it open to us to redefine the nature of gender, or declare that henceforth there will not be men and women, but Snarks or Bojums, or perhaps five genders. Yet strictly speaking, no more is it truly open to us to redefine the nature of justice entirely through the positive law, as though the law, in the style of Woody Allen's dictator, could declare that henceforth, "all girls under sixteen are now over sixteen," or that, contrary to every axiom of moral judgment, people may indeed be held responsible and blameworthy for acts they were powerless to affect.

True Disagreement?

But we may ask, why all the strain? Is there really any disagreement, any true disagreement, on the main choices that confront us on the conditions for begetting? If we traced the question back to some original ground, would there really be any dispute between these alternatives?: Is it better for children to be spawned in random relations, or is it better for them to be begotten in arrangements in which their parents are bound to their offspring by the ties of law as well nature? Would anyone seriously deny that it is altogether more wholesome, more preferable in principle, that parents would be as committed to the nurturance of their children as they are committed to each other as husband and wife? More people today are living together apart from marriage, but is there really any doubt that it is better for children to come into this world through families prepared to impart to children their names, and in giving them their names, taking responsibility for them?

But all of that does rather assume, once again, that the meaning and purpose of sexuality has always been bound up with the purpose of begetting. Of course, not all married couples are capable of bringing forth children, but the people who enter the homosexual life must assert, quite unambiguously, the utter detachment of sexuality from that purpose. I am quite aware of gays and lesbians who wish to adopt children and care for them; nothing I say discounts their presence or the generosity of their motives. But neither does it dislodge my point: The praise, or celebration, of the gay life must celebrate a notion of sexuality quite severed from that understanding in which sexuality is connected immanently to a responsibility for begetting, and nurturing, the next generation. We may recall that, in the *Crito*, Plato has the Laws of Athens standing, embodied, before Socrates, and putting the question: How do we know that you were committed to Athens and committed then to the laws of Athens? As Socrates imagines the scene, the Laws would find as "the crowning proof that you are satisfied with our city [that] you have begotten children in it."[20] He had been willing to risk raising children under these laws, and his children gave him a deeper stake in taking responsibility for the polity that would house and shape those children.

Whatever can be said then for the gay and lesbian life, it must be admitted, even by its votaries, that nothing in the logic or character of that life can replicate those words in Isaiah, spoken by God in relation to Israel, but words that could be spoken in turn by any parent who fills the moral definition of a parent. We may ask, is there anything in the end simpler, or more decisive—or more telling finally of the things that separate the homosexual life from that sexuality imprinted in our natures? Is there anything simpler or more decisive than those words that come back to us from Isaiah?: "Fear not: for I have redeemed thee, I have called thee by thy name, thou art mine."

9

HOMOSEXUALITY
AND THE COMMON GOOD

Michael Pakaluk

IT IS SOMETIMES CLAIMED that, if laws were uniformly changed
to prohibit discrimination based upon sexual orientation or
preference, or if same-sex partners were allowed by law to enter into contracts regarded as the equivalent of marriage and having similar privileges and rights, these changes would undermine
the family and society at large. My purpose in this paper is to spell
out some of the reasons why that claim is true, and what exactly
the claim means, that is, what the "undermining" of the family and
society would amount to in this case.

We should acknowledge that the claim strikes many people,
and not only "gay activists," as absurd. Fr. John F. Tuohey, described
as being an assistant professor of moral theology at the Catholic
University of America, provided a good example of this response in
an article in *America* magazine.[1] Fr. Tuohey is criticizing a letter
sent by the Vatican to American bishops, with the not very succinct title, "Some Considerations concerning the Catholic Response
to Legislative Proposals on the Non-Discrimination of Homosexual
Persons." That letter, echoing a 1986 Vatican document,[2] stated
that "the view that homosexual activity is equivalent to, or as acceptable as, the sexual expression of conjugal love has a direct impact on society's understanding of the nature and rights of the family

and puts them in jeopardy." Fr. Tuohey complains that "Nowhere does the statement attempt to show that recognizing the civil rights of gay and lesbian persons would harm the 'genuine' family or the common good." Indeed, "The absence of any evidence . . . that gay and lesbian persons pose a threat to society is easy to explain. No credible evidence exists. On the contrary, there is evidence to suggest exactly the opposite." He then describes the many contributions that homosexuals have made to their communities, implying that what they may do in private has no bearing on how they act as citizens and that, if so, they can hardly constitute any "threat" to anyone else.

Or, again, on a gay-activist web page, I encountered the following argument: "Giving gay couples the right to marry would not take away any of the rights heterosexual couples currently enjoy; it would only extend those rights and responsibilities to everyone in our society"—as if the proposed changes would only increase freedom, not limit it, and only add to the benefits people enjoy, not in any way diminish them. But, if so, the changes would leave everything else intact: heterosexual couples and families could continue thriving and flourishing as much, or as little, as they were before. This is the way some people look at the matter, then, and any claims to the contrary strike them as exaggerated, even hysterical, and absurd.

Before proceeding, we should make clear the various sorts of legislative change that are at stake:

1. the extension of anti-discrimination laws, making it illegal to discriminate, especially in matters of housing or hiring, on the basis of sexual orientation or activity;

2. the legal recognition of same-sex couples as equivalent to marriage;

3. permitting same-sex couples to adopt or to serve as foster parents;

4. the repeal of anti-sodomy laws.

I want to say something about the last of these points in order to put the subject aside, since, although important, it is not my primary concern. In fact, the claim is *not* often made that repealing anti-sodomy laws would undermine the family or society. Although two dozen states presently retain anti-sodomy laws, it is not uncommon even for social conservatives to regard these laws as unwise and dispensable on the grounds that they are in general unenforceable.

But I think that view is a mistake. It is better to retain such laws where they exist, unless it were clear that they would be repealed as part of a what was a larger, *de facto* societal compromise, for anti-sodomy laws have a valuable function, even if they are unenforceable. First, they constitute a kind of link with the past, a link to society as it was *before* the sexual revolution, when our insight into matters sexual was clearer. We should retain such laws, then, as a kind of deference to the wisdom of the past. We accept them "on authority," so to speak, even if we do not directly grasp their point and force. And then, also, unenforceable laws may have the function of expressing a view and instructing: Anti-sodomy laws are an expression, in law, of the view that homosexual activity is inherently wrong—and that is the key truth that we have to preserve in the debates over each of the points I mentioned. Unenforceable or unenforced laws can also play an indirect role in deciding matters that *are* "enforceable." For example, in child custody decisions, it may become relevant that one parent rather than the other regularly engages in activity that is contrary to some unenforced law—the child then goes to the one who does *not* fornicate, or commit adultery, or engage in sodomy.

It is important not to acquiesce in *bad* reasons for repealing anti-sodomy laws, for instance, because they are argued to be excluded by an alleged constitutional right to privacy, or because they are claimed to be exceptions to Mill's harm principle. In fact, it is only if we hold that the state *could*, licitly and in principle, retain anti-sodomy laws, that we can then regard the repeal of such laws as an element in a stable compromise. John Finnis has referred, approvingly, to what he calls the "modern European consensus" on homosexuality, that is, the legal arrangement whereby, roughly, *pri-*

vate homosexual acts are not proscribed, but public acts, and the public promotion of homosexuality, are proscribed. That arrangement, like indeed most stable social arrangements in which there are competing interests or desires, involves reciprocity: Society relinquishes legislation over homosexual acts in private, but those who engage in such acts relinquish any claim of right to them, which their public performance or advocacy would imply. Yet such an arrangement is not possible, once it is conceded, as it should not be, that society has no competence to legislate against homosexual acts in the first place.

PLUS ÇA CHANGE?

How can we make out the claim that the *other* sorts of legal changes *would* tend to undermine society or the family? A first step is to argue that the proposed changes would not be slight changes in degree—say, the extension of benefits or rights to a larger class—but rather changes in *kind*, of a very radical nature. This makes it more plausible, at least, that the changes might undermine society or the family: Presumably, a change that was not radical could not be the sort of thing that would pose such a threat. This, I take it, is the force of the argument that Hadley Arkes and others have advanced,[3] that if same-sex "marriages" were recognized, then there would be no reason, in principle, why a marriage should be between only two persons. There is a certain ambiguity in the current legal category of marriage. The old view remains vestigially that a marriage is the founding of a family; but alongside this is another competing view, that a marriage can be simply a long-term erotic friendship. The older view retains a kind of natural pride of place and in some sense overmasters the other. But once same-sex marriages are recognized, we resolve the ambiguity decisively in one direction, severing "marriage" from procreation—in which case there is no reason why only two should marry, any more than why only two should be friends. So the change, clearly, is a radical one—of the sort, we might suspect, which would be mischievous in unpredictable ways, even if its immediate effects do not appear so damaging. The change does not extend marriage but alters its nature.

That is the force, too, of the argument that, if anti-discrimination laws are extended to include sexual orientation, then we shall soon afterwards be met with affirmative action for professed homosexuals. Of course this will follow: If it is wrong, *now*, to take homosexuality into account in any decisions about hiring or housing, then it was wrong throughout past decades and centuries as well. But that is to say that homosexuals may claim a long history of unjust oppression, just as African-Americans and other minorities. And the recognized remedy for that sort of thing is affirmative action. It is clear, then, that we have, not a mere incremental change, which *allows* some additional citizens to do what they wish to do, but a radical change, namely, the mobilization of the entire apparatus of social justice, which originated in the civil rights movement, to *promote* and *advance* a certain way of life.

That is the first step, to argue that the proposed changes are radical, not slight. The second step is similar. We saw that proponents of gay rights legislation argue that the changes they favor would leave everything else in place, as before, while simply increasing the freedoms and benefits enjoyed by homosexuals. Therefore, one advances the argument to the contrary that the proposed changes would imply the use of the coercive power of the state, brought to bear against citizens who are not homosexual, precisely insofar as they act in support of marriage and the family as these are traditionally conceived. So, for instance, a Christian who lets a room in a small apartment building will no longer be allowed to refuse to provide, as he sees it, an "occasion for sin" (to use the traditional terminology) by renting to a same-sex couple: he finds his Christian sentiments blocked and checked by the force of law—by a law, one should recall, which was supposed merely to let others do what *they* wanted.[4] Or, again, parents who teach their children one thing about sexuality and the family will find that state funds are used, and regulations are established, directly in opposition to them in government schools, since, *of course*, if discrimination on the basis of sexual orientation is strictly analogous to that based on race, it will need to be similarly warned against in the schools, and this from the earliest ages.

The second step, then, is to argue that things are not at all left in place by the proposed changes; it is not simply a matter of allowing an additional view. And then it begins to appear even more plausible that the proposed changes could undermine society and the family—if, that is, they are radical and imply the use of coercive state power against dispositions and actions that we regard as *good*, that is, those of honest citizens acting in accordance with their religious convictions, or simply aiming to teach their children well.

THE COMMON GOOD

But this leads to the third step of the argument, which is the most fundamental and, in a sense, the most obvious, but also the most subtle. At this point we need to go back and point out that Fr. Tuohey was not correct when he made his complaint. The Vatican letter he criticized *did* give an argument, albeit a very compressed one, for how the proposed legislative changes would harm society and the family. It gave the argument, in fact, in the very passage I quoted earlier: "the *view* that homosexual activity is equivalent to, or as acceptable as, the sexual expression of conjugal love has a direct impact on society's *understanding* of the nature and rights of the family and puts them in jeopardy" (my emphasis). What is at stake, most fundamentally, is a *view*—how it is that society looks upon something—and the view that we have is a part of the common good, and it involves immediate and manifold consequences.

Let me explain what I mean by saying something about the notion of a "common good" and what it is for society to have a *view* or belief about something. (This is in fact to explore the ancient idea of *concordia*: agreement on practical matters which is constitutive of social unity and civic friendship.)

I shall assume that people form associations, any association whatsoever, to procure or achieve something which they could not get at all, or could not get easily, if they acted each on his own. In that case, what they get through their association, and the instruments they use together in getting this, are, we can say, "common goods." For instance, in a large town or city, it would be either impossible or very difficult for each person to get water on his own— the water source is too small, or too far away, and hauling buckets takes too much time. So the town builds a system of reservoirs and pipes to supply water. The reserved water would then be a common good, and so too the reservoirs and supply system, the common instruments for procuring that good.

It should be noted that rarely is a common good simply a "thing" or material object. Even a water supply system, of any but the crudest sort, needs engineers to oversee it and skilled workers to maintain it. Their knowledge and habits of work—their virtues—have to be counted as part of that common good. But then, also, very often a *belief* is a common good. To give a simple example: Some commandos synchronize their watches and agree to rendezvous at a certain time. They must all believe that doing so is essential to their accomplishing their task; if an enemy could somehow befuddle some of them about that, he would foil their mission. Or, less trivially, it is a common good for both husband and wife to regard their marriage as indissoluble and for them to tailor their actions accordingly. If one member of the couple changes his mind about that, they both fail to achieve what they associated together for in the first place. Or, to take a political example, and one closer to our purposes, Lincoln held that the shared belief, among citizens in a republic, in the principles expressed in the Declaration of Independence, was essential to the practice of democracy. Their common belief in those "axioms of democracy," as Lincoln called them, is, we might say, an important common good. The shared belief in them is essential if citizens are to work together and assist one another, in a coordinated fashion, in maintaining and building up a free society.

A belief is held in common, we should note, not simply when each member of a group happens to hold it, but rather when each is furthermore *aware* that the others hold it, and is aware that the others are aware that *he* holds it. Typically, the way in which this sort of agreement is achieved in political society is through a law, a public resolution having the force of law, or some practice itself regulated by law. For instance, it is only after a declaration of war is passed by the legislature that everyone in a society becomes aware that a particular nation is regarded as a hostile power in the minds of all other fellow citizens as well. The declaration of war at once expresses and brings about this consensus. There are in fact many things which we thus believe in common, and which we must so believe, if our type of government is to work and endure. For example, we all believe that a life of productive work is better than one of listless unemployment, that literacy is a great good, and so on. It is an important mark of beliefs that are held in common, that they are transmitted effortlessly, with hardly any need of explicit teaching (which, by the way, is precisely why it is easy to neglect them). In a modern liberal state, in fact, it is typically left to religion to refresh and reinvigorate the shared beliefs most necessary to the state's existence, and rightly so; the government for its part has aimed, generally, not to place itself at odds with the promotion or encouragement of these beliefs.

We can say that a law implies a certain belief if the law could not be regarded as desirable or appropriate, except on that belief; also, that a law implies the *falsity* of a belief if it could be regarded as desirable or appropriate, *only* given the falsity of that belief. It was Lincoln's point against Douglas, for instance, that Douglas's idea of self-government implied a rejection of the principles of the Declaration of Independence: to accept a law which left it up to individual states, as something indifferent, whether they would be free or slave, was to abandon a shared belief in the basic equality of human beings, in virtue of their humanity. Douglas's conception of self-government could be regarded as desirable only given the falsity of the principles of the Declaration; thus it implied the rejection of those principles.

Finally, we can distinguish between beliefs which it is in some sense *natural* to hold in common, because they are regarded, correctly, as fulfillments or completions of other things believed, and those which it is not natural to hold in common, and which can be sustained, then, only artificially and through devices of coercion.

For instance, the doctrine of communism, that all property should be held in common, proved itself to be unnatural, something which could not really be believed, and which therefore had to be upheld, if it was to be maintained at all, through extreme or illegitimate coercion. In this sense, the belief that the unborn child has a right to life is natural: It is the easy extension, to the unborn, of a belief we are prepared to hold as regards any human being. But the belief that a woman's so-called right to choose is more fundamental is like Douglas' view of self-government: It is unnatural and can only be maintained by the corruption of the institutions of medicine, the law, and the media.

Now, to apply these considerations to the case at hand. Consider first laws that would prohibit discrimination on the basis of sexual orientation. Such laws are, of course, modeled on civil rights legislation of the 1960s. Now it is necessary, if one is to *rule out* discrimination of some kinds as being inappropriate, to have in mind reasons on the basis of which discrimination, or the drawing of distinctions, or the assignment of rank, *would* be appropriate. You cannot rule out some types of features, as a basis of judgment, except to clear the way for others. The correct view in this matter was articulated by Martin Luther King, when he said famously that his ideal was a society in which people judged each other, not by the color of their skin, but by the content of their character. And of course matters that have a bearing on morality are precisely those that, potentially, should enter into decisions about how we are to associate with others and on what conditions. If we grant this, then to say that a certain characteristic is *not* one that should be used for drawing distinctions is to say that it is *not* related to questions of morality or character. Anyone, then, who believed that homosexual acts were morally wrong, and who accepted this sound understanding of the point of anti-discrimination laws, could *not* regard it as appropriate or desirable to proscribe by law all discrimination on that basis; thus, laws which proscribe such behavior imply the view—and indeed propose it as a shared belief—that homosexual acts are not morally wrong. (Actually, one is left with an alternative: *either* homosexual acts are not morally wrong, *or* the apparatus of social justice originating in the civil rights movement works to no coherent purpose.)

What follows from this? If homosexual acts are not morally wrong, then, obviously, it is not the case that sexual activity *ought* to be confined to marriage. But that it ought to be is the correct view of the matter, and one that is most consistent with other deeply held common beliefs. Thus, for a society to accept such non-discrimination laws is for it to reject the true view of sexuality and marriage. We might say, then, that under the guise of a slight change in the law, motivated, apparently, by a concern for fairness, such laws embody or express the basic belief of the sexual revolution. They, so to speak, enshrine the sexual revolution in law.

THE CULTURE WAR

Of course it might be objected at this point that, if there is any threat to the family or society in this regard, it comes, rather, from the sexual revolution itself, and the evident change in society's mores then, not from some consequent change in law which assumes, as a *fait accompli*, the changes already introduced by the sexual revolution. But this objection underestimates the importance of law and fails to take into account the dividedness of society, that is, that there is indeed a culture war over sexual morality, which has continued to this point, and which will not be brought to a conclusion until the sexual revolution attains full legitimacy. Law is to society as principle and conscience are to an individual. A man may be a repeat adulterer, but so long as he recognizes that his marriage vow is binding upon him, he can reform. There are actually few, if any, legal changes since the 1960s which so directly imply the falsity of the view that sexual activity should be confined to marriage, as do gay rights laws. To accept such laws is to reject the principle, the claim of "conscience," by which, perhaps, the mores of the sexual revolution *could* be reversed.

Furthermore, although it is difficult to live in a society such as ours presently is, in which the true view of marriage and sexuality is hardly ever affirmed, it is much more difficult to live in one in which it is explicitly denied, and this with the power of the state. Currently, parents who wish to teach chastity and marital fidelity to their children are like the townspeople who needed water in our example, but where the water supply system has been disabled by a social upheaval, so that those who want water have to find a bucket and a water source and haul it in on their own. But once the negation of what such parents believe gets embodied into law—and law, too, which has the appearance of being righteous and progressive— it is as if the town then poisons its water supply, so that one has to be concerned, not only with getting fresh water, but also with not drinking the fouled water.

Consider next laws that would recognize same-sex couples as marriages. I consider it a telling fact that one never hears anyone saying, simply, that the proposed change is outright *impossible*, that two persons of the same sex *cannot* be married, whatever the state may say about it. Really, the only healthy reaction to the idea of same-sex "marriage" would be a kind of chuckle at the absurdity of it, and an internal resolve to ignore, as though nothing at all, both this fiction and anything any government might say in support of it. It is as though the government were to declare monkeys to be men, or men not to be men. Well, we have not done so well in resisting this last idea—the government *has* declared some men not to be men, and we go along with it—so I suppose it is not surprising that there are no signs of the appropriate response to the idea of men marrying men.

What these reflections suggest is the following. No one who thought that marriage had an objective character, prior to the state, could regard it as appropriate or desirable that there be a law by which the state defined and indeed altered, as by fiat, the character of marriage. Thus, laws recognizing gay marriage imply the falsity of the view that marriage is an objective reality prior to the state. Note too that parental authority must stand or fall with marriage. If the bond of husband and wife is not by nature, then neither is the government of those who share in that bond over any children that might result. Thus, laws recognizing gay marriage imply, similarly, that parents have no objective and natural authority over their children, prior to that of the state.

We are familiar with the idea, and, as I have said, we have acquiesced in it, that belief in the inherent dignity of all human beings is a subjective preference, a whim or fancy, which some fringe members of society—the right-to-life extremists—may perhaps regard as decisive in their *own* lives, because they hold to particular religious beliefs which involve this belief as a consequence. To accept gay "marriage," similarly, is to endorse the position that the belief in the family as having its own nature prior to the state is a mere whim or preference, springing from a religious viewpoint, perhaps, which the state is not bound to honor—in fact, which it cannot honor, without violating the separation of church and state.

If, indeed, gay "marriage" were to be recognised in law—a state of affairs which would itself be regrettable, since the required beliefs underlying it would be "unnatural" beliefs, in the sense I have explained, and which therefore could only be sustained by illegitimate force and coercion—then I do not doubt that it would not be long before it became regarded as unjust, that *some* couples, the heterosexual ones, can have children, but others cannot—just as, presently, women who accept the "pro-choice" ideology regard it as unjust that *they* can bear children, but men cannot. As much as possible, then, in a society in which the proposed changes have been fully implemented, children will be raised directly by the state. That biological parents have some special claim over their children will be seen as some kind of mysterious superstition, perhaps even a disguised animus against others, which can in any case be easily trumped by the state's concern for what it would regard as the well-being and proper education of citizens.

These are some of the developments that may be in store for us—at least we cannot say that we would be tending to avoid them—if we endorse gay rights and gay marriage. Of course, it might be objected that this is all fantastical and preposterous. But I am certain that gay marriage and partial birth abortion would have seemed much more fantastical and preposterous in 1965. And in any case the burden has been discharged, the challenge overthrown. Why is it not absurd to hold that gay rights laws undermine society and the family? Because they imply beliefs which are incompatible with the common pursuit of goods which one wishes to obtain in marriage and family life. They remove a common good, a correct shared belief about the nature and good of marriage, which enables us to assist one another in realizing marriage and attaining its good, and they substitute—again, in the guise of something praiseworthy and just—a view which can only be sustained with coercion, and which will lead to suffering and unhappiness to the extent to which it is acted upon.

"Marriage" Hawaiian Style?

Gerard Bradley

T HE MOST COMPELLING CONSTITUTIONAL QUESTION involving homosexuality is the prospect of Hawaiian same-sex "marriages" spreading to and across the mainland, propelled by the Constitution's Full Faith and Credit Clause (FFCC). That provision, in relevant part, reads: "Full faith and credit shall be given in each state to the public acts, records, and judicial proceedings of every other state." The clause also authorizes Congress to regulate the "manner" and "effect" of fidelity, and Congress passed what it called the Defense of Marriage Act under this authority. Its purpose, and the purpose of some twenty-odd state laws which, like DOMA, restate that marriage is the union of one man and one woman, is to protect against the forced introduction of same-sex marriage by FFCC.

The prospect, more specifically, is that once any single state recognizes, as Hawaii is about to, relationships between persons of the same sex as "marriages," these couples *must* be recognized as married throughout the country, even where—as, for the moment everywhere—no same-sex couple could legally enter into a marriage. Hawaii could be to same-sex marriage what Nevada used to be to divorce. And all state policies limiting marriage to its traditional constituency will come to naught.

What can be done to protect against this tsunami? Will DOMA and cognate state laws form an impregnable dam against "same-sex marriage"? One problem—a possible hole in the dike—is the basic aim behind FFCC, which is interstate comity. If you are married, you were married in one state, but you are considered married in them all. When you go on vacation in another state and register at a motel, you register as a married couple even if you never before set foot in that state, know not a thing about its marriage laws, and would not attend the wedding of your best friend if it were held there. As Supreme Court Justice Robert Jackson said in 1948 in *Estin vs. Estin*, "if there is one thing that the people are entitled to expect from their lawmakers, it is rules of law that will enable individuals to tell whether they are married and, if so, to whom . . . the uncertainties that result are not merely technical; nor are they trivial: the lawfulness of their cohabitation, their children's legitimacy, their title to property, and even whether they are law-abiding persons or criminals." Jackson wrote when it mattered more than it does today with whom one spends the night. But even now the difference between bigamy and lawful marriage is the portable validity of a divorce decree. And the difference between marital love and unlawful sodomy is soon going to be how well Hawaiian marriages travel.

Two men or two women cannot now legally enter into a marriage in Hawaii or anywhere else. But a gender discrimination lawsuit against Hawaii has just about reached endgame, and the news is not good: All the Hawaiian courts so far have decided that the state cannot limit the legal status of marriage to couples of different genders. The Hawaii Supreme Court has yet to confirm the latest ruling of the inferior court there. But the high court's earlier opinion, to which I shall turn momentarily, leaves no room for doubt: same-sex marriage is just around the corner.

What did the Hawaii Supreme Court, in the case of Ninia Baehr (who wanted to marry Genora Dancel) versus John Lewin (the state official responsible for denying Baehr a marriage license), say? Not what you would expect. One would expect from all that has been reported about this decision, including what I have so far reported to you, that Hawaiian same-sex marriage is "gay marriage," with its implicit approval of homosexual sexual activity. Not at all: Hawaiian same-sex marriage turns out to be "no-sex" marriage. Footnote eleven of *Baehr vs. Miike** is particularly revealing: "'Homosexual' and 'same-sex' marriages are not synonymous; by the same token, a 'heterosexual' same-sex marriage is, in theory, not oxymoronic . . . . Parties to 'a union between a man and a woman' may or may not be homosexuals. Parties to a same-sex marriage could be either homosexuals or heterosexuals." The court later said that "it is immaterial" whether "the plaintiffs [that is, the same-sex couples, including Baehr and Doncel] are homosexuals." The court also pointed out that nowhere did the plaintiffs say they were homosexual (or heterosexual, for that matter).

The Hawaii Supreme Court discussed at length what most people have in mind when they speak of marriage. But marriage the court associated with the right of privacy located somewhere in the federal Constitution, and so called it the "federal construct" of marriage. This construct, the court correctly reported, "presently contemplates unions between men and women," and is associated with or defined by the "fundamental rights of procreation, childbirth, abortion and child rearing." (Of course, that sentence is grotesque, and even a false statement of the law: Single people possess all these rights too, except that husbands and fathers remain, by judicial dictate, notoriously outside the loop of the abortion decision. What the court meant by its assertion of this heterogeneous bundle and the "federal" right to marry as "the logical predicate[s]" of each other is anyone's guess.)

We can see that Hawaiian marriage swings free of the "federal construct," and of the idea that one essential feature of marriage is that it is a sexual, indeed reproductive, union (as the canonical and civil law requirements of gender complementarity and consummation attest). Let's call this, simply, marriage. Hawaiian "marriage" is radically divorced from it. The estrangement is most vividly il-

---

* Miike succeeded Lewin in office, and therefore became the defendant in the lawsuit.

lustrated in the court's response to arguments advanced on behalf of Miike. The state, as the court related the point, "contends that 'the fact that homosexual [sic—actually, same-sex*] partners cannot form a state-licensed marriage is not the product of impermissible discrimination' implicating equal protection considerations, but rather 'a function of their biologic inability as a couple to satisfy the definition of the status to which they aspire.'" The argument is, in other words, that given what marriage really is,—metaphysically, morally, pre-legally—persons of the same gender cannot marry. "We believe," said the court, that the argument is "circular and unpersuasive . . . . an exercise in tortured and conclusory sophistry."

The Hawaii Supreme Court articulated and imposed upon the people of that state an unsurpassably positivistic definition of marriage, one which could be related to the moral reality of the matter only by a sophist. The court's marriage was, in principle, *sexless*, and almost all about money. Calling it, revealingly, at one point a "legal partnership," the court listed fourteen specific benefits to which this "legally conferred status" is the gatekeeper. Twelve of them were clearly economic advantages; the other two—easier name changing and the evidentiary privilege for spousal communication—were relatively minor.

The relation of this legal counterfeit to the real thing is entirely accidental: Really married people may find Hawaiian "marriage" a commodious enough legal station, but the identity itself is not tied to, nor is it about, real marriage. Were this view of marriage to take hold, it might be the case that everyone was *legally* "married," but that no one *really* was.

CORPORATE MARRIAGE?

To what might we compare this new Hawaiian export? I would compare it to the relation between churches and corporations.

---

* Where the asterisk appears in the quotation the court referred readers to footnote eleven, cited above.

Churches are virtually required by practicalities to incorporate themselves under state law. They surely need some legal identity to acquire, hold, and sell property, to maintain a bank account, to carry on employment relations with workers, and so on. So, let us say that all churches are corporations (and if a few are not, my main point still holds). But not all corporations are churches. Most are not churches, even though nonreligious corporations incorporate for many of the reasons churches do: to carry on orderly economic relations with people both within and without the corporation. But note well: Though all churches are corporations there is nothing at all about that legal status that denotes or connotes the sacred. And that would still be true even if, in some small state, most or even all corporations in that locale were churches.

On this understanding of how Hawaiian "marriage" is (un)related to marriage and to the entity treated as marriage in the other states, what faith and credit is due island unions? The answer to which most sensible people in this debate are inclined is to treat heterosexual married couples differently than homosexual couples. This answer would develop and defend an exception to the general, and generally sound, rule of "married here, married everywhere." But persuading courts in each state to which island couples might travel that the exception is warranted will be exceedingly difficult. Besides having to defend the slight against "comity" (the traditional spirit of friendly accommodation among states), the argument would have to shoulder the additional burden of defending the rationality of what the Hawaii Supreme Court called circular and sophistical and what other courts may call the legal detritus of popular prejudice, influenced by sectarian doctrines.

William of Ockham was famously wrong about many important things, but his razor is still good to use: Why try to establish unnecessary premises? Question: What credit is due to Hawaiian marriages after whatever date the new regime takes legal effect? Answer: None. Not no credit for same-sex marriages, but credit for heterosexual marraiges; simply no credit for anyone. After the effective date the position of other states should not be that Hawaii has expanded the definition of marriage in some mischievous, incremental way. Rather, Hawaii should be seen as having, legally speaking, abolished marriage.

The situation would be much more clear if the Hawaii Supreme Court had named its creation accurately, not "marriage," but what in normal usage is called a "household." Then we could say with intuition and common sense in our sails that other states need not treat Hawaiian "householders" as if they are married. Just as we could, in legal terms and by analogy, say that no state is under a FFCC obligation to treat all out-of-state corporations as it treats in-state churches. Nike is not entitled to the favorable treatment that the Catholic Church might receive under state property tax laws, even though both are corporations. Similarly, Hawaiian "householders" would not be entitled to the special privileges that married couples enjoy in some destination state.

Same-sex couples, if they should marry after the effective date, can claim no marital status abroad. But so long as they leave the islands with an intent to settle, the imposition upon them would be trivial. Their new domicile state could set a registration provision for migrating couples eligible under its marriage laws to be married in-state, and call them married upon registration. Migrating same-sex couples would be in their present situation: unable to marry in the domicile state. Temporary travelers of all stripes would be legally unmarried.

These and other difficulties may stimulate the judicial reconsideration which this case so desperately needs. And this is probably the place to observe that the conduct of this trial by Hawaii authorities was disastrous. The state gave notice, after the Supreme Court opinion we have examined was handed down in 1993, that it would defend traditional marriage on several grounds. Included on this pretrial list were the treatment of Hawaiian marriages in other jurisdictions and, as the trial court phrased it, "the adverse effects, if any, which same-sex marriage would have on the institution of traditional marriage and how those adverse effects would impact on the community and society."

"The evidentiary record in this case," the trial court wrote of the last question, "is inadequate to thoughtfully examine and decide these significant issues." What of comity (or, if I am right, the lack thereof)? "[E]xcept for asking the court to take judicial notice of DOMA," the state "introduced little or no evidence with regard to this significant issue . . ." Hawaii instead tried the case entirely on a child-benefit theory, basically that traditional marriage is the "optimal" context in which to raise children. Leaving aside just what "optimal" means in this context, it should have been clear to the state's attorneys that, deprived as they were by the Hawaii Supreme Court of the premise essential to their case—that traditional marriage is true, sound, upright and that nothing else is marriage—they could prevail, if at all, only on some other grounds. Even so, execution of the ill-chosen strategy was unfortunate. Most of the state's expert witnesses were cross-examined so effectively that they ended up being better witnesses for the same-sex couples.

We can now see, ironically enough, that if the argument here is sound and if Hawaii will be seen as having abolished marriage, so much more likely is that catastrophe to be averted. The other question concerns the relationship of traditional marriage to the common good. It is a large one. Obviously any cogent answer to it will want to avail itself of a judicially denied premise—that marriage really is a distinct something which can be supported by all but which can actually be entered into only by persons of different genders. (And of course only some of them. Given what marriage is, minors and incompetents cannot marry, as our law of marriage has always recognized.) This rhetorical handicap does not foreclose dialectical arguments. The main line of a response will, it seems to me, aim to show that where the law divorces marriage from its reality, as the law of permissive divorce has done, that reality becomes less and less culturally sustainable, to the point where the reality is hardly available save to the heroic or otherwise deeply countercultural. Simply put, how many Catholic young adults getting married today really believe that marriage lasts, notwithstanding civil divorce, until death? The analogy here is not that someday, in a generation or so, same-sex marriage will be as common in Hawaii as belief in the impermanence of marriage is now. The analogy is tighter and deeper. For even after the battering it has

taken from contraception and abortion, marriage will be conclu-
sively separated from reproduction, as far as the law is concerned,
only by "marriage Hawaiian-style." Same-sex or no-sex, it will not
matter.

A final note, which is really an argument in the battle ahead in
Hawaii, and probably elsewhere. Imbibe deeply, if you will, the
idea of marriage as a free-standing civil status, "conferred" by the
state on relations of its choice, in the allegedly linear world created
by the occlusion of metaphysics and morality. Question: Will the
natural right of parents to direct and control the upbringing of their
children survive, much less flourish, there? Will this natural right
of parents be intelligible at all?

11

THE QUESTION OF MARRIAGE

David Orgon Coolidge

T
HE QUESTION OF MARRIAGE HAS ARRIVED. Every American citizen must now engage two controversies that require resolution: *Who* should decide what the law of marriage is? *What* should the law be? The meaning of marriage is being contested in many ways, at a variety of levels. The issue of "same-sex marriage" is only one of these, and ultimately, others may be just as important.[1] But the question, "Does marriage require a man and a woman?," is surely of lasting significance.

In 1996, the possibility of same-sex marriage seemed to burst upon the American scene. Suddenly the whole country heard about what was happening in the State of Hawaii and the implications of actions in Hawaii for the federal government and the other forty-nine states. Congress, the President, and mainland legal and advocacy groups were caught up in an intense debate, which culminated in the passage and signing of the federal Defense of Marriage Act.

Appearances, nevertheless, can be deceiving. The question of same-sex marriage has been debated on the margins of our culture for decades, surfacing in courts from time to time and then dropping back out of sight. The current crisis broke in Hawaii in 1993, yet took three years to come to the forefront of national attention. Now, similar lawsuits have spread to Alaska, Vermont, and New

York. The debate shows no signs of ending anytime soon and could be resolved before most people even notice what is happening.

Andrew Sullivan, perhaps the leading advocate of same-sex marriage, describes our present time as "The Marriage Moment."[2] He argues that "the issue of same-sex marriage is a civil rights matter and a religious matter. It is a question of politics and a question of culture. It interacts with people as citizens and as parents, as lovers and as relatives, as people of faith and as people of reason. It requires from each of us the most patient of dialogues and the most exacting of distinctions."[3] If Sullivan is correct, it is time to prepare ourselves to address the question. To participate responsibly in the debate, a citizen needs to know four things: what the marriage debate is about, what is happening around the country, what are the deeper issues and arguments; and finally what practical options there are for a person who wants to respond effectively to the campaign for same-sex marriage.

THE CENTER OF THE DEBATE

The present marriage debate is about *whether the American people have the right to define marriage as the union of a man and a woman.* The legal campaign for same-sex marriage is a transparent attempt to go around the people, through the courts, because there is no *political* support to legalize same-sex marriage. If there was any doubt about this, the recent passage of state constitutional amendments in Hawaii and Alaska should put the question to rest. The people of these states have rejected the attempt to redefine marriage through the courts. Yet the lawyers in these states who are campaigning for same-sex marriage insist that even these amendments are illegitimate.[4]

The challengers of the current law argue that the existing legal definition of marriage is irrational and prejudicial (their substantive point), and because of this, the courts' job is to overturn these majority-made laws (their process point). Those in favor of same-sex marriage are not necessarily arguing that the courts should always lead in social reform; they are arguing, more specifically, that the definition of marriage as the union of a man and a woman is substantively *indefensible* and therefore courts should intervene and overturn laws that rest upon this definition.

The defenders of the current law disagree. They argue that the existing legal definition of marriage is a reasonable exercise in self-government (their substantive point), and that those who disagree with it should not try to do an "end run" around the democratic process by persuading judges to overturn current laws (their process point). Those in favor of the existing law are not necessarily arguing that legislatures should never be constrained by the courts; they are arguing, more specifically, that the definition of marriage as the union of a man and a woman is substantively defensible and therefore legislatively permissible.

Who decides (the process) is not the same as what is decided (the substance). In constitutional law, however, for better or worse, process and substance are often closely related. Substantive characterizations of an issue are often linked to conclusions about the proper process. If both sides link their substantive assumptions to their view of the proper process for resolving the question, what then makes one view more legitimate than the other? The answer seems straightforward: one view (in favor of current law) allows for everyone to be involved, and does not rule its opponents' views out of order. The other (in favor of same-sex marriage), in contrast, *depends*, by definition, upon successfully convincing an elite to rule its opponents' views out of order.[5]

It is crucial for those who wish to defend the existing legal definition of marriage to understand that the campaign for same-sex marriage depends, at its core, upon convincing the courts that the current law is prejudicial and that those who support it are bigots. If advocates of same-sex marriage cannot convince a judge to take this point of view, then all that remains is a disagreement between otherwise legitimate opinions, something that should be resolved through the legislative process. In the normal democratic process, everybody (including gay and lesbian activists and their allies) should have a voice, but nobody (including those same activists) should be able to rule out points of view altogether.

The campaign to legalize same-sex marriage through the courts has at least four stages: Sue, Soften up the Public, Slash and Burn, and Sue Again.

Sue. First, nationally-prominent public interest lawyers, working with local gay and lesbian activists, target a specific jurisdiction with courts thought to be sympathetic to their cause. The state is usually one which is relatively liberal in its laws on same-sex couples and in which likely political opponents are relatively marginal or unorganized. A same-sex couple applies for a marriage license, knowing that it will be denied. Then they sue, claiming that the marriage law is unconstitutional on state or federal grounds

Soften up the Public. The second stage is a "public education campaign" by gay and lesbian activists, and their allies in the progressive community, to pressure the public to stay out of the contest. It begins with press interviews portraying the plaintiffs in a positive light. This way people will be more inclined to say to themselves, silently, "The judge ought to help those people." Comparisons will be made to earlier civil rights movements.

If any initial success is achieved in the courts, the case will be presented to the public as a "done deal." High-minded scholars will applaud the court's ruling as an "advance for civil rights," and will "remind" attorneys general, legislators, and citizens that the courts are the final interpreters of state and federal constitutions and that the court's word should be taken as the last word. The public will be "informed" that resistance is futile, because any attempt to override the courts will be declared unconstitutional by the U.S. Supreme Court ("You saw what happened in Colorado, didn't you?").[6] In this stage, there will be the appearance of a debate, but there will be as little actual debate as possible: if citizens make no objection, the campaign succeeds.

Slash and Burn. If, instead, dissenters organize and a genuine public debate begins, then things become ugly. In stage three, proponents of same-sex marriage actively attack their opponents as "bigots," "homophobes," and people who want to "impose their religious beliefs" on those who do not accept them. Those who are inclined to support current marriage law are put on notice that if they join the opposition, they will soon be branded as the equivalent of old-time Jim Crow racists. Through public attempts to discredit dissenters, the cost of supporting marriage will rise, and the faint of heart will head for political cover.

Sue Again. Despite all this, the legislature or the voters may pass a consitutional amendment to preempt or overturn the courts, as they have in Hawaii and Alaska. At this point, supporters of same-sex marriage will file *another* lawsuit, challenging the constitutionality of the amendment in state or federal court. They may also argue that such an amendment is irrelevant to the question of equal legal benefits for same-sex couples. This is their final attempt to rule their opponents' arguments out of order. In this way they hope to achieve a political victory, but without the normal political process of give-and-take.

This is not an abstract scenario.[7] The entire crisis in Hawaii was spawned in the courts, and the federal Defense of Marriage Act can be understood as a preemptive strike against possible overreaching by other courts. The forty-eight state legislatures which have taken up the marriage debate have done so in response to the Hawaii courts, and with an eye on future cases before their own courts. New lawsuits in Alaska, Vermont, and New York are fresh attempts to force the issue. The power of the courts is at the center of this debate.[8] For this reason alone, the campaign to redefine marriage is deeply troubling for the future of our democracy.[9]

FRONT LINES IN THE MARRIAGE DEBATE

Since the *Baehr v. Lewin* decision of the Hawaii Supreme Court in 1993[10], it has been clear that the states might be forced to recognize same-sex marriages. Under traditional legal principles, a marriage performed in one state is normally valid in another state, and federal law has traditionally chosen to draw its definition of marriage from state law. This being the case, if other states and the federal government wanted to avoid being forced to recognize the validity of same-sex marriages, they would have to take swift and unequivocal action to make this clear.

Before Hawaii, only a few state legislatures had passed marriage recognition legislation. But when Hawaii became embroiled in the debate over marriage, other legislatures began to respond. Since then, the U.S. Congress and virtually every state legislature has been caught up in the marriage debate.

Hawaii

Elsewhere, I have told the story of the crisis in Hawaii in some detail.[11] The drama began when three same-sex couples applied for marriage licenses, were denied, and filed a lawsuit. They claimed, for various reasons, that it was unconstitutional for Hawaii to exclude them. In their view, marriage was a civil right; giving the right to them was a question of simple fairness.

In 1993, a plurality of the Hawaii Supreme Court declared that the existing marriage law was a form of "sex discrimination" and could only be justified by showing a "compelling state interest."[12] Shorn of the legal jargon, this means that the Hawaii Supreme Court decided, for the first time in history, that with respect to marriage the burden of proof was on the state to justify the law, not the on same-sex couples who were challenging it. This set off a politically explosive chain-reaction of events in Hawaii that culminated in the recent passage of the marriage amendment to the Hawaii constitution.

But the drama in Hawaii is not over yet. In the courts, the law was found unconstitutional by a trial court in 1996 and was again appealed to the Hawaii Supreme Court.[13]

Meanwhile, among the people, there was a groundswell of opposition to the court's removing the question of marriage from the democratic process.[14] Opponents of same-sex marriage believe that marriage is a unique social institution that requires a man and a woman and that the Hawaii Constitution, properly interpreted, is consistent with this view. They have maintained that the people have the right to enact laws that reflect that belief. In their view, the Hawaii Supreme Court usurped the people's role.

It was clear that some form of Constitutional solution would be required if the Hawaii Supreme Court would not reverse itself. In April 1997, the state legislature passed a proposed Constitutional Amendment which reads: "The legislature shall have the power to reserve marriage to opposite-sex couples."[15] For eighteen months, between April 1997 and November 1998, the citizens of Hawaii waited for the opportunity to vote on the amendment. At any time during that period, the Hawaii Supreme Court could have pre-empted their vote by deciding the *Baehr* appeal. This time, however, it waited. On November 3, 1998 the amendment passed by more than a two-to-one margin (69 to 31 percent). Now the Hawaii Supreme Court can do what it is genuinely authorized to do: interpret the text. Both sides will present arguments before the Hawaii Supreme Court about the meaning of the marriage amendment and its applicaion to the *Baehr* case.

Alaska

In 1998, the debate over same-sex marriage descended upon Alaska, to everyone's surprise. A lawsuit had been filed several years earlier by a gay male couple who wanted a marriage license. The case had moved slowly, however. Suddenly, on February 27, 1998, Peter Michalski, an Anchorage Superior Court judge, declared that under the privacy clause of the Alaska State Constitution "the choice of a life partner is personal, intimate, and subject to the protection of the right to privacy." This was further than even the Hawaii Supreme Court had gone in 1993. He also agreed with the Hawaii Supreme Court that the existing marriage law was "sex discrimination" and ordered further hearings.

The Alaska legislature was in session when Judge Michalski issued his decision. The debate was fierce, but the response was swift. Before they adjourned, legislators passed a proposed state constitutional amendment to reverse his order and placed it on the November 3, 1998 ballot.

In July, opponents of the amendment filed suit before the election to try and stop the vote. They lost at the trial court level and appealed to the Alaska Supreme Court. That court chose to "edit" the amendment text by keeping the first sentence, but removing the second. This was a highly questionable act on their part, but the amendment did remain on the ballot: "To be valid or recognized in this State, a marriage may exist only between one man and one woman." On November 3, 1998, the amendment passed with 68 percent of the vote. Opponents of the amendment immediately vowed to continue their original suit and to challenge the amendment. The Attorney General and the legislature, each with their own lawyers, are busy fighting back.[16]

Vermont

Supporters of same-sex marriage launched a new lawsuit in Vermont in July of 1997 in response to the failure of their allies in Hawaii to stop the proposed constitutional amendment. The Vermont lawsuit mimics the Hawaii lawsuit: it is partly statutory, mostly constitutional, and again includes two female couples and one male couple. A public interest legal group from Boston, Gay and Lesbian Advocates and Defenders (GLAD), has served from the beginning as co-counsel in the case. The trial judge dismissed the case in December 1997, holding that the current marriage law has a rational basis. The plaintiffs immediately appealed the decision to the Vermont Supreme Court. In the course of 1998, briefs were filed, including an extensive set of amicus briefs on both sides. Oral argument was held on November 18, 1998. As of this writing, no decision has been issued.[17] Vermont is now *the* hope of the campaign for same-sex marriage.

Congress

In early May 1996, a group of federal legislators, realizing they had to preempt the Hawaii Supreme Court, introduced the Defense of Marriage Act. Its goal was to shield federal and state law from Hawaii's threatened redefinition of marriage. After hedging, President Clinton announced his support for the bill, to the dismay and then outrage of his supporters in the gay and lesbian community.

The White House, in explaining the President's support, put it in these terms: "This goes to the heart of what marriage is."[18]

The Defense of Marriage Act, as enacted, has two provisions: (1) it clarifies that the "effect" portion of the Full Faith and Credit Clause of the Constitution does not require that same-sex marriages be recognized by other states; and (2) it defines marriage, for purposes of federal law, as the union of one man and one woman.[19] Its opponents have vigorously attacked it as "either unnecessary or unconstitutional," not to mention portraying it as a mean-spirited statute driven by "animus."[20] Its defenders have applauded Congress for wisely exercising its power as guardian of federal law and as independent interpreter of the Constitution, as well as putting the courts on notice that they will meet considerable resistance if they try to redefine marriage and foist the new definition on the entire country. Both sides agree that a lot is at stake in the realm of federal law.[21] If some state legalizes "same-sex marriage," couples from other states will go to that state, marry, and return to their home states. If they claim to be married—perhaps by filing a joint tax return—and are denied, litigation will follow. As part of that litigation, there is sure to be an all-out challenge to the constitutionality of the Defense of Marriage Act.

State Legislatures

When Congress acted to address the potential legalization of "same-sex marriage," it only brought to a head, at the federal level, a debate already raging in the states. By the end of 1998, bills clarifying rules of marriage recognition had been introduced in forty-eight states, and of these, thirty had been enacted.[22]

The reason for these laws is relatively straightforward. The general legal rule is this: If a man and a woman are married in Nebraska and move to Illinois, Illinois treats them as married *because Nebraska* considers them married. The Full Faith and Credit Clause encourages this kind of policy, as do legal principles that have developed in common law and contemporary statutes. On the other hand, exceptions are permitted to this general rule, including what is known as the "public policy exception": If recognizing the Nebraska marriage would violate a "strong public policy" of Illinois, then Illinois may refuse to recognize the marriage.[23]

But who decides whether Illinois has a strong public policy? Usually, the question would be addressed in the course of a lawsuit. In this case, for instance, a judge would have to assess whether Illinois *really has* a strong public policy objection to Nebraska's marriage law. In making that assessment, the judge would likely give significant weight to any clear statements that Illinois has already made on the subject, especially statements in the form of statutes.

Therefore, legislation can give courts clear guidance about whether a state wishes to recognize same-sex marriages performed in another state. Unlike a lawsuit, the legislative process allows citizens a chance to participate in the debate over same-sex marriage. If a state goes on record, in advance, in opposition to recognizing same-sex marriage, then the people of that state will have given a clear signal to state agencies and courts about the proper response.

Generally speaking, the statutes which have passed have two or three elements. First, they reaffirm that, under the state's own laws, "same-sex marriages" are void (if the law is not explicit). Second, they clarify that their state will not recognize any "same-sex marriages" entered into in other jurisdictions. Finally, some statutes also contain language stating that no "incidents" of marital status will be recognized. Presumably, this language refers to rights, responsibilities, and benefits of a same-sex marriage which a court might otherwise recognize, even if it did not recognize the same-sex marriage as a marriage *per se*.[24]

There are interesting things to be observed in the debates and struggles going on in these legislative bodies. On the one hand, political support for traditional marriage is still relatively strong, even in states that have not yet enacted recognition statutes. Legislators generally recognize that they are dealing with something profound and are hesitant to endorse a radical change. In particular, they are instinctively suspicious of allowing another state to resolve the issue *for* them.

On the other hand, the cultural, political, and legal acceptance
of alternative sexual relationships, including those of same-sex
couples, is growing rapidly. Jurisdictions are continuing to debate,
and sometimes enact, sexual orientation "anti-discrimination" statutes, and domestic partnership policies are being adopted by both
public and private employers.[25]

In these legislative debates, one often finds three sides, rather
than two. Each legislative body has a core of legislators who support traditional marriage because they define it as a basic question
of "family values." Every legislative body also has a core of legislators who support same-sex marriage because they define the issue
as a basic question of "civil rights." In each legislature, there are
representatives with these views, and their positions are usually well-
known.

The "third side" is everybody else, bobbing and weaving somewhere in between, trying to find a way to present themselves as
both supporters of family values and civil rights. These are often
persons in leadership positions, trying to avoid partisan battles and
seeking to read which way the public wind is blowing. Some are
purely pragmatic; others are uncertain what to make of the marriage question as a policy matter. All are highly sensitive to its
political volatility.

In and out of government, this political "middle" is up for grabs.
Each clearly-identified side typically tries to convince its fence-
sitting audience of citizens, media, and fellow legislators that theirs
is the mainstream position, that the other side is "extremist." At
this point the rhetorical *casting* of the issue by advocates and editorial writers makes a big difference. Can the supporters of traditional marriage convince the undecided that their position is
pro-marriage, rather than anti-gay? Can the supporters of same-
sex marriage convince the waverers that their position is pro-marriage, rather than anti-family? Who can persuade others that they
care the most about the community and not just about their own
interest-group agenda?

It is instructive that, at the end of 1998, twenty states have not
yet passed marriage recognition legislation. While there are unique

circumstances in each state, there is something more at work. We may be in the midst of a seismic shift in how many Americans look at marriage, a way of viewing the issue which challenges *both* the so-called parties of family values and of civil rights. Supporters of the existing marriage law must address this shift if they want to remain contenders in the marriage debate.

WHAT IS MARRIAGE?

What is this seismic shift? We need to step back from the immediate, day-to-day arguments and strategies, and look more deeply at cultural trends. Disagreements about how to address the possibility of same-sex marriage reveal more fundamental divisions about what marriage "really" is and what the law of marriage should be. Amid all the technical legal arguments, Americans are debating this question *What is marriage?* In the words of Russell Shaw, "We now lack a single, universally agreed-upon model of marriage and family—an ideal to which everyone subscribes—and we're in bad trouble as a result."[26] To participate effectively in the public debate, it is important to understand these deeper issues.

Three Models of Marriage[27]

Put succinctly, the new view of marriage being adopted by an increasing number of cultural and legal decision-makers is that *marriage is an intimate, committed relationship. The purpose of marriage law is therefore to recognize and encourage intimate, committed relationships.* The following are the basic features of what I call the "Commitment" model:

1. Every individual seeks intimate relationships. Sex is a way of expressing intimacy.

2. Intimate relationships grow best within a framework of commitment.

3. Couples, children, society and government benefit from committed, rather than promiscuous relationships.

4. It is reasonable, therefore, for the law to encourage committed relationships.

5. Marriage is the central legal institution of commitment in American society. Therefore marriage—or something equivalent to it—should be open to any couple.

6. Attempts to resist this are irrational and bigoted. Where it seems prudent, courts should take the initiative and push the legal system in the right direction.

This model is not morally neutral.[28] It has a moral-legal norm, which appears to be that sex between intimate, committed partners is good; promiscuous or casual sex is bad.

This view of marriage can be contrasted with two more familiar approaches. The first undergirds the existing law, and has been the basis of Western law for centuries.[29] It is claimed by the supporters of family values and assumes that men and women "complement" each other, so we can call it the "Complementarity" model. It has these features:

1. Marriage is a unique *sexual community* based on the difference and union of the sexes. It is more than the creation of contracting individuals or of the State.

2. Marriage is also a *social institution* that links prior generations and future generations. It has an intergenerational mission.

3. Marriage is a *legal status* that is designed to preserve, protect and promote this institution, especially for the benefit of children, parents, and grandparents.

4. What the Constitution guarantees is the right of every individual to enter into that legal status. Due Process and Equal Protection are meant to *defend* marriage.

Complementarity does not mean that men and women are only half-persons or that all human qualities can be neatly divided into those that belong to one sex or the other. At best, it means that sexual community requires sexual difference, and insofar as marriage is a total sexual community, it is based upon sexual difference.

The fact that our marriage laws still require a man and a woman to obtain a marriage license is a reflection of these assumptions. The moral-legal norm at work is that marital sexual intercourse is good, nonmarital sexual intercourse is bad.

The second model of marriage is what I call the "Choice" model. It makes these assumptions:

1. Individuals should be free to choose their sexual partners.

2. Marriage is a socially-constructed institution which embodies certain views of sexuality, relationship, and family. These views should not be treated as normative.

3. The law should leave individuals free to contractually create their own relationships, and restrict itself to enforcing agreements and addressing injuries.

4. Constitutional law should enforce individual rights to freely-contracted relationships, over against legislative attempts to restrict the range of options.

This model assumes that marriage is a contract between individuals with no intrinsic meaning, utterly subject to redefinition. What we call "marriage" is merely a licensing procedure in order to track and regulate those who have entered into contracts. While the Choice model claims to be neutral, it exalts the autonomous individual above all other values or laws. The moral-legal norm of Choice is that sexual expression is good, sexual repression is bad.[30] Pushed to its logical conclusion, the Choice model suggests that the State should get out of the marriage-licensing business altogether, and leave people to freely-contracted relationships.

Although the Commitment model is now competing for dominance, it is the conflict between Complementarity and Choice that has defined much of our culture over the past century.[31]

Second Thoughts

During the so-called "Sexual Revolution" of the 1960s, many in the heterosexual community changed their view of marriage from the Complementarity to the Choice model.[32] They no longer understood marriage as an institution meant to be total, exclusive, life-long, and procreative. The idea that sex, marriage, and children are somehow connected was rejected, and the new ideal proposed was one of equal individual sexual choice. This became an influential movement in our culture and remains so to the present day.[33]

The early gay liberation movement was very much part of this trend. It joined the general sexual revolution in its call for individual autonomy in matters of sex and considered marriage irredeemably "heterosexist" and incompatible with freedom from sexual and social oppression. There continue to be prominent scholars, activists, and grassroots leaders in the "gay, lesbian, bisexual, and transgendered" movement who hold this view.[34] These old-fashioned gay liberationists are often quoted by their opponents in the family values camp.

Arguably, we are now in an era of "Second Thoughts." As the returns have come in from the sexual revolution, many in the mainstream have come to see the limits of a Choice model of marriage. Whether as a consequence of the epidemic of divorce or the abandonment of children, today many people say they are more interested in commitment and stability, in responsibilities as well as rights—especially where children are involved.[35] They say they are willing to abandon "neutrality" and promote accountability. This "communitarian" mood we see so much of is the root of the Commitment model of marriage. Yet Commitment is clearly not Complementarity because it does not depend upon the difference and integration of the sexes. However, Commitment does claim to be less individualistic than Choice.

These second thoughts have also appeared in the gay and lesbian community. The early years of liberation were challenged by the tragedy of AIDS; many have seen through the emptiness of the bar scene; and the idea of "coupling" has become more popular. Notice how Professor Eskridge subtitles his book, *The Case for Same-Sex Marriage: From Sexual Liberty to Civilized Commitment*.[36] A movement has developed which advocates faithful, long-term same-sex relationships. Andrew Sullivan is one of those most identified with this viewpoint.[37]

There is also a practical incentive for this view: it is more appealing to the mainstream. It builds bridges more readily within liberal religious communities to gay and lesbian movements, who in turn are closely linked to progressive heterosexual religious leaders.[38] These liberal religious communities talk of commitment and have responded very positively to the idea of blessing "covenant relationships" as equal or parallel to marriage. Yet while the Commitment model connects with the mainstream, it does not totally alienate advocates of Choice. Many of those who take a Choice view of marriage and might reject marriage for themselves have now closed ranks with advocates of Commitment in order to support legal efforts for same-sex marriage. Choice advocates see it, though, as an interim step in the transformation of family law.

The result of this new emphasis on long-term relationships is a kind of "gay communitarianism." Instead of saying, "Marriage is for heterosexuals; let us go our own way," these advocates say, "If marriage is such a good thing, let us have it too—we want to be accepted as full members of the community." This argument is proving to have increasing appeal among some segments of the public.[39]

The Appeal of the Commitment Model

We must concede that the Commitment model has many attractive features. It fits the companionate ideal of marriage which is so popular in American culture generally. We are quite used to thinking of married persons, in Pepper Schwartz's well-known words, as "American Couples."[40] In addition, it is hard to disagree with love, commitment, and stability, generally stated. The case for same-sex marriage, with this shift of focus, plays much better in the public debate.

The Commitment model claims to encourage long-term relationships and societal stability, while discarding such "baggage" as the view that men and women are different in significant (and therefore legally relevant) respects. Instead, the Commitment model re-characterizes marriage as a *relational* institution, rather than a sexual one, and presents same-sex marriage as an *extension*, rather than a redefinition, of that institution.

As a result of these developments, there are now constituencies within both the heterosexual and homosexual communities that have discovered each other and are making common cause on behalf of redefining marriage as Commitment. To be sure, the heterosexuals in this crowd are more likely to support domestic partnerships than same-sex marriage (Ann Landers, for instance) whereas the homosexuals are more likely to support same-sex marriage than domestic partnerships (Deb Price, for instance). But this is a matter of political calculation, I think, rather than principle. The underlying point of view is the same.[41]

This approach fits prevailing trends. Consider a typical way of telling the story of our culture: "A generation ago, our marriage law was very traditional. Then we told people to 'do their own thing.' The results are in: We need more realism and accountability in marriage and family law." The topic could be gay liberation, teen pregnancy, promiscuity, no-fault divorce, child support, child custody, or any number of other issues.

According to this story, the 1950s model of sex, marriage and family was "too strict," the 1960s model was "too radical," and now, our culture and law need to land "somewhere in the middle." But everything depends on how one defines "the middle." Probably the Christian Coalition and the Children's Defense Fund would agree that intimacy and accountability ought to go hand in hand, culturally and legally. But this tells us everything and nothing. It expresses a mood, but not a coherent point of view. It does not tell us how the persons involved would apply their views to specific issues.

To sharpen the question: Is same-sex marriage merely an extension of the so-called 1950s model? Or does it exemplify the 1960s model? Or is it, instead, a valid element of some yet-to-be-defined "new middle"? Legislators, governors, and judges are being confronted with precisely this question, even though they may not realize it.

The advocates of same-sex marriage do realize this and are adjusting their strategy. In Hawaii, the litigators employed lots of "rights talk," emphasizing legal equality, but were vulnerable to the charge that they care nothing for the views of the people. In Vermont, the litigators are using more "relationship talk," emphasizing family values, and their tone is broadly moral, rather than narrowly legal: "We are here, we are your neighbors, we are committed just like you are, we raise children just like you do, we won't harm anybody. Therefore we should have the rights, responsibilities, and benefits that you have." Once the issue is framed in this way, advocates of same-sex marriage can portray their opponents as people "against our families," and advocates can encourage progressives to "side with our families."

In the marriage debate, Commitment may be sold as a "third way" for those in the political middle to present themselves as both in favor of family values and civil rights. It may appear a synthesis of the best of both Complementarity and Choice: a blend of order and liberty, family without rigidity or anarchy, an inclusive approach to the marriage "tradition." Consider that Lincoln's Birthday, conveniently close to Valentine's Day, is now the annual occasion for nationwide events promoting same-sex marriage. In San Francisco, the All Our Families Coalition sponsors National Freedom to Marry Day. In the words of Kate Kendall, Executive Director of the National Center for Lesbian Rights: "Having our relationships legally recognized is not about special rights or undermining the 'traditional' American family. Allowing lesbians and gay men the same right to marry as every other couple promotes such core family values as stability and security for our children."[42]

The Weakness of the Commitment Model

Because of our divided hearts and often compromised lives, we can be taken in by ambiguous rhetoric. Indeed, ambiguity may be the key to the appeal of the Commitment model. Jean Bethke Elshtain has put it as clearly as anyone: "These days, talk about community and connectedness sounds very appealing, especially if the talk does not threaten to demand very much. But whenever general talk of community turns to specific notions of strengthening our core civic institutions—such as marriage, for example—the attractiveness seems to fade and a certain sourness often sets in."[43] Mindful of this dynamic, we need to ask some hard questions about the Commitment model.

There are at least three kinds of questions we might ask. The first concerns the intellectual content of the model. For instance, is this model really making a claim about human nature, in which case there is something to discuss? Or is it purely a strategic reinterpretation of tradition for political purposes? How does the Commitment model relate sex, marriage, and children? Purely as a matter of choice? Purely as a matter of relationship? If so, isn't Commitment just as drastic a redefinition of marriage as the Choice model?

Second, it should be observed that the public policy implications of the Commitment model look very much like those of the Choice model. Those who talk about commitment still do not acknowledge the right of the American people to decide the legal definition of marriage. They keep us busy talking while their lawyers continue their march through the courts.

Finally, I wonder whether the Commitment model is truly accepted by the gay and lesbian cultural and political community, except as another choice for those who may prefer it. Evidence for this observation can be found in the January 20, 1998, issue of the *Advocate*, "the national gay & lesbian newsmagazine." One of its featured pieces is Andrew Sullivan's "The Marriage Moment," which I have already mentioned. Sullivan exalts commitment and criticizes promiscuity, even if his use of these terms is not entirely clear.

Yet the same issue includes another feature article, "Portraits: Gay Sex in the Face of AIDS."[44] It presents profiles of the sex lives of seven gay men, listing the number of their "sex partners in 1997." The first man profiled is an "activist, porn star, hustler," who says he had "as many as 150" partners in 1997. The subtitle of his excerpt is, "Freedom means sex for erotic film star." Another is a New York City schoolteacher who explains that he came to the United States from Puerto Rico because having sex with whomever he wants is "what America is about." He had "hundreds" of sex partners in

1997. Another is a man who cruises the internet for those interested in "leather, kink, and master-slave relationships." He says "The issue is not how many sex partners you have. If they do it responsibly [e.g., with a condom], then I don't feel that's a bad thing." Another is a twenty-three-year-old man who describes sexual freedom as a "right and privilege," and had fifteen sex partners in 1997. Then there is a thirty-year-old former drag queen who "honestly can't say" how many people he had sex with. He criticizes "reckless promiscuity," but then adds that no one should "regulate where I f— and how I f—." The sixth is a man who had nine sex partners. Two of these encounters involved "unprotected" sex.

Only *one* of the seven men profiled had just one "sex partner." This man, an activist from Austin, Texas, has this to say: "Unfortunately, the history of gay men has been defined by what they do in bed." In the 1960s and 1970s, he says, promiscuity was "a calling card for activism." Now that some believe AIDS may be cured, he sees promiscuity on the rise again. He faults those who fail to understand that "sex, like guns, can be a tool, a weapon." Criticizing the rise in unsafe sex, he says, "It amazes me how gay men in this country are so selfish."[45] His is the lone voice which questions, in *any* manner, the reigning ethic of "choice." It is not even clear whether he questions the ethic, or just wants to remind us of its danger in a world with AIDS.

Considering that the *Advocate* is now widely viewed as a mainstream magazine and is available at local bookstores, what message about commitment does this article convey? Each of the men profiled speaks for himself, not officially for the *Advocate*. But isn't the magazine telling teenagers and young adults that this is what it means to be a gay man today? At least this suggests that Sullivan's preference for monogamy (however he defines it) is merely another option. But if Commitment is merely an option, rather than a moral imperative, it is not Commitment, it is Virtually Choice.[46] This suggests that domestic partnership is the legal category that corresponds most logically to the Commitment model, since it is more flexible and carries less "baggage."

Indeed, at a certain point the boundaries of Commitment and Choice begin to blur. Some legal scholars blend them effortlessly. David Chambers, a prominent law professor at the University of Michigan, has this to say about the meaning of same-sex marriage:

> If the law of marriage can be seen as facilitating the opportunities of two people to live an emotional life that they find satisfying—rather than as imposing a view of proper relationships—the law ought to be able to achieve the same for units of more than two. . .it seems at least as likely that the effect of permitting same-sex marriage will be to make society more receptive to the further evolution of the law. By ceasing to conceive of marriage as a partnership composed of one person of each sex, the state may become more receptive to units of three or more (all of which, of course, include at least two persons of the same sex) and to units composed of two people of the same sex but who are bound by friendship alone. All desirable changes in family law need not be made at once.[47]

The question each citizen has to answer is: Do we want to go down this road or not?

How Should We Respond?

For those of us who support the definition of marriage as the union of a man and a woman, a response to the challenge of the marriage debate is absolutely critical. Here I will try to lay out what I see as the crucial points in the debate, first rebutting arguments for same-sex marriage and then adding some positive arguments for reaffirming marriage as a union of a man and woman.

Arguments Against the Current Definition of Marriage

1. *Same-sex marriage should be legalized because, after all, marriage is an intimate, committed relationship. Same-sex couples can be intimate and committed like anyone else.*

This is a fairly direct argument based on a claim about what marriage is. The proper response to this, first of all, is *not* to argue about whether same-sex couples can be intimate or committed. Of course they can. Instead, it is best to respond that this may be *one* view of marriage, but the law expresses a different view: It assumes that there is something unique about a male-female sexual community. Those who disagree and think the law should be different, should argue for it like everybody else. They should approach the legislature with their proposals, instead of running to the courts. In a forum that allows for genuine citizen participation, we can fairly debate the issues.

2. *Supporters of the existing law believe that the only purpose of marriage is procreation. Either they should forbid marriage for opposite-sex couples who cannot or will not have children, or they should let same-sex couples marry, too.*

This common argument is based on a misrepresentation of the traditional view of marriage. It suggests that if marriage is solely for "baby-breeding," then only those able and willing to have babies should be allowed to marry. But the initial premise is false, so the implications are as well. The traditional understanding does not view marriage in such crudely functional terms. It views marriage, first of all, as a *community* of the sexes, and second, it sees this community as having, as *part* of its natural role, the nurturing of the next generation. This is not an argument from biology; it includes biology, but it is about persons in community. A couple who are infertile, for whatever reason, can still enter into a total sexual union, and thereby form a genuine marriage. Their marriage may not have all the *effects* that often concern the law—the law will have less to regulate in their marriage, if children are not involved—but it will still be a marriage.

3. *Gay and lesbian people are a persecuted minority. Marriage statutes should be actively overturned because they are based on a systemic bias against gays, lesbians, and other sexual minorities.*

This argument *sounds* legal, but it is really political. No Supreme Court has ever held that homosexuals are a persecuted minority deserving special constitutional consideration. This is just an argument that the courts *should* adopt this general point of view. Even if a court did come to this general conclusion—some court may, at some point—it would not follow that *marriage* laws were motivated by a desire to harm. Hard as it is for advocates of same-sex marriage to believe, marriage laws could actually be motivated by a view that marriage is a special sexual community that deserves *preference* in the law. Non-marital sexual relationships of *all* kinds can be (and are) legally distinguished from marriages.

If an advocate concedes this, she must concede that the issue is controversial, and that the traditional point of view is one legitimate point of view. At this point, you then remind her that if both points of view are legitimate, then they should be debated and resolved in a more democratic forum than the courts.

4. *Thirty years ago, interracial marriage was illegal, and the courts struck it down. No one questions whether that was a good idea. Today, same-sex marriage is illegal, and the courts should strike it down too. It's the same principle: the freedom to marry.*

The hidden premise of this argument is that just as racial differences are as irrelevant to marriage as sexual differences. It follows that just as the courts took the initiative to strike down bans on interracial marriage, they should strike down bans on same-sex marriage.

But the premise is dubious, both historically and philosophically. As a historical matter, the general law of marriage thirty years ago did not rest on racial differences. For over a millenium, it had been understood in the West that marriage was the union of a man and a woman.[48] "Anti-miscegenation" laws were legal aberrations, outside the mainstream, that developed during slavery. They were, as the lawyers call them, "badges and incidents" of slavery, segregation, and racism.[49]

The premise behind this argument is dubious, too. It assumes that sex (or what it often calls "gender") is as "socially constructed" as race. But most Americans do not believe this, and there is no reason that they should. "Race" is a social category that has a connection to skin color in some cultures but not in others. Sex, on the other hand, is a biological category that applies across cultures. To put it bluntly, there are no cultures in which men bear children, or in which women impregnate men. To be sure, sex has *added* meanings in *every* culture, some of them positive, some negative. But sexual difference and marriage are realities in every culture, not mere "social constructions."

Because the premises of this argument are flawed, it does *not* follow that the courts should strike down existing marriage laws. In *Loving v. Virginia*, the 1967 decision that overturned bans on interracial marriage, the Supreme Court spoke movingly of the freedom to marry.[50] But no one seriously argues that by "marry" they meant anything other than men and women marrying. The only way to extend the word "marry" to include same-sex couples is to redefine it, by smuggling in the whole set of dubious assumptions that we have identified. Short of that, the interracial analogy fails.

So when you hear the "same as race" argument, I suggest two responses. First, ask the advocates of same-sex marriage *how* it is, exactly, that sex is the same as race. Let them explain that sex and marriage are culturally constructed. Let them explain how marriage has nothing to do with sexual difference. Then let them tell you what marriage "really" is, and see whether anyone who does not share their ideology is persuaded.

Second, realize the real purpose of using the race analogy: to cast you as a bigot. It is not to have a philosophical conversation about "essentialism" and "social constructionism." If the advocates of same-sex marriage can tar everyone who disagrees with them as the equivalent of a racist, then people will be intimidated. When this happens, their strategy is more likely to succeed.

5. *Supporters of 'traditional' marriage are mostly religiously motivated citizens who want to impose their religious views on others. This is both immoral and unconstitutional, because civil marriage should be*

*based on secular views, and America is based on separation of church
and state. Religious people can hold their views in private.*

This argument sounds legal, but is actually makes several highly
debatable claims about religion, politics, and law. *If* America is
based on the separation of church and state, and *if* marriage law
may only be based on "secular" views, and *if* supporters of traditional marriage simply want to "impose their religious views" on
others, then perhaps the argument has force. But none of these
premises is self-evident

First of all, the First Amendment guarantees citizens religious
liberty, which surely includes the right to advocate political and
legal views based on one's religious convictions. It does not include a religious test for arguments—indeed, it prohibits religious
tests for officeholders of any kind. How religious one's political-
legal arguments should be, in order to persuade those of differing
views, is a mixture of principle and prudence which requires the
best judgment of each religious believer.

Second, the view that marriage laws must be based on only
"secular" views is only one point of view, and a dubious one at best.
It assumes that secular views exist which are entirely "uncontami-
nated" by religious ones—and that if they exist, they are a good
basis for making laws. This is certainly the view of some prominent legal scholars, but it has no *constitutional* force.

Third, religious people are involved in the debate about *civil*
marriage because they care about the welfare of society, not merely
the well-being of their own religious community. This is an hon-
orable tradition in American life, no more "authoritarian" than any
other such tradition. And of course, as the advocates of same-sex
marriage never tire of telling us, there are religious people on both
sides of the issue.

So ironically, the viewpoint behind this (anti-religious) argument is itself intolerant. It assumes one true answer to the question of how religion and politics may relate and imposes that answer
in the guise of constitutional doctrine. Show it for what it is.

Besides these kinds of arguments, there are more practical ones which are often made.

6. *Same-sex marriage won't make any real difference to society anyway.*

Proponents of same-sex marriage argue that its legalization will make no real difference. They paraphrase the now-famous words of Congressman Barney Frank, "What difference does it make to you if my partner and I can get married? How does it change your life in any real way?"[51] At the same time, these advocates claim that legalizing same-sex marriage will be a tremendous achievement. In Andrew Sullivan's equally memorable words, "If nothing else were done at all, and gay marriage were legalized, ninety percent of the political work necessary to achieve gay and lesbian equality would have been achieved. It is ultimately the only reform that truly matters."[52] Which is it? "No difference" or "Ninety percent"?

Of course the legalization of same-sex marriage will have dramatic effects; it is supposed to. The real debate is about whether these effects will be good.

For instance, legalizing same-sex marriage will send a new *moral message* to Americans about marriage: Marriage is based solely upon emotional and economic attachment, and those who disagree with this view are bigots who should not be allowed to "discriminate" against others.

It will also have a *legal impact*. This includes federal benefits, but the main effects will be at the state level, in the areas of marriage-related benefits, anti-discrimination laws based on marital status, adoption and child custody laws, public and private school curricula, nonprofit contracts with State and local government, private groups using public facilities, and professional licensing standards for lawyers, doctors, social workers and teachers, among others.

Finally, this moral message and legal impact cannot help but have profound *societal effects* over the long run. Those parents and associations who disagree with legalized same-sex marriage will be further alienated from mainstream America and its central institutions. There will be less support for marriage benefits in the workplace; benefits will be reduced, and more and more employers will give benefits only to individuals, leaving families to fend for themselves. Meanwhile, young people will grow up imbibing the official view that there is nothing special about the male-female family unit; it is only one item on the sexual smorgasboard of life. They will feel that they must experiment sexually in order to discover "who they really are." But since there will be no real answer to that question, the result will be deep confusion and many broken lives.

To some, these travails will be a sign of a transition to a more inclusive society; to others, they will be evidence of a society without standards, descending into chaos, prepared to suppress its own tradition of civic participation in the name of "equality."

7. Same-sex marriage will be not be harmful for children, it will be good for them.

Proponents of "same-sex marriage" argue that children need "parents," not a mother and a father. In some cases they claim that children in same-sex households get a *superior* upbringing. Using a stockpile of carefully-constructed research, they argue that studies "prove" these facts. These studies, however, use biased samples and have other significant methodological flaws.[53] In addition, the whole argument assumes that the *normative* issue of what kind of upbringing children need can be *scientifically* resolved, without introducing any substantive assumptions. This is logically false, because science and its uses are not morally neutral.[54]

Most people still believe that a child is best raised by a mother and father (ideally, in most cases, his or her own mother and father), because in a household that includes both sexes, a child learns something important about relating to each sex.[55] Those who do *not* believe, however, that there is anything unique to be learned from one sex or the other, are hardly about to conduct studies investigating the impact of these differences. Instead, they are likely to conduct studies that conclude there is "no difference" between opposite-sex and same-sex parenting. Most people are naturally suspicious of such "scientific" results. They should be.[56] They should also be skeptical of the claim that judges have any special expertise in evaluating such studies. If nothing else is to be learned from the 1996 same-sex marriage trial in Honolulu, this is it.[57]

8. *Same-sex marriage will not open a Pandora's box, for instance, to polygamy.*

This is another argument about societal effects. Most proponents of same-sex marriage laugh off the question, or label it a diversion from the "real" issue. But the question of polygamy is not a diversion, because it highlights a perfectly legitimate substantive question: Once one drops the definition of marriage as the union of one man and one woman, why limit marriage to two people? Professor Chambers made precisely this point. Some gays and lesbians are personally interested in multiple partners, and some are not. There is no "pro-polygamy" movement on a grand scale. But that is not the issue: there is a logical implication here, and logical implications are especially powerful in legal settings. A change in the law based on the introduction of a new principle can begin "small" and quickly become "large," while its proponents deny responsibility for the results. In the case of America today, simple sexual anarchy is probably more likely than "polygamy," but anything could happen, and once the floodgates are opened, anything probably will happen. If and when it does, then the question will be whether there is any principled basis for opposing it. Supporters of the existing law have a valid basis for worrying that same-sex marriage will open a "Pandora's Box" and be unable to close it.

9. *The law should come to terms with the reality of gay and lesbian families.*

There *do* exist, in growing numbers, same-sex couples with children, who argue that they need greater legal protections. They argue, therefore, that legalizing "same-sex marriage" would have *beneficial* societal effects for children—their own children. This is perhaps the hardest argument to address, because we are no longer speaking in the abstract. We are called to live at peace with our neighbors, and treat them well, even if they establish households whose values we deeply question. The welfare of all our children should be at the heart of our considerations of the public good.

Yet tolerance does not require endorsement. Same-sex marriage is endorsement. Whenever a same-sex couple "have children," recall that somebody is missing: the other parent. Even if the other parent is somehow present in the child's life, perhaps as a visitor or friend, he or she has been excluded in a basic way. While the custodial parent should (and does) normally have legal rights, society has no general duty to promote child-rearing in settings that deliberately exclude a mother or father. Children who are born in these settings deserve our love and compassion, just like children living in other kinds of non-marital households. But their mere existence does not in itself establish their goodness. Legalized same-sex marriage would strongly legitimate such households.

Having said this, how should the law relate to "gay and lesbian families"? Are there ways to address wisely the concrete issues which arise in these settings, without generally endorsing them? The answer has to be yes, and it is a matter of working out how, on a trial-and-error basis. Legal means have been developed to deal with children living in other sorts of non-traditional settings. While upholding general principles, the law must also address particular circumstances. How it will do this, in coming years, remains to be seen, and we have a duty to be involved. What we should *not* do, however, is to legalize same-sex marriage as a moral, political, and legal shortcut. This is not required, and it would not be wise.

10. *If fidelity is good, and promiscuity is bad, why not encourage fidelity by legalizing same-sex marriage?*

This is an especially attractive argument. Praise of fidelity and criticism of promiscuity is superficially reassuring. Unfortunately, it is not persuasive.

Short answers to the argument are that homosexuals do not really mean "monogamy" in the same sense supporters of current marriage do and that, in any case, there is no reason to call monogamous same-sex relationships "marriages." Now let us consider each element of this response.

Despite claims to the contrary, there *is* truth to the first response. Studies have repeatedly shown that the majority of gay male couples neither practice nor value sexual fidelity.[58] Even those who do seem to define "fidelity" in a very elastic manner. Andrew Sullivan's landmark book, *Virtually Normal*, is perhaps the most eloquent statement of the argument that "we're just like you, we want the same things, let us in." Yet, as most reviewers of the book noted, even this most prominent spokesperson for same-sex marriage urges heterosexuals to learn from homosexuals an appreciation of the need for extramarital "outlets."[59] Richard Mohr, another prominent advocate, even more openly celebrates the value of "flexibility" in same-sex unions.[60] In short, the leading advocates of "same-sex marriage" appear to want to redefine "monogamy" in a way that makes room for infidelity.

Second, even if these advocates were to agree that "monogamy" means real exclusivity, that would be no reason to legalize "same-sex marriage." Sexual fidelity is part of a larger vision of marriage. Despite all the changes of recent times, the law still assumes that marriage is the vow to enter a lifelong *and* monogamous *and* male-female community. The fact alone that a sexual relationship is monogamous does not, therefore, make it into a "marriage."

If marriage is *inherently* the union of a man and a woman, then it cannot (morally) and should not (legally) be redefined in order to achieve some *instrumental* public policy goal. If one is seeking other ways to reduce promiscuity among gays and lesbians, the spectrum of means—depending on one's viewpoint—ranges from enacting domestic partnership laws to making funding available for practitioners of reparative therapy [61]

In other words, it is not that "monogamy" is a public value, and that marriage laws exist as a mere means of promoting monogamy. It is the other way around: Because of what marriage is, it should be monogamous. A man and woman can only offer themselves fully to one other person. Marriage, understood as the union of one man and one woman, is thus the touchstone from which concepts of *marital* "fidelity" and "monogamy" themselves take their bearings.

The alternative—defining marriage as Commitment—undercuts appeals to "monogamy" and "fidelity." If all genital sexual relationships are a matter of degree, rather than a matter of kind, then there is no "bright line" separating sex within marriage and sex outside of marriage. There is no morally significant difference between marital and non-marital sex. Instead, there is merely a "sliding scale," in which some relationships are more or less "close" . or "distant."

This set of assumptions, if adopted, clearly undercuts the critique of "promiscuity" which is supposed to be the attractive feature of the Commitment model. By removing the moral element and replacing it with a relational or utilitarian one, "monogamy" and "fidelity" become subject to redefinition based on "the relationship," or one's individual preference or calculations. Whatever else may be said about these views, they are *different* from the view that monogamy and fidelity are principles which are *necessary* to the institution of marriage, and therefore to marriage law.

Arguments for the Current Definition of Marriage

Now it is time to add some reasons for existing marriage laws, without repeating what has already been stated above. Ultimately, the case for the current definition of marriage is a positive one. It is not based on overcoming arguments set forth by its opponents, but on the enduring reality of marriage itself.

1. *Marriage is a unique, male-female sexual community with many public effects. For this reason, marriage deserves recognition, protection and benefits under the law.*

First, the current marriage law, as we observed earlier, assumes that there are two sexes, male and female. Is this a reasonable assumption? Yes, although there are those who question it.[62] It further assumes that the sexual organs of men and women are designed to go together, at least for reproductive purposes. Is this a reasonable assumption? Yes, although there are those who question this, too.[63] Third, it assumes that the sexual union of male and female creates not only a reproductive unit, but a unique human community. Is this a reasonable assumption? Yes, although supporters of same-sex marriage vigorously dispute this.[64] Fourth, it assumes that this marital community makes an indispensable contribution to the well-being of the larger society, particularly by uniting and extending the generations. Is this a reasonable assumption? Yes, although supporters of same-sex marriage argue that there is nothing special about the procreation and nurture of children that requires a husband and wife.[65] Finally, the law assumes that it is in society's interest to preserve, protect, and promote this marital community through its laws. Is this a reasonable assumption? Yes, if one grants the earlier assumptions. Not if one contests them.

To call the current law of marriage "irrational" or "discriminatory" because it does not include same-sex couples is really just to present one's argument for a different point of view. That is why the question of marriage belongs among the people and their elected representatives, rather than among a judicial elite. The ideas that men and women do not form a unique sexual community, that the procreation and nurture of children have no natural connection to one another, and that marriage makes no distinctive contribution to the larger social order, sound even more "irrational" to most Americans. In a culture where one person's rationality is another's prejudice, the idea that the current law of the entire world is "obviously irrational" is *itself* irrational. Compared to such views, the opinion that marriage is a distinctive form of human community is entirely sensible.[66]

2. *The law should continue to encourage men and women to enter into* marital *sexual relationships.*

It has three tools at its disposal: it can promote, it can permit, and

it can prohibit.[67] The law *promotes* behavior by giving it endorsement, recognition, protections, and public benefits. Our current
marriage laws do this with definitions, licensing, rights and responsibilities, and subsidies. The law also *permits* behaviors which it
does not endorse, but does not criminalize. States which have repealed their adultery, sodomy, and fornication statutes, for instance,
have not thereby given their endorsement to extramarital, homosexual, or premarital sex. They have merely decided that they will
not devote government resources to enforcing penalties for these
kinds of behavior. A state may accomplish the same result by leaving a law on the books, and using it only sparingly. Finally, the law
also *prohibits* behaviors it judges to be not only immoral, but so
unhealthy for society that it chooses to discourage them in advance,
rather than leaving choice to the individual. In all states, this still
includes, for example, prohibitions on incest, bigamy, and under-
age marriages, and many now ban marriage between same-sex partners.

   If what same-sex couples want is privacy, it is available to them
in most states, some formally (by leaving adult consensual sex un-
regulated) others informally (by not enforcing bans).[68] The law also
leaves many areas, for example in contracts, to the private judge-
ment of individuals. Various issues relating to same-sex sexual (or
non-sexual) relationships can be addressed this way. The law need
not necessarily endorse or override a specific agreement between
private parties.

   But one can already hear the objections from the other side.
By adopting a clear preference for marriage, and leaving other sexual
relationships in the zone of "permission," the law is "doing violence." It is "marginalizing" sexual "outsiders," communicating to
these persons that they are "worthless." Andrew Sullivan makes
many of these claims. He claims that he "knows in his heart" that
same-sex sexual relationships must be good.[69] He believes that persons have a variety of "orientations," some heterosexual, some homosexual, and that the only prospect for a homosexual person to
have a full and happy life is for her to enter into intimate, lasting

sexual relationships with another person of the same sex.[70] Therefore, as long as society withholds its full acceptance of these relationships, it will send a message to homosexuals that they are
"incapable of real love, unworthy of real commitment, incompe-
tent to achieve what every heterosexual in this country and indeed
the world regards as the most important and satisfying and significant thing in their lives." Condemned to miserable and loveless
lives, persons with same-sex desires will express their despair in
destructive ways, according to Sullivan.[71]

Others, including myself, disagree. We question the view that
sexual desires are the key to identifying one's sexual identity. We
question the view that "sexual orientation" is as significant as being
male or female. In our view, many factors may contribute to same-
sex sexual attraction. But at bottom, each person is meant to have
healthy sexual relationships with members of the opposite sex, and
healthy non-sexual relationships with members of the same sex.
Since *these* are the kinds of relationships that are best for a person,
other kinds should not be encouraged.[72] To be sure, people get
themselves into same-sex sexual relationships, like other kinds of
non-marital sexual relationships. Like any such relationship, they
may have long-term consequences that need to be legally addressed.
But it is not in the best interest of these persons, or the community
around them, for these relationships to be legally endorsed. To do
so would only promote a movement that seeks full acceptance of
"gay, lesbian, bisexual, and transgendered identity" and is willing
to redefine marriage to get it.[73]

Does this then mean, as Sullivan claims, that persons with this
viewpoint, including myself, really *do* believe that homosexuals are
"incapable of real love, unworthy of real commitment, incompe-
tent to achieve what every heterosexual in this country and indeed
the world regards as the most important and satisfying and significant thing in their lives"? Not at all. This could only be true if one
accepts the assumptions that appear to lie behind Sullivan's claim.

For instance, he appears to assume that sexual love is necessary
for "real" love or "real" commitment. But this is not true. Sexual

love is only one of many forms of love. True love among family, friends, and associates in shared tasks does not require intercourse or orgasm, and I doubt that Sullivan would claim it does. Yet these are genuine forms of real and committed love.

Sullivan also appears to assume that anyone who does not marry is missing what would be "the most important and satisfying and significant thing in their lives." But this is not true either. Marriage is no panacea for anyone's need for "satisfaction" or "significance"—in fact it often requires sacrifices that force one to set aside those very needs. Again, I am sure that Sullivan knows this. Meanwhile, many unmarried persons live equally satisfying and significant lives, sustained by deep and lasting friendships.

Finally, Sullivan appears to assume that homosexuals are forever denied the desire or opportunity to enter into marriage, because they cannot marry their preferred same-sex partner. But this, too, is not true. Some persons with same-sex desires are able to discover genuine sexual desire for the opposite sex, develop relationships, and eventually enter male-female marriages. Any laws or policies which would make this *less* likely only end up harming those they claim to serve.[74]

I do not believe that persons who struggle with same-sex desires are incapable of true love or real commitment. I believe that these persons are precious individuals, created in the image of God, who deserve respect as my neighbors and fellow-citizens. Here I am arguing, as one citizen to another, about what that respect requires.

An Example of Arguments in Action

Soon after the same-sex couples filed their recent lawsuit in Vermont, the Attorney General of Vermont filed a "Motion to Dismiss." After responding to some of the arguments we have already discussed, this well-crafted reply proceeded to offer seven reasons that Vermont's marriage law has, using the terms of legal jargon, a "rational basis"[75]:

1. "The State has an interest in promoting the institution of marriage in its current form because it unites men and women." Marriage, the Attorney General says, "is an institution which uniquely celebrates the complementarity of the sexes." Therefore, "it symbolizes to all society the value of bridging differences and working together," and it "instructs the young of the value of uniting male and female qualities and contributions in the same institution."

2. "The State has an interest in promoting child-rearing in a setting which provides both male and female role models." Since "marriages are built on male and female inclusion, they provide special advantages to raising children." This is because "Children see and experience the innate and unique abilities and characteristics that each sex possesses and contributes to their combined endeavor. Children, thus, learn lessons for later life by seeing both parents working together in child-rearing."

3. "The State has an interest in furthering the links between procreation and child-rearing." Vermont has seen a growth in single-parent households, and though many single parents do a good job, "they do not have all the benefits of families with two parents." Because "same-sex couples cannot conceive a child on their own," the Legislature could reasonably conclude that "increased creation of children through technologically or third-party assisted reproduction" tends "to further separate the connection between procreation and parental responsibilities."

4. "The State has an interest in preserving marriage as an institution." Marriage is under attack today, and "the Legislature could conceivably have concluded that expanding marriage to include same-sex unions would destabilize the institution of marriage." If same-sex couples are allowed to marry, for instance, "the conception of marriage as a precursor to raising a family will thus be diminished. In its place will come marriage as a tax status, a means to obtain economic benefits." While one can debate whether this is better or worse, "the Legislature could rationally conclude that the change will make the institution weaker."

5. "The State has an interest in ensuring that its marriages are recognized in other states and in not expending resources to sort out conflict-of-law issues among its sister states." If Vermont is forced to marry same-sex couples, when these couples move to other states they are likely to file suit to attempt to gain recognition of the validity of their marriages. Not only may this impair the legality of those marriages, it will potentially drag the state into "expending scarce judicial and government attorney resources on deciding the myriad questions of whether certain marriages, divorces, or related family orders are valid."

6. "The State has an interest in using the law to make normative statements." "No matter how modern we may believe our society to be," the Attorney General says, "the law still has a role in reflecting and shaping value judgments." Vermont's laws embody these judgments in various ways: by prohibiting bigamy, by criminalizing prostitution, by criminalizing sexual relations with individuals under age sixteen. Likewise, it may define marriage as the union of a man and a woman.

7. "The State has an interest in minimizing the use of surrogacy contracts and sperm donors to avoid, inter alia [among other things], increased child custody and visitation disputes." Because "Same-sex couples biologically require a third person's assistance or contribution to conceive a child," the state could conclude that the legalization of same-sex marriage "would lead to an increase in technologically assisted conception." Conception by means of sperm donors or gestational surrogates is controversial, and "the custody issues that can arise are significant, and the State has an interest in keeping the number of those disputes within reasonable bounds." The resulting impact "on the resources of the court system from increased litigation of this sort is obvious. The State has a rational justification for avoiding these issues by denying marriage to same-sex couples."

In summary, "The numerous justifications for the present legislative scheme are not based upon out-moded views of men and women," according to the Attorney General. "Rather, they are grounded upon the rich physical and psychological differences between the sexes that exist to this very day." For this reason, Vermont (or any other state) may reasonably enact such a marriage law, and there are no "constitutional" grounds for declaring it "invidious" or "irrational."

These are not the only arguments that can be offered for the "rationality" of a state's marriage law, but legally speaking, they are among the most important. Depending on their own beliefs, judges will find all of them persuasive, or only some of them, or perhaps none of them. Even if we question whether judges should be debating these arguments at all, our duty is to make the best arguments we can. We cannot control the outcome, we can only respond as it occurs.[76]

CONCLUSION

Our newspapers, airwaves, and civic arenas are filled with claims and counter-claims about family, equality, and the needs of children. The static level is rising, and we may be headed for a showdown before the next millennium begins.

Culturally and intellectually, the question of marriage goes as deep as any question can. It engages our deepest convictions about life, love, and law. It stretches our minds and hearts.

Legally, the contest over same-sex marriage is a classic example of the conflict between two understandings of the relationship between the people and the courts. The one side considers itself the defender of *civil rights*. It sees a constitution as a charter of individual rights, views the people as a dangerous majority, and believes that courts should interpret a constitution in a way that advances individual rights *over against* the social and legal institutions adopted and enacted by the people and their elected representatives. It views the courts as the preferred forum for social reform, because they are seen as *less* political.

The other side considers itself the defender of *civil society*. It sees the constitution as a charter of political self-government and believes that the courts should interpret the constitution in a way that *respects* the people's social and legal institutions, unless they openly contradict the meaning of the constitution. It views the legislative branch as a better forum for social reform, because it is *more* political.

These debates will continue. Neither side is going away. Whoever is "victor" at any given time will still have to contend with the "vanquished." People will continue to live their very imperfect lives, seeking some balance between justice and compassion, between truth and liberty.

In the meantime, if one believes that a good society requires a critical mass of healthy male-female marriages with children, then any policies that redefine, and thereby weaken, that basic unit are a bad idea. I believe that same-sex marriage is a bad idea, not because same-sex couples are bad people, but because same-sex marriage is not marriage. A genuinely pluralistic society must do justice to individuals. But it must also do justice to marriage.

How we ultimately answer the question of marriage will depend on the quality of our citizenship. However the contest turns out, the effects will be felt for generations to come.

LOVE, NO MATTER WHAT

Richard John Neuhaus

THE QUESTION "WHERE DO WE GO FROM HERE?" should not be taken to imply that there is a clear path, or even an unclear path, toward a "solution" of the problems addressed in this volume. The unruly passions of human sexuality are a permanent feature of the human condition. Individually and in our several communities, we can only try to cope with them better than we have in the past. Toward that end we should pray for an increased measure of all four cardinal virtues: prudence, temperance, fortitude, and justice. These must inform where we go from here.

Prudence is the wisdom to understand the nature of the homosexual impulse and its organized insurgency in our public life. Temperance is the refusal to panic, and the tempering of any illusion that either the impulse or the insurgency will disappear. Fortitude—also known by the name of that fine organization, Courage—means we decline to be intimidated by opponents and brace ourselves for the duration, which will likely be a very long time.

Then there is justice. It must be unmistakably clear that ours is a concern for justice. Justice for people, especially young people, caught in sexual perplexity and assailed from within and without by pressures to consign themselves to a way of life that is marked by compulsion, loneliness, depression, and disease. Justice also for the integrity of our public life, which requires that truth be spoken with candor and disagreements be engaged with civility. Justice, finally, for millions of Americans—mothers, fathers, and children— who need all the support they can get to sustain in the present and transmit to the future the "little platoon" of love and fidelity that the family is meant to be.

Prudence, temperance, fortitude, and justice. The subject of "Homosexuality and American Public Life" has many dimensions— dimensions of politics, public policy, medicine, and education. But without these virtues all our efforts will end up in frustration, despair, or never-ending polemics. In that event, it is not so important that we would lose. The real losers would be the sexually perplexed whom we would help, the democracy that we cherish, and the families that claim our support.

In preparing for today, I looked again at the statement of the Ramsey Colloquim, "The Homosexual Movement," published in the March 1994 issue of *First Things*. It still strikes me as a singularly coherent and persuasive account of the task ahead, and I warmly recommend it to your consideration. Make no mistake about it: The task is daunting, and we must brace ourselves for a work of many years. This long-term view may be discouraging to some. John Maynard Keynes famously said that in the long run we're all dead. Not so incidentally, he was homosexual, and the remark reflects the history-limiting horizon of a sterile worldview divorced from the promise and peril of successor generations.

It is said that we who challenge the homosexual insurgency are traditionalists clinging to the past. And it is true that we would respect those who came before us, as we hope to be respected by those who come after us. But our cause is for the future: the future of our children and children's children and the future of the human project itself. Next only to religious communities of ultimate promise, the ever-fragile community that we call family is the primary bearer of hope for the future.

It is in families that ordinary people participate as procreators in the continuing creation of life. It is in families that ordinary people make history, and do so much more palpably and believably than do the movers and shakers who presumably make the history of this or any other time. Family is a synonym for history, of continuity through time, and for most people family is their most audacious and sacrificial commitment to the communal hope that in the long run we will not all be dead. The history-limiting horizon of a sexual revolution that is captive to the immediacies of desire is in the service of what Pope John Paul II has aptly called "the culture of death." In the great contest that has now been joined, ours is the party of "the culture of life."

In reading again the statement, "The Homosexual Movement," I wondered about the course of the contest over these last several years. This volume testifies to the failure of the homosexual insurgency to silence its critics. Thoughtful people with a moderately healthy backbone are no longer intimidated by the charge of "homophobia." Along with the epithets of "racism" and "sexism," the charge has lost its force by promiscuous over-use. Not everywhere, to be sure. In most colleges and universities thirty years ago, a faculty member who publicly announced that he thought homosexuality a good thing would have invited suspicion and censure. In the same schools today, he is likely in deep trouble if he offers less than unqualified approval of the homosexual movement. So there is no doubt that the insurgency has made advances. But we would be making a very big mistake if we measured cultural change by fashions in the academy. The academy today is in large part a reservation for the lost tribes of radicalisms past.

The homosexual movement is usually dated from the "Stonewall Riot" of 1969. That is almost thirty years ago. As with the radicalism of an ossified civil rights establishment, and with the splintered leaderships of the several feminisms, the direction of the homosexual movement has become uncertain. In the entertainment politics of contemporary America, thirty years is a long time to play the role of the avant garde. After a while, people come to recognize that everything changes except the avant garde.

I am inclined to the view that 1993, proclaimed as the Year of the Gays, was the high point of the effort to persuade the American people that homosexuality is, all in all, a good thing. President

Clinton called for gays in the military. A huge gay pride march on Washington declared definitive cultural victory. In movies, theater, and television, on the cover of almost every popular magazine, the homosexual insurgency was exultantly championed that year. One may wonder whether it made much difference where making a difference really counts, namely, whether parents are any more welcoming of the prospect that their children may be homosexual.

Between gay advocates who present the movement as one of radical cultural change and those who want to "mainstream" homosexuality into existing social patterns, there seems to be something of a stand-off. Groups such as ACT-UP are in disarray, and the Mass at St. Patrick's has not been disrupted for some time. It is true that there are still the gay pride parades here and there, but they no longer have the shock of novelty and most people, including many homosexuals, decorously avert their eyes in embarrassment for the paraders. The advocates of "mainstreaming," such as Andrew Sullivan and Bruce Bowers, sometimes seem to be doing no more than endorsing the attitude of the Victorian lady who said they can do what they want so long as they don't frighten the horses. Of course their modesty of language and demeanor is misleading, as is evident in their demand for same-sex marriage.

My point is that the homosexual movement is not the unstoppable counter-cultural juggernaut that its champions and many of its opponents once thought it to be. The movement has suffered severe setbacks. It is, for instance, hard to overestimate the significance of the shattering of the myth of Kinsey's ten percent. Although those of us who live in places such as New York and Washington may find it hard to believe, we are dealing with a deviancy from the heterosexual norm that probably involves no more than two percent of the male population, and it seems that half of them do not want to make a public issue of it.

Consider, too, that after three decades of strenuous effort and high confidence of victory, the demand for the formal approval of homosexuality has been turned back again and again also in the liberal oldline Protestant churches. Only the small and rapidly disappearing United Church of Christ has approved the ordination of the homogenitally active. The Episcopal Church threatened officially to do so last summer but in the end did not.

Please do not misunderstand. I am not saying that the movement has been stopped. Not by a long shot. But it is not in unchallenged ascendancy. The strategy of the movement was caught most precisely in the lines of Alexander Pope:

> *Vice is a monster of so frightful mien,*
> *As to be hated needs but to be seen;*
> *Yet seen too oft, familiar with her face,*
> *We first endure, then pity, then embrace.*

To endure, that is the goal of tolerance. To pity, that is the goal of compassion. To embrace, that is the goal of affirmation. Those are the three strategic steps. Despite the overwhelming support of what presume to be the major culture-forming institutions of our society, and most particularly the support of the media, the American people have not been induced to take the fateful step of affirming homosexuality as a good thing.

Yes, it may be objected, but what about the first step of tolerance? Well, what about it? I hope it is agreed that we neither could nor should put consenting adults in jail for homosexual acts. In addition, we do well to remember that there has always been—in major cities and in certain lines of work—a substantial homosexual subculture. Sophisticated heterosexual New Yorkers of, say, the 1920s were probably less troubled by the homosexual phenomenon than their counterparts are today. It was not then demanded that they commit themselves to homosexuality as an ideological crusade. Homosexuality was then viewed as a deviance to be socially tolerated, but not morally approved.

It was once called the love that dare not speak its name, and many have observed that it has now become the neurosis that doesn't know when to shut up. But there is more to it than that. There was and there is a gay world and a straight world, and both the terms and the borders are set mainly by the gay world. Within the subcultural world of its own making, the name of the desire was not only spoken but exuberantly celebrated. Then the borders were declared abolished, and gays, or at least some gays, set out to re-make the world.

Of course, those who oppose the homosexualizing of the world—which means redefining sexuality as the servicing of de-sire—will be accused of saying that people should go back into the closet. They may call that world a closet if they choose. What we are saying is that a small minority that is at odds—whether by choice or circumstance or a combination of both—with the constituting institution of society and the right ordering of human sexuality have not the right to remake the world in the image of their dis-sent. We are saying that, so long as this is an approximately free and democratic society, they cannot push into the closet those who would defend the world we have received and pass it on to coming generations.

I am suggesting that 1993 may have been the high point of the insurgency's effort to win, as it is said, the hearts and minds of the American people. That effort has had only very modest success. It is true that there are data indicating a greater "acceptance" of ho-mosexuals and homosexuality. Acceptance is an ambiguous term, and I am sure it applies more to homosexual persons than to ho-mosexuality. Nor is such acceptance necessarily a bad thing. On the part of parents in particular, it is often acceptance with a bro-ken heart—acceptance of a son or daughter with foreboding about what is in store for them, acceptance despite shattered dreams of grandchildren that will not be. Such acceptance is not untouched by those three other virtues, commonly called the theological vir-tues, of faith, hope, and charity. Keeping faith with those for whom we care, despite all. Holding on to hope for change, refusing to believe that the youthful announcement of homosexual identity is the final word. And above all charity, which simply means love. Love, no matter what.

If this is what is meant by a popular increase in "acceptance," then I say we should be thankful for it. What has not happened is that the American people have not been persuaded that homosexu-ality is a good or even a morally neutral thing. Many have been momentarily intimidated into not expressing their objections and misgivings, but they have not been persuaded, and I do not believe they will be persuaded. On the contrary, they were frontally assaulted by a proposition that most of them had never had occasion to think about, and did not want to think about. They had good reason not to think about it. The philosopher Sidney Hook, late in life, asked a friend, "But what do they actually *do?*" When told, he recoiled in disbelief and declared, "But that's disgusting!"

Sidney Hook's response—reinforced by habit, moral teaching, and devotion to marriage and family—is the response of most people. It is a response that is largely intuitive and pre-articulate. People were told, and many came to believe, that they should be ashamed of themselves for their irrational prejudice. Many intellectuals—those who belong to what has aptly been described as the herd of independent minds—readily believed it and eagerly performed the appropriate rituals of self-denigration to expiate their sin of homophobia. But for others, what was intuitive and pre-articulate is increasingly being thought through and articulated. They will no longer be silenced.

"Can't we talk about it?" That seemingly innocent question is a mantra of the homosexual movement. The assumption is that the more people talk and think about it, the more affirmative they will be. The leaders of the movement may come to rue the day that they invited the American people to think long hard thoughts about homosexuality. Examining the way of life that is captive to the immediacies of homoerotic desire—a way of dissolution, deception, despair, and early death—more and more people will find the reasons and the words for a response that was at first intuitive and pre-articulate.

To be sure, the advocates of the movement say that the pathologies of the gay subculture—which at least some readily acknowledge—would be remedied by the general acceptance of homosexuality. The opponents say that such acceptance would only guarantee the spread of the pathologies. I do not think the American people are prepared to gamble on who is right. Certainly there is nothing in historical experience or common sense to suggest that pathologies are remedied by integrating them into society, while there is abundant reason to believe that such pathologies will further debase a society that has lost its capacity to censure. Already in our society it is too often the case that moral judgment is the duty that dare not speak its name.

Having failed in the arena of politics where we democratically deliberate how we ought to order our life together, the homosexual movement has no choice but to vest its hopes in courts, government regulations, professional organizations, and the bureaucracies of the public school system. In these arenas their victories have been substantial, and they aspire to much more. In all these arenas, the movement must be challenged at every step—fearlessly, calmly, reasonably, relentlessly. The good of innumerable individuals, and the common good, depend on it. The outcome of that challenge is uncertain. We cannot know what the future holds. We must do what we can. Eliot said it in "East Coker," "For us there is only the trying; the rest is not our business."

Finally, we will not understand what is happening or be able to do much about it unless we recognize the cultural erosion of what can only be called a spiritual sensibility—a sensibility that we are all flawed creatures living in a fragile world that cannot survive without forbearance and forgiveness. A young man to whom I was explaining the Church's teaching about disordered sexual desire responded with the plaintive cry, "But the Church is still saying there is something wrong with me!" Well yes—and with me, and with all of us. But we must never define ourselves —not entirely, not most importantly—by what is wrong with us. Who we are, our identity, is more than that, much more than that. We are defined not by the disorder of our desires but by the right ordering of our loves and loyalties, and at the end of the day we must all ask forgiveness for loves and loyalties betrayed. Without forbearance and forgiveness, we are all hopelessly lost.

Perhaps you saw it too, the story about this new organization of physically disabled people who criticize the movie actor Christopher Reeve because he wants to be cured. The group wants to promote what it calls "disability pride." "I can't walk and I'm glad I can't walk," declared one young woman. "I don't want to walk.

Disability is good!" We must hope that she does not really believe that. While being sensitive to the poignancy of her defiance, we must refuse her demand that we believe that. Her disability is not good; it is very sad, but she is more than her disability. We support her in her struggle, and help her not at all by pretending that it is not a struggle. Of that truth we must also persuade our homosexual brothers and sisters. We must do so humbly, in painful awareness of our different but often more severe disabilities. But we must also do so firmly, knowing that they are not helped and many lives are ruined by their effort to impose upon others their defiant denial of the troubling truth.

"Can't we talk about it?" they ask. Well yes, we are talking about it, and we will continue to talk about it. Although some seem determined to view us as their enemies, we will refuse to view them as our enemies. We will talk about it with them, and with whomever else is willing to talk. We will talk about it, God willing, in a manner that is informed by the classical virtues of prudence, temperance, courage, and justice. And we will talk about it in a manner that is graced by the virtues of faith, hope, and love. Love above all. Love, no matter what.

Notes

1 The Biology of Homosexuality: Science or Politics?

1. J. M. Bailey et al., "Heritable Factors Influence Sexual Orientations in Women," *Archives of General Psychiatry* 50: 217-23. Note the title. Even though the authors admit that any possible heritable factors contribute only 25 percent to a homosexual predisposition, the article is titled as though trumpeting a headline discovery. It was picked up that way by sympathetic media outlets.

2. A lower score on this scale means a less negative attitude toward homosexuality.

3. Piskur and Degelman, "Attitudes Toward Homosexuals," 1219-25; my emphasis. See also K. E. Ernulf, "Cross-National Analysis."

4. E. Dejowski, "Public Endorsement of Restrictions on Three Aspects of Free Expression by Homosexuals: Sociodemographic and Trends Analysis 1973-1988," *Journal of Homosexuality* 23 (1992): 1-18.

5. For an excellent nontechnical critique of the limitations of genetics research into many areas of human behavior, see J. Horgan, "Eugenics Revisited," *Scientific American* (June 1993): 123-31.

6. D. A. Hay, "Genetics in the Analysis of Behaviour," *Neuroscience and Biobehavioral Review* 4 (1980): 489-508.

7. J. A. Egeland et al., "Bipolar Affective Disorders Linked to DNA Markers on Chromosome 11," *Nature* 325, no. 6107 (1987): 783-87.

8. C. D. Mellon, "Genetic Linkage Studies in Bipolar Disorder: A Review," *Psychiatric Development* 7, no. 2 (1989): 143-58.

9. J. R. De Paulo, Jr. et al., "The New Genetics of Bipolar Affective Disorder: Clinical Implications," *Clinical Chemistry* 35, no. 7 (supplemental) (1989): B28-32.

10. M. Barinaga, "Manic Depression Gene Put in Limbo," *Science* 246, no. 4932 (1989): 886-87.

11. M. Robertson, "False Start on Manic Depression," *Nature* 342, no. 6247 (1989): 222.

12. E. I. Ginns et al., "Update on the Search for DNA Markers Linked to Manic-Depressive Illness in the Old Order Amish," *Journal of Psychiatric Research* 26, no. 4 (1992): 305-8; E. Gandini, "Genetics of Affective Disorders," *Journal of Psychiatric Research* 26, no. 4 (1992): 271-77; J. Mendlewicz, S. Sevy, and K. Mendelbaum, "Minireview: Molecular Genetics in AVective Illness," *Life Sciences* 52, no. 3 (1993): 231-42; J. Hebebrand and K. Hennighausen, "A Critical Analysis of Data Presented in Eight Studies Favouring X-linkage of Bipolar Illness with Special Emphasis on Formal Genetic Aspects" *American Journal of Human Genetics* 90, no. 3 (1992): 289-93; S. Jensen et al., "Linkage Analysis of the D1 Dopamine Receptor Gene and Manic Depression in Six Families," *Human Heredity* 42, no. 5 (1989): 269-75, S. D. Detera-Wadleigh et al., "A Systematic Search for a Bipolar Predisposing Locus on Chromosome 5," *Neuropsychopharmacology* 6, no. 4 (1992): 219-29; P. Mitchell et al., "Exclusion of Close Linkage of Bipolar Disorder to Dopamine D1 and D2 Receptor Gene Markers," *Journal of AVective Disorders* 25, no. 1 (1992): 1-11; A. Law et al., "Genetic Linkage Analysis of Bipolar Affective Disorder in an Old Order Amish Pedigree," *American Journal of Human Genetics* 88, no. 5 (1992): 562-68; M. M. Nothen et al., "Lack of Association Between Dopamine D1 and D2 Receptor Genes and Bipolar Affective Disorder," *American Journal of Psychiatry* 149, no. 2 (1992): 199-201; J. Hebebrand, "A Critical Appraisal of X-linked Bipolar Illness: Evidence for the Assumed Mode of Inheritance Is Lacking," *British Journal of Psychiatry* 160, no. 1 (1992), p, 7-11; W. Byerley et al., "Tyrosine Hydroxylase Gene Not Linked to Manic-Depression in Seven of Eight Pedigrees," *Human Heredity* 42, no. 4 (1992): 259-63; J. Mendlewicz et al., "Absence of Linkage Between Chromosome 11p15 Markers and Manic-Depressive Illness in a Belgian Pedigree." *American Journal of Psychiatry* 148, no. 12 (1991): 1683-87; D. L. Pauls et al., "Linkage of Bipolar Affective Disorders to Markers on Chromosome 11p Is Excluded in a Second Lateral Extension of Amish Pedigree 110." *Genomics* 11, no. 3 (1991): 730-36; M. Baron, "X-linkage and Manic-Depressive Illness: A Reassessment," *Soc. Biology* 38, nos. 3-4 (1991): 179-88; A. J. Pakstis et al., "Status of the Search for a Major Genetic Locus for AVective Disorder in the Old Order Amish," *American Journal of Human Genetics* 87, no. 4 (1991): 475-83; D. Holmes et al., "No Evidence for a Susceptibility Locus Predisposing to Manic Depression in the Region of the Dopamine (D2) Receptor Gene," *British Journal of Psychiatry* 158, no. 1 (1991): 635-41; E. S. Gershon, "Marker Genotyping Errors in Old Data on X-linkage in Bipolar Illness," Comment on *Biological Psychiatry* 29, no. 7 (1 April 1991): 721-29, in *Biological Psychiatry* 29, no. 7 (1 April 1991): 730-31; S. Nanko et al., "Linkage Analysis of AVective Disorder Using DNA Markers on Chromosomes 11 and X," *Japanese Journal of Psychiatry and Neurology* 45, no. 1 (1991): 53-56; P. Mitchell et al., "Close Linkage of Bipolar Disorder to Chromosome 11 Markers Is Excluded in Two Large Australian Pedigrees." *Journal of AVective Disorders* 21, no. 1 (1991): 23-32; M. Gill et al., "Tyrosine Hydroxylase Polymorphisms and Bipolar AVective Disorder," *Journal of Psychiatric Research* 25, no. 4 (1991): 179-84; P. V. Gejman et al., "Manic Depressive Illness not Linked to Factor IX Region in an Independent Series of Pedigrees," *Genomics* 8, no. 4 (1990): 648-55; S. V. Faraone. W. S. Kremen, and M. T. Tsuang, "Genetic Transmission of Major Affective Disorders:

Quantitative Models and Linkage Analyses," *Psychological Bulletin* 108, no. 1 (1990): 109-27; J. Korner, J. Fritze, and P. Propping, "RFLP Alleles at the Tyrosine Hydroxylase Locus: No Association Found to Affective Disorders," *Psychiatry Research* 32, no. 3 (1990): 275-80; W. H. Berrettini et al., "X-chromosome Markers and Manic-Depressive Illness: Rejection of Linkage to Xq28 in Nine Bipolar Pedigrees," Comment in *Archives of General Psychiatry* 48, no. 7 (July 1991): 671-75 and *Archives of General Psychiatry* 47, no. 4 (1990): 366-73; M. J. Owen and M. J. Mullan, "Molecular Genetic Studies of Manic-Depression and Schizophrenia," *Trends in Neuroscience* 13, no. 1 (1990): 29-31; E. S. Gershon, "Recent Developments in Genetics of Manic-Depressive Illness," *Journal of Clinical Psychiatry* 50, no. 1 (1989), supplement 4-7 and discussion 45-47; K.R. Merikangas, M. A. Spence, and D. J. Kupfer "Linkage Studies of Bipolar Disorder: Methodologic and Analytic Issues" (Report of MacArthur Foundation Workshop on Linkage and Clinical Features in Affective Disorders), *Archives of General Psychiatry* 46, no. 12 (1989): 1137-41; J. R. Kelsoe et al., "Re-evaluation of the Linkage Relationship Between Chromosome 11p loci and the Gene for Bipolar Affective Disorder in the Old Order Amish." *Nature* 342, no. 6247 (1989): 238-43.

13. As much as we have learned, there is still so much more that we do not know that it is fair to say that we still know little.

14. E. S. Gershon and R. O. Rieder, "Major Disorders of Mind and Brain," *Scientific American* 267, no. 3 (1992): 126-33.

15. As reported by E. T. Fuller, *Psychiatric Times*, 21 November 1993.

16. E. O. Laumann, J. H. Gagnon, R. T. Michael, S. Michaels. *The Social Organization of Sexuality: Sexual Practices in the United States*. Chicago: University of Chicago Press (1994), 317.

17. Ibid., 318

18. D. Buss, "The Strategies of Human Mating." *American Scientist* 82, no. 3 (1994): 238-249.

19. W. J. Gadpaille, "Cross-species and Cross-cultural Contributions to Understanding Homosexual Activity," *Archives of General Psychiatry* 37, no. 3 (1980): 349-356. The author comments: "Some forms of homosexual activity are widespread if not ubiquitous among studied mammals, occur invariably in all reported subhuman primates, and are present in most human cultures. Homo Sapiens is the only species, however, in which adult preferential or obligatory homosexuality occurs naturally. . . ." And with respect to there being many diVerent kinds of homosexuality, they remark: "The data suggest that preferential or obligatory homosexuality in adulthood, in the presence of available and receptive heterosexual partners, is qualitatively rather than quantitatively distinct from all other manifestations of homosexual activity, and that quantitative incidence rating scales obscure meaningful understanding of this dimension of homosexual behavior."

20. M. Hemmat and P. Eggleston, "Competitive Interactions in *Drosophila Melanogaster*: Recurrent Selection for Aggression and Response," *Heredity* (Edinburgh) 60 (1988): 129-37, part 1; D. A. Hay, "Genetics in the Analysis of Behaviour," *Neuroscience and Biobehavioral Review* 4, no. 4 (1980): 489-508.

21. S. Holzberg and J. H. Schroder, "The Inheritance of Aggressiveness in the Convict Cichlid Fish, *Cichlasoma nigrofasciatum* (Pisces: Cichlidae)," *Animal Behaviour* 23, no. 3 (1975): 625-31.

22. D. Buchenauer, "Genetic Behavioral Aspects of Agricultural Animals

[Verhaltensgenetische Aspekte bei landwirtschaftlichen Nutztieren]," *Deutsche Tierarztliche Wochenschrift* 97, no. 6 (1990): 247-49.

23. D. E. Bernon and P. B. Siegel, "Mating Frequency in Male Japanese Quail: Crosses Among Selected and Unselected Lines," *Canadian Journal of Genetic Cytology* 25, no. 5 (1983): 450-56.

24. D. K. Belyaev, A. O. Ruvinsky, and L. N. Trut, "Inherited Activation-Inactivation of the Star Gene in Foxes: Its Bearing on the Problem of Domestication," *Heredity* 72, no. 4 (1981): 267-74.

25. A. Didier-Erickson, S. C. Maxson, and S. Ogawa, "Differential Effect of the DBA1 and C57BL10 Y Chromosomes on the Response to Social or Other Stimuli for OVense," *Behavioral Genetics* 19, no. 5 (1989): 675-83; E. M. Weerts et al., "Increased GABA-dependent Chloride Uptake in Mice Selectively Bred for Low Aggressive Behavior," *Psychopharmacology* 108, nos. 1-2 (1992): 196-204; R. F. Benus et al., "Heritable Variation for Aggression as a Reflection of Individual Coping Strategies," *Experientia* 47, no. 10 (1991): 1008-19; J. M. Petitto et al., "Genetic Differences in Social Behavior: Relation to Natural Killer Cell Function and Susceptibility to Tumor Development," *Neuropsychopharmacology* 8, no. 1 (1993): 35-43; E. M. Nikulina and N. S. Kapralova, "The Role of Dopamine Receptors in Controlling Mouse Aggressivity: The Genotype Dependence [Rol' dofaminovykh retseptorov v kontrole agressivnosti myshei: zavisimost' ot genotipa]," *Zh Vyssh Nerv Deiat* 41, no. 4 (1991): 734-40 (Abstract); E. M. Nikulina and N. K. Popova, "Genetic Analysis of Predator Aggressiveness in Mice [Geneticheskii analiz agressivnosti khishchnika u myshei]," *Genetika* 19, no. 7 (1983): 1105-10; G. A. van Oortmerssen and T. C. Bakker, "ArtiWcial Selection for Short and Long Attack Latencies in Wild *Mus musculus domesticus*," *Behavioral Genetics* 11, no. 2 (1981): 115-26.

26. R. F. Benus et al., "Heritable Variation for Aggression as a Reflection of Individual Coping Strategies," *Experientia* 47, no. 10 (1991): 1008-19.

27. H. A. van der Steen et al., "Aggressive Behavior of Sows at Parturition" *Journal of Animal Science* 66, no. 2 (1988): 271-79. Published erratum appears in *Journal of Animal Science* 66, no. 10 (1988): 2711.

28. A. M. Santillan-Doherty, J. L. Diaz, and R. Mondragon-Ceballos, "Synergistic Effects of Kinship, Sex and Rank in the Behavioral Interactions of Captive Stump-Tailed Macaques," *Folia Primatologia* (Basel) 56, no. 4 (1991): 177-89; M. J. Raleigh et al., "Serotonergic Mechanisms Promote Dominance Acquisition in Adult Male Vervet Monkeys," *Brain Research* 559, no. 2 (1991): 181-90; M. L. Boccia, "Comparison of the Physical Characteristics of Grooming in Two Species of Macaques (*Macaca nemestrina* and *M. radiata*)," *Journal of Comparative Psychology* 103, no. 2 (1989): 177-83; X. Valderrama, S. Srikosamatara, J. G. Robinson, "Infanticide in Wedge-Capped Capuchin Monkeys, *Cebus olivaceus*," *Folia Primatologia* (Basel) 54, nos. 3-4 (1990): 171-76; A. Troisi et al., "Maternal Aggression by Lactating Group-Living Japanese Macaque Females," *Hormone and Behaviour* 22, no. 4 (1988): 444-52.

29. P. Netter and S. Neuhauser-Metternich, "Types of Aggressiveness and Catecholamine Response in Essential Hypertensives and Healthy Controls," *Journal of Psychosomatic Research* 35, nos. 4-5 (1991): 409-19; R. Plutchik and H. Van Praag, "The Measurement of Suicidality, Aggressivity and Impulsivity," *Progress*

in Neuropsychopharmacology and Biological Psychiatry 13, no 1 (1989), supplement S23-34; J. P. Rushton et al., "Altruism and Aggression: The Heritability of Individual DiVerences," *Journal of Personality and Social Psychology* 50, no. 6 (1986): 1192-98; J. P. Rushton and S. Erdle, "Evidence for an Aggressive (and Delinquent) Personality," *British Journal of Social Psychology* 26 (1987): 87-89, part 1; J. P. Rushton, "Distal-proximal Approaches to Aggression: A Rejoinder to Campbell, Muncer and Bibel," *British Journal of Social Psychology* 26 (1987): 185-86, part 2; J. C. Meininger et al., "Genetics or Environment? Type A Behavior and Cardiovascular Risk Factors in Twin Children," *Nursing Research* 37, no. 6 (1988): 341-46; S. A. Mednick and K. M. Finello, "Biological Factors and Crime: Implications for Forensic Psychiatry," *International Journal of Law and Psychiatry* 6, no. 1 (1983): 1-15; K. A. Matthews et al., "Familial Resemblance in Components of the Type A Behavior Pattern: A Reanalysis of the California Type A Twin Study," *Psychosomatic Medicine* 46, no. 6 (1984): 512-22; H.G. Brunner et al., "Abnormal Behavior Associated With a Point Mutation in the Structural Gene for Monoamine Oxidase A," *Science* 262 (1993): 578-80.

This last study is especially interesting because the identified genetic mutation is associated not only with elevated levels of aggression (impulsive violence, arson, and attempted rape) but with increased paraphilac sexual behavior as well (exhibitionism). This study suggests therefore not so much a gene for aggression per se but for decreased impulse control altogether. The gene may therefore not cause the behaviors but release them.

30. B. Kerem et al. "Identification of the Cystic Fibrosis Gene: Genetic Analysis," *Science* 245, no. 4922 (1989): 1073-80; M. Wagner, M. Schloesser, and J. Reiss, "Cystic Fibrosis: A Gene at the End of the Road," *Mol Biol Med* 7, no. 4 (1990): 359-64.

31. C. Anderson, "Genome Project to Tackle Mass Screening," *Nature* 348, no. 6302 (1990): 569; C. L. Christian, "Discovery of the Gene Defect in Cystic Fibrosis: Implications for Diagnosis and Treatment," *Clinical Perinatology* 17, no. 4 (1990): 779-91; H. R. Colten, "Screening for Cystic Fibrosis; Public Policy and Personal Choices," *The New England Journal of Medicine* 322, no. 5 (February 1990): 328-29; "Is Population Screening for Cystic Fibrosis Appropriate Now?" *American Journal of Human Genetics* 46, no. 2 (1990): 394-95; C. R. Newton et al., "Amplification Refractory Mutation System for Prenatal Diagnosis and Carrier Assessment in Cystic Fibrosis," *Lancet* 2 (23-30 December 1989): 1481-83; L. P. ten Kate, "Carrier Screening in CF," *Nature* 342, no. 6246 (9 November 1989): 131, 471-73; M. J. Smith, "An Evaluation of Population Screening for Carriers of Cystic Fibrosis," *Public Health Medicine* 14, no. 3 (1992): 257-63; C. Anderson, "Widespread CF Testing Inevitable, Congressional Report Finds," *Nature* 358, no. 6387 (1992): 529.

32. W. Poller et al., "Sequence Analysis of the Cystic Fibrosis Gene in Patients With Disseminated Bronchiectatic Lung Disease: Application in the Identification of a Cystic Fibrosis Patient With Atypical Clinical Course," *Klinische Wochenschrift* 69, no. 14 (1991): 657-63; A. L. Beaudet, "Genetic Testing for Cystic Fibrosis," *Pediatric Clinics of North America* 39, no. 2 (April 1992): 213-28; W. C. Spence et al., "Neonatal Screening for Cystic Fibrosis: Addition of Molecular Diagnostics to Increase SpeciWcity," *Biochemical Medicine and Meta-*

bolic Biology 49, no. 2 (1993): 200-211; L. Cremonesi et al., "Four New Mutations of the CFTR Gene (541delC, R347H, R352Q, E585X) Detected by DGGE Analysis in Italian CF Patients, Associated With DiVerent Clinical Phenotypes," *Human Mutations* 1, no. 4 (1992): 314-19; B. Mercier et al., "Detection of More Than 94% Cystic Fibrosis Mutations in a Sample of Belgian Population and Identification of Four Novel Mutations. *Human Mutations* 2, no. 1 (1993): 16-20; M. Schwartz, "[Cystic Wbrosis. From clinical diagnosis to a mutation specific test]," *Ugeskrift For Laeger* 155, no. 5 (1993): 292-95; M. Nemeti et al., "The Occurrence of Various Non-Delta F508 CFTR Gene Mutations Among Hungarian Cystic Fibrosis Patients," *American Journal of Human Genetics* 89, no. 2 (1992): 245-46; N. Ghanem et al., "Exhaustive Screening of Exon 10 CFTR Gene Mutations and Polymorphisms by Denaturing Gradient Gel Electrophoresis: Applications to Genetic Counselling in Cystic Fibrosis," *Mol Cell Probes* 6, no. 2 (1992): 27-31; M. Super and M. J. Schwarz, "Mutations of the Cystic Fibrosis Gene Locus Within the Population of the Northwest of England," *European Journal of Pediatrics* 151, no. 2 (1992): 108-11; J. Plieth et al., "Single-Strand Conformation Polymorphism (SSCP) Analysis of Exon 11 of the CFTR Gene Reliably Detects More Than One Third of Non-Delta F508 Mutations in German Cystic Fibrosis Patients," *American Journal of Human Genetics* 88, no. 3 (1992): 283-87.

33. Science Section, 1. My emphasis. ". . . over 100 disease-causing mutations have now been identified. [April, 1992] Although at least some of these determine the incidence of pancreatic disease, there is no association between a particular mutation and the severity of lung and liver disease." R. A. Knight, "Genetics of Cystic Fibrosis," *British Journal of Hospital Medicine* 47, no. 7 (1992): 502-6. Also, for example: "Adults with CF [cystic fibrosis] followed in a university center were assessed for the presence of the most common CF gene mutation, delta-F508. Excluding one member of a sibling pair, 29 of 55 subjects had two copies of delta-F508 (homozygotes), 23 had one copy of delta-F508 with the other CF mutation not identiWed (complex heterozygotes) and three were lacking delta-F508. A wide range of clinical severity was seen among individuals carrying two copies of the delta-F508 gene, who are genetically identical at the CF gene locus. The number of individuals diagnosed with CF as adults was signiWcantly lower in the homozygote group (1 of 29) as compared with the heterozygote group (7 of 24). No diVerences were detected between groups in pulmonary function, non-pulmonary complications or overall clinical severity. These results suggest that environmental or background genetic factors contribute signiWcantly to the variability in pulmonary and other complications seen among individuals with CF." W. Burke et al., "Variable Severity of Pulmonary Disease in Adults with Identical Cystic Fibrosis Mutations," *Chest* 102, no. 2 (1992): 506-9.

34. "Cystic Fibrosis Surprise: Genetic Screening Falters," *New York Times*, 16 November 1993; my emphasis.

35. Ibid.

36. Mann, "Behavioral Genetics in Transition," 1687.

37. Ibid., 1688.

38. S. LeVay, "A Difference in Hypothalamic Structure Between Heterosexual and Homosexual Men," *Science* 253 (1991): 1034-37.

39. D. Swaab and M. Hofman, "An Enlarged Suprachiasmatic Nucleus in Homosexual Men," *Brain Research* 537 (1990): 141-48.

40. L. Allen, et al., "Sexual Orientation and the Size of the Anterior Commissure in the Human Brain," *Proceedings of the National Academy of Science of the United States of America* 89, no. 15 (1992): 7199-7202.

41. S. Demeter et al., "Morphometric analysis of the human corpus callosum and anterior commissure," *Human Neurobiology* 6 (1988): 219-26.

42. G. Gabbard, "Psychodynamic Psychiatry in the 'Decade of the Brain'," *American Journal of Psychiatry*, 149, no. 8 (1992): 991-98.

43. D. Deam et al., "Alpha₁-Antitrypsin Phenotypes in Homosexual Men," *Pathology* 21 (1989): 91-92.

44. R. Post, "Transduction of Psychosocial Stress into the Neurobiology of Recurrent Affective Disorder," *American Journal of Psychiatry* 148, no. 8 (1992): 999-1010.

45. Gabbard, "Psychodynamic Psychiatry."

46. Reported in D. Gelman, "Born or Bred?" *Newsweek*, 24 February 1992: 46-53.

47. J. Maddox, "Is Homosexuality Hardwired?" *Nature* 353 (September 1991): 13.

48. P. Billings and J. Beckwith, "Born Gay?" *Technology Review*, July 1993: 60. Paul Billings, M.D., is the former chief of the Division of Genetic Medicine at California PaciWc Medical Center in Palo Alto, California and is now head of Internal Medicine at the Palo Alto Veteran's Administration Hospital; Jonathan Beckwith, M.D., is American Cancer Society Research Professor in the Department of Microbiology and Molecular Genetics at Harvard Medical School.

49. Ibid., 60.

50. Ibid., 61.

51. F. J. Kallmann, "Comparative Twin Study on the Genetic Aspects of Male Homosexuality," *Journal of Nervous and Mental Disease* 118 (1952): 283-298.

52. F. J. Kallmann quoted in J. D. Ranier, A. MesnikoV, L. C. Kolb, and A. Carr, "Homosexuality and Heterosexuality in Identical Twins," *Psychosomatic Medicine* 22 (1960): 251-259.

53. W. Pomeroy, *Dr. Kinsey and the Institute for Sex Research* (New York: Harper and Row, 1972), 97-137.

54. E. Eckert et al., "Homosexuality in Monozygotic Twins Reared Apart," *British Journal of Psychiatry* 148 (1986): 421-25.

55. P. Cameron et al., "Effect of Homosexuality Upon Public Health and Social Order," *Psychological Reports* 64, no. 3, part 2 (1989): 1167-79.

56. See D. W. Whitehead, "Dan Quayle Was Right," *The Atlantic Monthly* 271, no. 4: 47-84, for an excellent, lay-oriented summary of this reversal. Among others, Whitehead cites Sara McLanahan, now a sociologist at Princeton: "I'd gone to graduate school in the days when the politically correct argument was that single-parent families were just another family form, and it was fine." She acknowledges now that "Evidence on intergenerational poverty indicates that, indeed, offspring from single mother families are far more likely to be poor and to form mother-only families than are offspring who live with two parents most of their pre-adult lives." (62). Whitehead and McLanahan are just two of the

many, more often than not female, researchers who have broken out of the destructive seventies mindset. Perhaps the most well-known is Judith Wallerstein, director of the long-term, and still ongoing, California Children of Divorce Study. Her 1989 book, written with Sandra Blakeslee, *Second Chances: Men, Women, and Children a Decade after Divorce*, blew the lid off the divorce-as-personal-fulWllment-the-kids-will-be-fine fantasy.

57. E. Coleman et al., "Sexual and Intimacy Dysfunction Among Homosexual Men and Women," *Psychiatric Medicine* (United States) 10, no. 2 (1992): 257-71.

58. L. S. Doll et al., "Self-Reported Childhood and Adolescent Sexual Abuse Among Adult Homosexual Bisexual Men," *Child Abuse and Neglect* 16, no 6 (1992): 855-64.

59. D. M. Greenberg, J. M. Bradford, and S. Curry, "A Comparison of Sexual Victimization in the Childhoods of Pedophiles and Hebephiles," *Journal of Forensic Science* (United States) 38, no. 2 (March 1993): 432-36.

60. R. Goy and B. McEwen, *Sexual DiVerentiation of the Brain* (Cambridge, Mass.: MIT Press, 1980).

61. From *Dangerous Diagnostics*, as cited in the *Wall Street Journal*, 16 July 1993: B1.

62. The baseline prevalence rate of homosexuality aVects the calculations for the following reason: If homosexuality were very common, for the sake of illustration say 90 percent, then most of a high concordance rate among twins would simply be due to how prevalent it is regardless of genetics. In this case, a 90 percent concordance rate for identical twins would imply no additional genetic loading, the concordance rate for unrelated pairs of individuals would be just as high. On the other hand, if homosexuality were extraordinarily rare, one in a million, say, then even a small diVerential in the concordance rate would point toward genetic factors.

63. M. King and E. McDonald, "Homosexuals Who Are Twins: A Study of 46 Probands," *British Journal of Psychiatry* 160 (1992): 407-9; J. M. Bailey and R.C. Pillard, "A Genetic Study of Male Sexual Orientation," *Archives of General Psychiatry* 48 (1991), 1089-96; Bailey et al., "Heritable Factors," 217-23.

64. W. Byne and B. Parsons, "Human Sexual Orientation: The Biologic Theories Reappraised," *Archives of General Psychiatry* 50, no. 3: 228-39.

65. Bailey and Pillard, "Male Sexual Orientation."

66. See my comments below about and the statements of William Byne, the senior author of the article, that suggest his disinterested status. Of interest as well has been the hostile response of the gay activist community to his critique of recent biological research.

67. Bailey and Pillard, "Male Sexual Orientation." I was recently asked to discuss these authors' Wndings on a local television program. The invitation was issued because the station had learned that Bailey and Pillard had discovered that "homosexuality is genetic." The producers were shocked to read in the article itself the researchers' own admission of how the study pointed, rather, to the great importance of nongenetic factors, and of the researchers disappointment in the outcome.

68. E. Eckert et al., "Homosexuality in Monozygotic Twins Reared Apart," *British Journal of Psychiatry* 148 (1986): 421-25.

69. Byne and Parsons, "Human Sexual Orientation," 230.

70. Endnote needed; my emphasis.

71. Theodore Lidz, "Reply to 'A Genetic Study of Male Sexual Orientation'," *Archives of General Psychiatry* 50, no. 3 (1993): 240.

72. Doll et al., "Self-reported Abuse."

73. Billings and Beckwith, "Born Gay?" 60.

74. Ibid., 61.

75. Bailey et al., "Heritable Factors," 217-23.

76. Quoted by J. Horgan, "Eugenics Revisited," *Scientific American,* June 1993: 123.

77. C. Mann, "Genes and Behavior," *Science* 264 (1994), 1686-89.

78. J. P. Rushton, "Race Evolution and Behavior: A Life History Perspective." (1994), New Brunswick: Transaction Publishers, 47

79. Ibid.

80. W. Byne, "Science and Belief: Psychobiological Research on Sexual Orientation," *Journal of Homosexuality,* in press.

81. D. Jefferson, "Studying the Biology of Sexual Orientation Has Political Fallout," *Wall Street Journal,* 12 August 1993: 1.

82. Lidz, "Reply to 'Male Sexual Orientation'."

83. D. Rosenthal, P. H. Wender, and S. S. Kety, "Schizophrenics' OVspring Reared in Adoptive Homes," in *The Transmission of Schizophrenia,* D. Rosenthal and S.S. Kety, eds. (Elmsford, N.Y.: Pergamon Press, 1968).

84. P. Tienary, A. Sorri, and I. Lhati, "Interaction of Genetic and Psychosocial Factors in Schizophrenia," *Schizophrenia Bulletin* 13 (1987): 477-84.

85. Lidz, "Reply to 'Male Sexual Orientation'," 240; my emphasis.

86. Practical insignificance is not the same thing as statistical insignificance. A 10 percent greater likelihood of having something whose baseline incidence is 1 percent translates into an increased risk of an additional one chance in a thousand. Most people intuitively grasp the point when it affects them directly. One example is in regard to speed limits: between 55 and 70 miles an hour the likelihood of having a fatal accident may double. Statistically, it is a very significant, indeed 100 percent, increase. Nonetheless, most people continue to drive as though this statistic had no practical significance. Why? Because the baseline likelihood of dying in an automobile accident is so low, say one chance in a hundred thousand per trip. Doubling that rate translates into an increased risk of only an additional one chance in a hundred thousand.

87. These, by the way, have yet to be found. The same issue of *Archives of General Psychiatry* that contains Bailey and Pillard's newest research on female homosexuality, Lidz's reply to their first article, and Bailey and Pillard's reply to Lidz also contains three articles reporting yet further failures to identify a genetic locus for schizophrenia.

88. F. E. Bloom, "Advancing a Neurodevelopmental Etiology for Schizophrenia," *Archives of General Psychology* 50, no. 3 (1993), 224-27.

89. J. M. Bailey and R. C. Pillard, "In reply," *Archives of General Psychiatry* 50, no. 3 (1993).

90. As one research scientist commented to me about this incident: "Yes, beware of scientists wedded to their hypotheses; a good scientist tries to kill his hypothesis."

91. Byne and Parsons, "Human Sexual Orientation." See introductory comments to chapter 6.

92. T. Wiesel, "Genetics and Behavior," *Science* 264 (1994): 1647; my emphasis.

93. J. Knop et al., "A 30-year Follow-up Study of the Sons of Alcoholic Men," *Acta Psychiatrica* (Denmark) 370 (1993): 48-53; K. S. Kendler et al., "A Population-Based Twin Study of Alcoholism in Women," *Journal of the American Medical Association* 268, no. 14 (1992): 1877-82; J. B. Peterson et al., "Cognitive Dysfunction and the Inherited Predisposition to Alcoholism," *Journal of Studies in Alcoholism* 53, no. 2 (1992): 54-60.

94. Another example of how genes indirectly lead to behavioral patterns is found among Orientals. No gene exists that codes for a preference for an Oriental style of cooking. And yet careful study shows that there is a very strong genetic association to such a preference. This is because Orientals lack the gene that codes for the enzyme lactase, which breaks down the lactose found in all milk products. When lactose is not broken down, milk products cause diarrhea. Oriental cooking styles have thus developed around a milk restriction similar to that required by anyone with a lactose intolerance.

95. S. Y. Hill et al., "Cardiac Responsivity in Individuals at High Risk for Alcoholism," *Journal of Studies in Alcoholism* 53, no. 4 (1992): 378-88; P. R. Finn et al., "Sensation Seeking, Stress Reactivity, and Alcohol Dampening Discriminate the Density of a Family History of Alcoholism," *Alcohol Clinical and Experimental Research* 16, no. 3 (1992): 585-90.

96. Valium is the parent compound of a class of chemicals, benzodiazepines, that are widely used as anti-anxiety agents, muscle-relaxants, sleeping medications, and anesthetics. Other examples of this class, of which there are about forty, are Ativan, Dalmane, Halcion, and Librium. All are "cleaner" than alcohol, however, and associated with fewer "hangover" effects. This is because their breakdown products are either themselves different benzodiazepines or essentially inactive. Some of the breakdown products of alcohol, however, have adverse side eVects. Prior to the invention of synthetic agents, alcohol was widely used in hospital, sometimes intravenously, to calm nerves, dull pain, suppress seizures, and cause sleep. D. S. Cowley et al., "Response to Diazepam in Sons of Alcoholics," *Alcohol Clinical and Experimental Research* 16, no. 6 (1992): 1057-63.

97. N. el-Guabely et al., "Adult Children of Alcoholics in Treatment Programs for Anxiety Disorders and Substance Abuse," *Canadian Journal of Psychiatry* 37, no. 8 (1992): 544-48; S. M. Mirin et al., "Psychopathology In Drug Abusers and Their Families," *Comparative Psychiatry* 32, no. 1 (1991): 6-51; M.W. Otto et al., "Alcohol Dependence In Panic Disorder Patients," *Journal of Psychiatric Research* 26, no, 1 (1992): 29-38; G. Winokur and W. Coryell, "Familial Subtypes of Unipolar Depression: A Prospective Study of Familial Pure Depressive Disease Compared to Depressive Spectrum Disease," *Biological Psychiatry* 32, no. 11 (1992): 1012-18.

98. D. S. Cowley et al., "Response to Diazepam."

99. D. S. Cowley et al., "Response to Diazepam"; S. Y. Hill et al., "Cardiac Responsivity"; P. R. Finn et al., "Sensation Seeking."

100. See C. Holden, "A Cautionary Genetic Tale: The Sobering Story of D2," *Science* 264: 1696-97.

101. See Bailey and Pillard, "Male Sexual Orientation," and surrounding discussion.

102. The dramatic influence of the intrauterine environment on behavior is demonstrated well by a recent article in *Science* on spotted hyenas. In this species, maternal androgens are so elevated during pregnancy, especially when the fetus is female, that adult females are heavier and more aggressive than males, have fused vaginal labia that form a "scrotum," and have a clitoris that is fully erectile and as large as the male penis. Native tradition in the Savannah long held that there were only males in this species. And as we might guess, the females in this species dominate the males. Incidentally, this is yet another example of how genetic structure influences aggression. In this case genetics aVects behavior not only directly on a species-wide basis, but also indirectly through hormonal mechanisms.

The typically masculine aggression that is "hard-wired" into this animal (into both males and females, but especially females) is biologically determined and fierce. Unlike other carnivores, infant hyenas are born with fully erupted and efficient teeth, open eyes with fully functioning rapid tracking and focusing mechanisms, and the capability for perfectly coordinated adult-type motor action. Within an hour of birth a newborn pup can mount a full-fledged "bite-shake attack", the adult hunting pattern, in which she bites and grips the neck of her opponent, shaking it violently to death.

The unfortunate opponent in this case is usually the same-sex twin, especially when the twins are two females. (Hyena female twins, it seems, lack "twin narcissism"!) In most cases, the first female twin to emerge will kill the second one just as she begins to emerge from the birth canal, before she can even leave the amniotic sac. Not surprisingly, the chief characteristic of members of this species is their extraordinary skill and efficiency as predatory killers. They can even successfully chase off lions from a kill, failing only when the lion is an unusually experienced and dominant male. The individual hyena requires no instruction in aggression. L. Frank, S. Glickman, and P. Licht, "Fatal Sibling Aggression, Precocial Development and Androgens in Neonatal Spotted Hyenas," *Science* 252 (1991): 702-4.

103. G. Dorner et al., "Gene- and Environment-Dependent Neuroendocrine Etiogenesis of Homosexuality and Transsexualism," *Experimental and Clinical Endocrinology* 98, no. 2 (1991): 141-50.

104. See Byne and Parsons, "Human Sexual Orientation," for a summary of counterWndings and conclusions.

105. This unexpectedly renewed possibility that homosexuality is truly a physical, brain-based illness may sound strange and perhaps offensive to those who first hear it. But the idea follows the general observation that most aspects of normal human behavior are purposeful. Thus, from an evolutionary perspective, which emphasizes the development of characteristics that help protect the individual and propagate the species, homosexuality seems to have no adaptive purpose. Indeed, the strikingly higher rate of the many medical illnesses associated with sodomy is consistent with just the opposite.

106. A. Galaburda, et al., "Right-Left Asymmetries in the Brain," *Science* 199, no. 4331 (1974): 852-56; N. Geschwind, "Anatomical Asymmetry as the Basis for Cerebral Dominance," *Federal Proceedings* 37, no. 9 (1978): 2263-66; A.

Galaburda and N. Geschwind, "Anatomical Asymmetries in the Adult and Developing Brain and their Implications for Function," *Advances in Pediatrics* 28 (1991): 271-292.

107. P. Satz, et al., "Hand Preference in Homosexual Men," *Cortex* 27 (1991): 295-306.

108. C. McCormick, S. Witelson, and E. Kingstone, "Left-Handedness in Homosexual Men and Women: Neuroendocrine Implications," *Psychoneuroendocrinology* 15, no. 1 (1990): 69-79.

109. J. M. Bailey et al., "A Test of the Maternal Stress Theory of Human Male Homosexuality," *Archives of Sexual Behavior* 20, no. 3 (1991): 277-93.

110. N. Risch, E. Squires-Wheeler, and J. B. K. Bronya, "Male Sexual Orientation and Genetic Evidence," *Science* 262 (1993): 2063-65.

111. A. I. Gladkova, "The Reproductive Function of Female Rats During Overcrowding," *Fiziologia Zhournali SSSR* 78, no. 5 (May 1992): 86-92 [English Abstract]; W. J. Zielinski and J. G. Vandenbergh, "Effect of Intrauterine Position and Social Density on Age of First Reproduction in Wild-Type Female House Mice (*Mus musculus*)," *Journal of Comparative Psychology* 105, no. 2 (1991): 134-39; F. Goudey-Perriere et al., "Indolamines in the Cockroach *Blaberus craniifer Burm.* nervous system, II. Fed and Crowded Young Males in Comparison with Females," *Comparative Biochemistry and Physiology* 100, no. 3 (1991): 457-61; J. A. Creighton and P. F. Chevins, "Stressful Crowding During Pregnancy Advances Onset of Offspring Adrenocortical Rhythm," *Experimental Biology* 48, no. 1 (1988): 57-62; V. G. Swarnakumari and R. Madhavi, "The Effects of Crowding on Adults of *Philophthalmus nocturnus* Grown in Domestic Chicks," *Journal of Helminthology* 66, no. 4 (December 1992): 255-59; G. R. Jansen and R. Binard, "Effect of Dietary Protein and Environmental Factors on Lactation Performance in Rats," *Physiology and Behavior* 50, no. 2 (1991): 297-304; A. D. Pickering et al., "Effects of Acute and Chronic Stress on the Levels of Circulating Growth Hormone in the Rainbow Trout, *Oncorhynchus mykiss*," *General and Comparative Endocrinology* 83, no. 1 (1991): 86-93; W. J. Zielinski, J. G. Vandenbergh, and M. M. Montano, "EVects of Social Stress and Intrauterine Position on Sexual Phenotype in Wild-Type House Mice (*Mus musculus*)," *Physiology and Behavior* 49, no. 1 (January 1991): 117-23; K. B. Firestone, K. V. Thompson, and C. S. Carter, "Female-Female Interactions and Social Stress in Prairie Voles," *Behavioral and Neural Biology* 55, no. 1 (1991), 31-41; P. W. Harvey and P. F. Chevins, "Crowding During Pregnancy Delays Puberty and Alters Estrous Cycles of Female Offspring in Mice," *Experientia* 43, no 3 (1987): 306-8.

112. King and McDonald, "Homosexuals Who Are Twins," 407-9.

113. D. H. Hamer et al., "A Linkage Between DNA Markers on the X-chromosome and Male Sexual Orientation," *Science* 261, no. 5119: 321-27.

114. "Research Points Toward a Gay Gene," *Wall Street Journal*, 16 July 1993.

115. Risch, et al., "Male Sexual Orientation and Genetic Evidence."

116. Unsurprisingly, a much smaller percentage of homosexual men have children than do heterosexual men. A. P. Bell and M. S. Weinberg, *Homosexualities: A Study of Diversity among Men and Women* (New York: Simon and Schuster, 1978).

117. It was precisely the failure to Wnd such conWrming data that torpedoed the "bipolar gene."

118. Risch et al., "Male Sexual Orientation and Genetic Evidence."

119. D. H. Hamer et al., "Response to N. Risch et al.," *Science* 262 (1993): 2065.

120. Ibid.

121. Mann, "Genes and Behavior," 1687.

122. Byne and Parsons, "Human Sexual Orientation," 228-39; my emphasis.

2 The Development of a Homosexual Orientation

1. M. S. Lundy and G. A. Rekers, "Homosexuality: Development, Risks, Parental Values, and Controversies," in *Handbook of Child and Adolescent Sexual Problems*, ed. G. A. Rekers (New York: Lexington Books/Jossey-Bass, 1995), 290-312.

2. A. P. Bell and M. S. Weinberg, *Homosexualities: A Study of Diversity Among Men and Women* (New York: Simon & Schuster, 1978).

3. See note 1 above.

4. See note 1 above.

5. I. Bieber et al., *Homosexuality: A Psychoanalytic Study* (New York: Basic Books, 1962); D. J. West, "Parental Relationships in Male Homosexuality," *International Journal of Social Psychiatry* 5 (1959): 85-97; R. B. Evans, "Childhood Parental Relationships of Homosexual Men," *Journal of Consulting and Clinical Psychology* 33 (1969): 129-135; E. Hooker, "Male Homosexuality in the Rorschach," *Journal of Projective Techniques* 22 (1958): 33-53, "What is a Criterion?," *Journal of Projective Techniques* 22 (1959): 278-281, and "Parental Relationships and Male Homosexuality in Patient and Non-patient Samples," *Journal of Consulting and Clinical Psychology* 33 (1969): 140-142.

6. M. T. Saghir and E. Robins, *Male and Female Homosexuality: A Comprehensive Investigation* (Baltimore, Md.: Williams & Wilkens Co., 1973).

7. E. Bene, "On the Genesis of Male Homosexuality: An Attempt at Clarifying the Role of Parents," *British Journal of Psychiatry* 111 (1965): 803-813; L. B. Apperson and W. G. McAdoo, "Parental Factors in the Childhood of Homosexuals," *Journal of Abnormal Psychology* 73 (1968): 201-206.

8. D. G. Brown, "Homosexuality and Family Dynamics," *Bulletin of the Menninger Clinic* 27 (1963): 227-232.

9. Evans; C. H. Jonas, "An Objective Approach to the Personality and Environment in Homosexuality," *Psychiatric Quarterly* 18 (1944): 626-641; L. M. Terman and C. C. Miles, *Sex and Personality* (New York: Russell & Russell, 1968).

10. Bieber et al.; Evans; E. R. Holeman and G. Winokur, "Effeminate Homosexuality: A Disease of Childhood," *American Journal of Orthopsychiatry* 35 (1965): 48-56; F. L. Whitam, "Childhood Indicators of Male Homosexuality," *Archives of Sexual Behavior* 6 (1977): 89-96.

11. Whitam, "Childhood Indicators," 89-96.

12. Ibid., 93.

13. Ibid., 94.

14. F. L. Whitam and M. Zent, "A Cross-culture Assessment of Early Cross-gender Behavior and Familial Factors in Male Homosexuality," *Archives of Sexual Behavior* 13 (1984): 427-439.

15. M. T. Saghir and E. Robins, "Male and Female Homosexuality-natural History," *Comprehensive Psychiatry* 12 (1971): 503-510.

16. T. Roesler and R. W. Deisher, "Youthful Male Homosexuality: Homosexual Experience and the Process of Developing Homosexual Identity in Males Age 16 to 22 years," *Journal of the American Medical Association* 219 (1972): 1018-1023.

17. A. P. Bell, M. S. Weinberg, and S. K. Hammersmith, *Sexual Preference: Its Development in Men and Women* (Bloomington, Ind.: University Press, 1981).

18. Ibid., 81.

19. Ibid., 99.

20. Ibid., 84.

21. D. Shrier and R. L. Johnson, "Sexual Victimization of Boys: An Ongoing Study of an Adolescent Medicine Clinic Population," *Journal of the National Medical Association* 80, no. 1 (1988): 1189-1193.

22. Ibid.

23. Ibid., 1192.

24. P. Cameron and K. Cameron, "Homosexual Parents," *Adolescence* 31, no. 124 (1996): 757-776.

25. P. H. Van Wyk and C. S. Geist, "Psychosocial Development of Heterosexual, Bisexual, and Homosexual Behavior," *Archives of Sexual Behavior* 13 (1984): 505-544.

26. Ibid., 505.

27. Ibid., 541.

28. Bell and Weinberg, *Homosexualities*.

29. S. Schafer, "Socio-sexual Behavior in Male and Female Homosexuals: A Study in Sex Differences," *Archives of Sexual Behavior* 6 (1977): 362.

30. Judd Marmor, ed., *Homosexual Behavior: A Modern Reappraisal* (New York: Basic Books, 1980), 17.

31. Saghir and Robins, *Male and Female Homosexuality*.

32. Ibid., 504.

33. Saghir and Robins, *"Male and Female Homosexuality"*.

34. F. E. Kenyon, "Studies in Female Homosexuality: Social and Psychiatric Aspects," *British Journal of Psychiatry* 144 (1968): 1337-1350.

35. Kenyon; J. Loney, "Family Dynamics in Homosexual Women," *Archives of Sexual Behavior* 2 (1973): 343-350; Saghir and Robins, *Male and Female Homosexuality*; M. Siegelman, "Parental Background of Homosexual and Heterosexual Women," *British Journal of Psychiatry* 124 (1974): 14-21.

36. Bene; R. H. Gundlach and B. F. Reiss, "Self and Sexual Identity in the Female: A Study of Female Homosexuals," in *New Directions in Mental Health*, ed. B. F. Reiss (New York: Grune & Stratton, 1968); H. E. Kaye et al., "Homosexuality in Women," *Archives of General Psychiatry* 17 (1967): 626-634; Kenyon; M. W. Kremer and A. H. Rifkin, "The Early Development of Homosexuality: A Study of Adolescent Lesbians," *American Journal of Psychiatry* 126 (1969): 91-96; Loney; K. Poole, "The Etiology of Gender Identity and the Lesbian," *Journal of Social Psychology* 87 (1972): 51-57; Siegelman; M. L. Thompson et al., "Parent-child Relationships and Sexual Identity in Male and Female Homosexuals and Heterosexuals," *Journal of Consulting and Clinical Psychology* 41 (1973): 120-127.

37. Kremer and Rifkin.

38. Gundlach and Reiss; Poole; Siegelman; Thompson et al.

39. D. W. Swanson et al., "Clinical Features of the Female Homosexual Patient," *Journal of Nervous and Mental Disease* 155 (1972): 199-124.

40. Kaye et al.

41. D. H. Rosen, *Lesbianish: A Study of Female Homosexuality* (Springfield, Ill.: C. C. Thomas, 1974).

42. Bell, Weinberg, and Hammersmith.

43. R. Blanchard and K. Freund, "Measuring Masculine Gender Identity in Females," *Journal of Consulting and Clinical Psychology* 51 (1983): 205-214.

44. Van Wyk and Geist.

45. K. J. Zucker, "Cross-gender Identified Children," in *Transexualism and Gender Identity*, ed. B. W. Steiner (Springfield, Ill.: C. C. Thomas, 1985).

46. H. Bakwin, "Deviant Gender-role Behavior in Children: Relation to Homosexual," *Pediatrics* 41 (1968): 620-629.

47. P. S. Lebovitz, "Feminine Behavior in Boys: Aspects of Its Outcome," *American Journal of Psychiatry* 128 (1972): 1283-1289.

48. B. Zuger, "Early Effeminate Behavior in Boys: Outcome and Significance for Homosexuality," *Journal of Nervous Mental Disorders* 172 (1984): 90-97.

49. B. Zuger, "Effeminate Behavior Preset in Boys from Childhood: The Additional Years of Follow-70," *Comprehensive Psychiatry* 19 (1978): 363-369.

50. R. Green, "Gender Identity in Childhood and Later Sexual Orientation: Follow-up of 78 Males," *American Journal of Psychiatry* 142, no. 3 (1985): 339-341.

51. G. A. Rekers et al., "Family Correlated of Male Childhood Gender Disturbance," *Journal of Genetic Psychology* 142 (1983): 31-42; G. A Rekers, "Fathers at Home: Why the Intact Family is Important to Children and the Nation," *Persuasion at Work* 9, no. 4 (1986): 1-7.

52. Bakwin; R. Green, *Sexual Identity Conflict in Children and Adults* (Baltimore, Md.: Penguin, 1974), and "Childhood Cross-gender Behavior and Subsequent Sexual Preference," *American Journal of Psychiatry* 136 (1979): 106-108.

53. G. A. Rekers and S. Mead, "Female Sex-role Deviance: Early Identification and Developmental Intervention," *Journal of Clinical Child Psychology* 9, no. 3 (1980): 199-203.

54. E. M. Pattison and M. L. Pattison, " 'Ex-gays': Religiously Meditated Change in Homosexuals," *American Journal of Psychiatry* 137, no.12 (1980): 1553-1562.

55. M. Kirkpatrick, "Clinical Implications of Lesbian Mother Studies," *Journal of Homosexuality* 14 (1987): 201-211.

56. Ibid., 202.

57. J. F. Harvey, "Homosexuality and Hope: New Thinking in Pastoral Care," in *Hope for Homosexuality*, ed. P. F. Fagan (Washington, D. C.: Center for Child and Family Policy of the Free Congress Research and Education Foundation, 1988), 65-77: Exodus International North America, P.O. Box 77652, Seattle, WA 98177, Phone: (206) 784-7799.

58. J. M. Bailey and R. C. Pillard, "A Genetic Study of Male Sexual Orientation," *Archives of General Psychiatry* 48 (1991): 1089-1096; W. Byne and B. Par-

sons, "Human Sexual Orientation: The Biologic Theories Reappraised," *Archives of General Psychiatry* 50 (1993): 228-239; S. LaVay, "A Difference in Hypothalamic Structure between Heterosexual and Homosexual Men," *Science* 253 (1991): 1034-1037.

    59. Byne and Parsons, 228.

    60. Ibid., 236-237.

    61. R.C. Friedman, *Male Homosexuality: A Contemporary Psychoanalytic Perspective* (New Haven, Conn.: Yale University Press, 1968).

    62. A. A. Ehrhardt, "Psychosexual Adjustment in Adolescence in Patients with Congenital Abnormalities of Their Sex Organs," in *Genetic Mechanisms of Sexual Development*, eds. H. L. Vallet and I. H. Porter (New York: Academic Press, 1979), 473-484; H. F. L. Meyer-Bahlburg, "Sex Hormones and Male Homosexuality in Comparative Perspective," *Archives of Sexual Behavior* 6 (1977): 297-325, and *Neurobehavioral Effect of Prenatal Origin: Sex Hormones, Drugs and Chemical Risks to the Fetus and Newborn* (New York: Alan R. Liss, 1980); G. A. Rekers et al., "Genetic and Physical Studies of Male Children with Psychological Gender Disturbances," *Psychological Medicine* 9 (1979): 373-375.

    63. G. Dorner et al., "A Neuroendocrine Predisposition for Homosexuality," *Archives of Sexual Behavior* 4 (1975): 1-8; A. A. Ehrhardt and S. W. Baker, "Fetal Androgen, Human Central Nervous System Differentiation, and Behavior Sex Differences," in *Sex Differences in Behavior*, eds. R. C. Friedman, R. M. Richart, and R. L. Vande Wiele (New York: John Wiley, 1974), 33-51; C. Hutt, "Biological Bases of Psychological Sex Differences," *American Journal of Diseases in Childhood* 132 (1978): 170-177; J. Money and M. Shwartz, "Dating, Romantic and Nonromantic Friendships, and Sexuality in 17 Early-treated Adrenogential Females, Aged 16-25," in *Congenital Adrenal Hyperplasia*, eds. P. A. Lee et al. (Baltimore, Md.: University Park Press, 1977), 419-431.

    64. J. L. Sheler, "Spiritual America," *U. S. News and World Report* 116, no. 13 (1994): 48-59.

    65. J. Dallas, "Born Gay?" *Christianity Today* (June 22 1992): 20-23.

    66. J. White, *Eros Defiled* (Downer's Grove, Ill: InterVarsity Press, 1977) 111.

    67. Ibid.

    68. Ibid.

    69. Dallas, 23.

    70. G. A Rekers, "Atypical Gender Development and Psychosocial Adjustment," *Journal of Applied Behavioral Analysis* 10 (1977): 560.

    71. P. M. Bentler, "A Typology of Transsexualism: Gender Identity Theory and Data," *Archives of Sexual Behavior* 5 (1976): 567-584; J. Money, "Sexual Dimorphism and Homosexual Gender Identity," *Psychological Bulletin* 74 (1970): 425-440, and "Critique of Dr. Zuger's Manuscript," *Psychosomatic Medicine* 32 (1970): 463-465; J. Money and A. A. Ehrhardt, *Man and Woman, Boy and Girl: The Difference and Dimorphism of Gender Identity from Conception to Maturity* (Baltimore, Md.: Johns Hopkins University Press, 1972); G. A. Rekers, "Gender Identity Problems," in *Handbook of Clinical Behavior Therapy with Children*, eds. P. H. Borstein and A. E. Kazdin (Homewood, Ill: Dorsey Press, 1985): 658-699.

    72. For example, S. J. Bradley et al., "Gender Identity Problems of Children and Adolescents," *Canadian Psychiatric Association Journal* 23 (1978): 175-198.

73. G. A Rekers, *Handbook of Child and Adolescent Sexual Problems* (New York: Lexington Books/Jossey-Bass, 1995).

74. M. S. Lundy and G. A Rekers, "Homosexuality: Presentation, Evaluation and Clinical Decision Making," and "Homosexuality in Adolescence: Interventions and Ethical Consideration," in *Handbook of Child and Adolescent Sexual Problems*, ed. G. A. Rekers (New York: Lexington Books/Jossey-Bass, 1995), 313-340, 341-377.

75. D. H. Barlow, "Increasing Heterosexual Responsiveness in the Treatment of Sexual Deviation: A Review of the Clinical and Experimental Evidence," *Behavior Therapy* 4 (1973): 655-761; J. E. Bates et al., "Intervention with Families of Gender-disturbed Boys," *American Journal of Orthopsychiatry* 45 (1975): 150-157; P. M. Bentler, "A Note on the Treatment of Adolescent Sexual Problems," *Journal of Child Psychology and Psychiatry* 9 (1968): 125-129; A. Canton-Dutari, "Combined Intervention for Controlling Unwanted Homosexual Behavior," *Archives of Sexual Behavior* 3 (1974): 367-371; M. P. Feldman and M. J. MacCulloch, *Homosexual Behavior: Theory and Assessment* (Oxford: Permagon, 1971); K. Freund, "A Laboratory Method for Diagnosing Predominance of Homo- or Hetero-erotic Interest in the Male," *Behavior Research and Therapy* 1 (1968): 85-93; K. N. Ginsburg, "The 'Meat-rack': A Study of the Male Homosexual Prostitute," *American Journal of Psychotherapy* 21 (1967): 170-185; S. Gold and I. L. Neufeld, "A Learning Approach to the Treatment of Homosexuality," *Behavior Research and Therapy* 2 (1965): 201-204; S. H. Herman, D. H. Barlow, and W. S. Agras, "An Experimental Analysis of Classical Conditioning as a Method of Increasing Heterosexual Arousal in Homosexuals," *Behavior Therapy* 5 (1974): 33-47; M. Marlowe, "The Assessment and Treatment of Gender-disturbed Boys by Guidance Counselors," *Personnel and Guidance Journal* 58 (1979): 128-132; N. McConaghy, "Subjective and Penile Plethysmograph Responses Following Aversion-relief and Apomorphine Aversion Therapy for Homosexual Impulses," *British Journal of Psychiatry* 115 (1969): 723-730, "Penile Response Conditioning and Its Relationship to Aversion Therapy in Homosexuals," *Behavior Therapy* 1 (1970): 213-221, and "Aversive and Positive Conditioning Treatments of Homosexuality," *Behavior Research and Therapy* 13 (1975): 309-319; R. D. Myrick, "The Counselor-Consultant and the Effeminate Boy," *Pers Guide Journal* 48 (1970): 355-361; K. D. Pruett and E. K. Dahl, "Psychotherapy of Gender Identity Conflict in Young Boys," *Journal of American Academy of Child Psychiatry* 21 (1982): 65-70; G. A. Rekers, "Assessment and Treatment of Childhood Gender Problems," in *Advances in Clinical Child Psychology*, vol. 1, eds. B. B. Lahey and A. E. Kazdin (New York: Plenum, 1977), 267-306, "Sexual Problems: Behavior Modification," in *Handbook of Treatment of Mental Disorders in Childhood and Adolescence*, ed. B. B. Wolman (Englewood Cliffs, N.J.: Prentice Hall, 1978), 268-296, "Therapies Dealing with the Child's Sexual Difficulties," in *Enfance et Sexualite/childhood and Sexuality*, ed. J. M. Samson (Montreal and Paris: Les Editions Etudes Vivantes, Inc., 1980), 525-538, "Play Therapy with Cross-gender Identified Children," in *Handbook of Play Therapy*, eds. C. E. Schaefer and K. J. O'Connor (New York: John Wiley and Sons, 1983), 369-385, "Gender Identity Problems", " Inadequate Sex Role Differentiation in Childhood: The Family and Gender Identity Disorders," *Journal of Family and Culture*, no. 3 (1986): 8-37, and *Handbook of Child and Adolescent Sexual*

Problems; G. A. Rekers et al., "Child Gender Disturbances: A Clinical Rationale for Intervention," *Psychotherapy: Theory, Research and Practice* 14 (1977): 2-11; G. A. Rekers et al., Sex-role Stereotypy and Professional Intervention for Childhood Gender Disturbances," *Professional Psychology* 9 (1973): 127-136; D. H. Russell, "On the Psychopathology of Boy Prostitutes," *International Journal of Offender Therapy* 15, no. 1 (1971): 49-52; L. G. Slater and C. H. Melville, "A Re-educative Approach to Homosexual Behavior: A Case Study and Treatment Recommendations," *Psychotherapy: Theory, Research and Practice* 9 (1972): 166-167; M. Shearer, "Homosexuality and the Pediatrician, Early Recognition and Preventive Counseling," *Clinical Pediatrics* 5 (1966): 514-518.

3   The Origins and Therapy of Same-Sex Attraction Disorder

1. Many of the points that follow represent a summary of my contribution to John Harvey, ed., *The Truth About Homosexuality* (San Francisco: Ignatius Press, 1996).

2. There are a number of other meditative or spiritual techniques that can be of tremendous benefit during this stage of the healing process. Additional insights about the value of meditation in healing can be gleaned from *Timeless Healing*, a fine book by Herbert Benson, a Harvard Internist .

5   The AIDS Pandemic

1. Where more recent data were not available, this introduction relies on "Status And Trends Of The Global HIV/AIDS Pandemic," Satellite Symposium, XI International Conference on AIDS, Vancouver, July 1996. By late 1998, a successor to this report should be available online through the National Library of Medicine at http://www.nlm.nih.gov/aidswww.htm

2. All the preceding data is from the Centers for Disease Control and Prevention, *HIV/AIDS Surveillance Report*, 1996; 8 (no.2). Because of reporting delays, complete figures for 1997 will not be available until late 1998. Updated surveillance data is available from the CDC website at http://www.cdc.gov/ndhstp/hiv_aids/stats/hasrlink.htm

3. All subtypes of HIV-1 infect circulating T4 lymphocytes quite efficiently, and can easily establish HIV infection if injected directly into the blood.

6   Thomas Aquinas on Homosexuality

1. John Boswell, *Christianity, Social Tolerance, and Homosexuality: Gay People in Western Europe from the Beginning of the Christian Era to the Fourteenth Century* (Chicago: University of Chicago Press, 1980), 319.

2. Ibid., 328

3. See John Harvey's review of Boswell in *Linacre Quarterly* (Aug. 1981): 265-275; Bruce Williams, "Homosexuality and Christianity: A Review Discussion,"

The Thomist 46:4 (1982): 609-25; Glen Olsen, "The Gay Middle Ages: A Response to Professor Boswell," *Communio* (Summer 1981): 119-38; Warren Johansson et. al., *Homosexuality, Intolerance, and Christianity: A Critical Examination of John Boswell's Work* (Gay Academic Union, P.O. Box 480, Lenox Hill Station, New York, NY. 10021).

4. See Boswell, 324-5.

5. For a brief but thorough defense of Aquinas in respect to the naturalistic fallacy see, Ralph McInerny, "The Primacy of Theoretical Knowledge: Some Remarks on John Finnis," in *Aquinas on Human Action: A Theory of Practice* (Notre Dame: U. of Notre Dame Press, 1990), 184-192.

6. I speak of homosexual acts here rather than homosexuality because for Aquinas morality is a matter of action. When I speak here of homosexual acts, I am using the phrase as a abbreviation for "homosexual acts of sexual intercourse."

7. St. Thomas Aquinas, *Summa Contra Gentiles: Book Three: Providence, Part II*, trans. by Vernon J. Bourke (Notre Dame: U. of Notre Dame Press, 1975), 143. Hereafter, SCG.

8. Ibid.

9. St. Thomas Aquinas, *Summa Theologiae*, I-II, 92:1. Hereafter, ST.

10. If sex were only for the purpose of the preservation of the species in the sense of keeping the species going, there would have been no need for reproduction in paradise, since Adam and Eve were never going to die. But Aquinas argues that there would have been generation of offspring in paradise for the purposes of the multiplication of individuals. (ST. I-II, 98:1, reply 2)

11. Boswell 322; cf. SCG III, 122 makes another remark that suggests that he misunderstands Aquinas's claims. He claims that in Aquinas 's advocacy in behalf of the preservation of the species was based on the ethical premise "that the physical increase of the human species constitutes a major moral good" (322). This certainly is not the view of Aquinas; he makes it very clear that the mere physical increase of the species is not a good (SCG III, 122); parents should bring forth children to raise them to share eternity with God—not to populate the earth.

12. SCG III, 122

13. ST, I-II 90:3

14. Boswell (322) finds Aquinas to be inconsistent in his rejection of homosexuality because it involves the waste of semen whereas Aquinas considers nocturnal emissions to be sinless because they are the result of natural causes (ST I-II, 154:5, resp.). Boswell fails to inform his readers that Aquinas does think that while nocturnal emissions themselves are never sins (because they are not the result of a deliberate act) but they can be sinful because of their cause, e.g., because of gluttony, drunkenness or deliberate thoughts about carnal pleasures that may have left some "trace or inclination" in the soul.

15. SCG III 122 5; ST, I-II, 94:3

16. SCG III, 22. Boswell claims that Aquinas held heterosexual promiscuity to be worse than gluttony only because it could result in serious harm to the a child conceived of the union (321). He then questions why Aquinas should find homosexual acts to grievous since they do not produce an uncared-for child. He also believes that to be consistent Aquinas should classify homosexual acts as

mere intemperance on the order of drunkenness. Boswell is wrong to think that the only reason Aquinas objects to heterosexual promiscuity is because of the harm that may be experienced by an uncared-for child. Aquinas does not give a full statement of his evaluation of acts upon every mention of them; he makes a point that is adequate to meet his immediate concerns.

17. Boswell, 319.

18. Ibid., 321.

19. Ibid., 323, n. 71.

20. Ibid., 320, n. 63.

21. Anthony C. Daly, S.J., "Aquinas on Disordered Pleasures and Conditions," *The Thomist* 56:4 (Oct. 1992): 583-612 gives an excellent review of the relevant texts on this issue.

22. ST, I-II, 31:7

23. Boswell, 326-8.

24. Ibid., 328.

25. For an excellent discussion of these texts, see Daly.

26. See Aquinas's Commentary on Aristotle's *Nicomachean Ethics* 7.5.

27. Boswell, 326-7, and n. 87.

7 "Same-Sex Marriage" and "Moral Neutrality"

1. The late John Boswell, for example, claimed that brother/sister-making rituals found in certain early medieval Christian manuscripts were meant to give ecclesiastical recognition and approval to homosexual relationships. See *Same-Sex Unions in Premodern Europe* (New York: Villard Books, 1994). However, as Robin Darling Young has observed, "the reviews [of Boswell's work] after the early burst of hopeful publicity, have been notably skeptical—even from sources one would expect to be favorable." "Gay Marriage: Reimagining Church History," *First Things*, No. 47 (November, 1994): 48. Darling herself concludes that Boswell's "painfully strained effort to recruit Christian history in support of the homosexual cause that he favors is not only a failure, but an embarrassing one." Id.

2. Germain Grisez, "The Christian Family as Fulfillment of Sacramental Marriage," paper delivered to the Society of Christian Ethics Annual Conference, September 9, 1995.

3. Adulterous acts, for example, may be reproductive in type (and even in effect) but are intrinsically nonmarital.

4. Securely grasping this point, and noticing its significance, Hadley Arkes has remarked that "'sexuality' refers to that part of our nature that has as its end the purpose of begetting. In comparison, the other forms of 'sexuality' may be taken as minor burlesques or even mockeries of the true thing." Now, Professor Arkes is not here suggesting that sexual acts, in what he calls "the strict sense of 'sexuality,'" must be *motivated* by a desire to reproduce; rather, his point is that such acts, even where motivated by a desire for bodily union, must be reproductive in type if such union is to be achieved. This, I believe, makes sense of what Stephen Macedo and other liberal critics of Arkes's writings on marriage and

sexual morality find to be the puzzling statement that "[e]very act of genital stimulation simply cannot count as a sexual act." See Hadley Arkes, "Questions of Principle, Not Predictions: A Reply to Stephen Macedo," *Georgetown Law Journal*, 84 (1995): 323.

5. This is by no means to suggest that married couples cannot instrumentalize and thus degrade their sexual relationship. See Robert P. George and Gerard V. Bradley, "Marriage and the Liberal Imagination," *Georgetown Law Journal*, 84 (1995): 301-320, esp. 303, n. 9.

6. On person-body dualism, its implications for ethics, and its philosophical untenability, see John Finnis, Joseph M. Boyle, Jr., and Germain Grisez, *Nuclear Deterrence, Morality and Realism* (Oxford: Oxford University Press, 1987), 304-09; and Patrick Lee, "Human Beings Are Animals," in Robert P. George, ed., *Natural Law and Moral Inquiry: Ethics, Metaphysics, and Politics in the Work of Germain Grisez* (Washington, D.C.: Georgetown University Press, forthcoming).

7. John Finnis, "Law, Morality, and Sexual Orientation," in John Corvino, ed., *Same Sex: Debating the Ethics, Science, and Culture of Homosexuality* (Lanham, Md.: Rowman and Littlefield, 1997), sec. III.

8. See George and Bradley, 307-09.

9. Ibid., 304.

10. I am not here suggesting that traditional ethics denies that it is legitimate for people to "desire" or "want" children. I am merely explicating the sense in which children may be desired or wanted by prospective parents under a description which, consistently with the norms of traditional ethics, does not reduce them to the status of "products" to be brought into existence at their parents' will and for their ends, but rather treats them as "persons" who are to be welcomed by them as perfective participants in the organic community established by their marriage. See George and Bradley, 306, n. 21. Also see Leon Kass, "The Wisdom of Repugnance: Why We Should Ban the Cloning of Humans," *The New Republic* (June 2, 1997): 17-26, esp. 23-24.

11. Stephen Macedo, "Homosexuality and the Conservative Mind," *Georgetown Law Journal*, 84 (1995): 278.

12. Ibid., 278.

13. Ibid., 280.

14. John Finnis, "Law, Morality, and 'Sexual Orientation,'" in John Corvino, ed., *Same Sex: Debating the Ethics, Science, and Culture of Homosexuality* (Lanham, MD: Rowman and Littlefield, forthcoming, 1997), sec. V.

15. Ibid.

16. John Finnis has carefully explained the point: "Sexual acts which are marital are "of the reproductive kind" because in willing such an act one wills sexual behaviour which is (a) the very same as causes generation (intended or unintended) in every case of human *sexual* reproduction, and (b) the very same as one would will if one were intending precisely sexual reproduction as a goal of a particular marital sexual act. This kind of act is a "natural kind," in the morally relevant sense of "natural," not ... if and only if one is intending or attempting to produce and *outcome*, viz. reproduction or procreation. Rather it is a distinct rational kind—and therefore in the morally relevant sense a natural kind—because (i) in engaging in it one is intending a *marital* act, (ii) its being of the

reproductive kind is a necessary though not sufficient condition of its being marital, and (iii) marriage is a rational and natural kind of institution. One's reason for action—one's rational motive—is precisely the complex good of marriage. Finnis, "Law, Morality, and 'Sexual Orientation,'" sec. V.

17. Stephen Macedo, "Reply to Critics," *Georgetown Law Journal*, 84 (1995): 335 ·

18. Ibid., 335.

19. Joseph Raz, *The Morality of Freedom* (Oxford: Clarendon Press, 1986), 162.

8 HOMOSEXUALITY AND THE LAW

1. See my testimony, in Hearings on the Defense of Marriage Act of 1996, Subcommittee on the Constitution, Committee on the Judiciary, U.S. House of Representatives; 104th Cong., 2nd Sess., May 15, 1996, 87-117, especially, 87, 99.

2. "The Homosexual Movement," A Response by the Ramsey Colloquium, *First Things* (March 1994): 15-20.

3. Ibid., 19. See also, Arkes, "Letter to the Protestant Advisor" [Open Letter to Rev. Deene Clark on the question of homosexuality], *Crisis* (November 1994): 6-8.

4. A fuller argument is developed in Arkes, "Questions of Principle, Not Predictions: A Reply to [Stephen] Macedo," 84 *Georgetown Law Review* 321 (1995). See also Arkes, "The Closet Straight," *National Review* (July 5, 1993).

5. See Andrew Sullivan, "The Politics of Homosexuality: A New Case for a New Beginning," *New Republic* (May 10, 1993): 32.

6. "If it is constitutionally permissible for a State to make homosexual conduct criminal, surely it is constitutionally permissible for a State to enact other laws merely *disfavoring* homosexual conduct." *Romer v. Evans*, 134 L Ed 2d855, at 871 (1996).

7. For the exposition of this point, among others, see my own piece, "Gay Marriage and the Courts: Roe v. Wade II?," *The Weekly Standard* (November 20, 1995): 37-39.

8. For a fuller statement on this point, or on the experience that stands behind it, see my piece in the Symposium in *First Things* on "The End of Democracy": "A Culture Corrupted," *First Things* (November 1996): 32-33.

9. *Romer v. Evans*, 134 L Ed 2d 855, at 865-66.

10. See ibid., 878.

11. Akhil Reed Amar, "Attainder and Amendment 2: Romer's Rightness," 95 *Michigan Law Review* 166 (October 1996).

12. See *United States v. Lovett*, 328 U.S. 303 (1946).

13. 4 Wallace 277 (1867).

14. 4 Wallace 333 (1867).

15. See *Nixon v. Administrator of General Services*, 433 U.S. 425, at 433-34. If the category were defined as "presidents who resigned from office," or "presidents who had been pardoned," it would have been clear that the Congress was attaching punishments to attributes that clearly could not warrant penalties.

16. John Locke , *Second Treatise on Civil Government*, par. 143.
17. See *United States v. Brown*, 381 U.S. 437 (1965).
18. See Amar, *supra*, note 11, at 225, 232.
19. Ibid., at 231-32.
20. Plato, *Crito*, 52c.

9 HOMOSEXUALITY AND THE COMMON GOOD

1. "The C.D.F. and Homosexuals: Rewriting the Moral Tradition," in *America*, 167, n.6, September 12, 1992.
2. Congregation for the Doctrine of the Faith, "Letter to the Bishops of the Catholic Church on the Pastoral Care of Homosexual Persons," Rome, October 1, 1986, no.9.
3. See for instance Hadley Arkes, "The Implications of Gay Marriage," presented at a July 2, 1996 Capitol Hill briefing regarding the Defense of Marriage Act (DOMA).
4. See Richard Duncan, "Who Wants to Stop the Church: Homosexual Rights Legislation, Public Policy, and Religious Freedom," *Notre Dame Law Review* 69:3.

11 THE QUESTION OF MARRIAGE

1. I put the term "same-sex marriage" in quotation marks here because, as the reader will discover, I believe that same-sex unions are not marriages, and should not be called marriages. I realize that this may be deeply offensive to those who disagree with my viewpoint, and regret this. In focusing this essay on the issue of same-sex marriage, I do not mean to discount the serious impact of instant divorce, adultery, illegitimacy and fatherlessness in our culture. These, it should be explicitly stated, are problems created by "straights." See Barbara Dafoe Whitehead, *The Divorce Culture* (New York: Alfred A. Knopf, 1996); Maggie Gallagher, *The Abolition of Marriage* (Washington, D.C.: Regnery, 1996); and David Popenoe, Jean Bethke Elshtain, and David Blankenhorn (eds.), *Promises to Keep: The Decline and Renewal of Marriage in America* (Lanham, Md.: Rowman & Littlefield, 1996).
2. Andrew Sullivan, "The Marriage Moment," *The Advocate* (January 20, 1998), 59-67. This article is a poignant reflection on the meaning of marriage in an era when AIDS may be receding.
3. Andrew Sullivan, ed., *Same-Sex Marriage: Pro and Con, a Reader* (New York: Vintage, 1997), xxiv.
4. On November 3, 1998, the voters of Hawaii enacted the following amendment to the Hawaii Constitution: "The legislature shall have the power to reserve marriage to opposite-sex couples." H.B. 117, S.D. 1, C.D. 1, Conf. Comm. Rept. No. 1 (Apr. 18, 1997). Yes votes were 69 percent, No votes were 29 percent, and 2 percent were blank ballots, which are counted as No votes under Hawaii law. The response of the lawyer for the plaintiffs in Hawaii was very straightfor-

ward: "Dan Foley, the attorney for the three gay couples whose lawsuit led to the 1993 decision, said the vote shows that civil rights questions should not be put before the electorate." Jean Christensen, "Marriage vote holds painful message; Gays disappointed by same-sex tally," *Honolulu Advertiser* (Nov. 5, 1998), A1, A7.

The same day, the voters of Alaska enacted the following amendment to the Alaska Constitution: "To be valid or recognized in this State, a marriage may exist only between one man and one woman." S.J.R. 42, 20th Leg. (Alaska 1998), as modified by Bess, Dodd and Legislature v. Ulmer, Nos. S-08811, S-08812, S-08821, Preliminary Opinion and Order, slip op. at 5-7 (Ak. Sept. 22, 1998). [I will see if this latter decision is now reported, which will make it shorter.]

5. I discuss this point in some detail in my article, "Playing the *Loving* Card: Same-Sex and the Politics of Analogy," *BYU Journal of Public Law* 12 (1998): 201.

6. This is a reference to the U.S. Supreme Court's decision in *Romer v. Evans*, 116 S.Ct. 1620 (1996), in which the Court overturned an amendment to the Colorado State Constitution on the grounds that Amendment 2 had made homosexuals "a stranger to the laws" of the State. *Romer* is now routinely invoked by advocates of same-sex marriage as a threatened basis for a lawsuit, whenever a State considers a bill that would not recognize same-sex marriages.

7. See, for instance, the effective handbook, *To Have and To Hold: Organizing for Our Right to Marry* (Washington, D.C.: National Gay & Lesbian Task Force Policy Institute, 1995).

8. On November 5, 1997, Martin Rice <lambda@aloha.net>, vice-chair of the Democratic Party in Hawaii, sent a national survey of litigation opportunities to the Marriage List, an online strategy listserv for advocates of "same-sex marriage." Entitled "Potential Status of SSM in the U.S.," it was posted on the List in its edited Marriage Digest <marriage-edit@abacus.oxy.edu>. Similar surveys and analyses are being carried out on a State-by-State basis by the Marriage Project, sponsored by the Lambda Legal Defense & Education Fund, Inc., based in New York.

9. On the importance of popular participation in fundamental lawmaking, see Mitchell S. Muncy, ed., *The End of Democracy? The Judicial Usurpation of Politics* (Dallas: Spence Publishing, 1997); Mary Ann Glendon, *A Nation Under Lawyers* (New York: Farrar, Straus & Giroux, 1994); and Richard D. Parker, *"Here, The People Rule": A Constitutional Populist Manifesto* (Cambridge, Mass.: Harvard University Press, 1994). The important trilogy by Christopher Wolfe offers a paradigm of how constitutional interpretation can be both principled and modest, without resorting to either an amoral positivism or a purely results-oriented activism. See his books *The Rise of Modern Judicial Review*, rev. ed. (Lanham, Md.: Littlefield & Adams, 1994), *How To Read the Constitution* (Lanham, Md.: Rowman & Littlefield, 1996), and *Judicial Activism*, rev. ed. (Lanham, Md.: Rowman & Littlefield, 1997).

10. *Baehr v. Lewin*, 852 P.2d 44 (1993).

11. David Orgon Coolidge, "Same-Sex Marriage: As Hawaii Goes . . .," *First Things* 33 (April 1997); *Same-Sex Marriage?* (Crossroads Monograph Series in Faith and Public Policy, 1996, rev. ed. 1997); "Same-Sex Marriage? *Baehr v. Miike* and the Meaning of Marriage," *South Texas Law Review* 1 (1997), and "The

Hawaii Marriage Amendment: Its Origins, Meaning, and Constitutionality," *University of Hawaii Law Review* (forthcoming, 1998).

12. The Court's plurality opinion has been described by a prominent legal scholar as one of the ten worst State Supreme Court decisions in American history. Bernard Schwartz, *A Book of Legal Lists: The Best and Worst in American Law* (New York: Oxford University Press, 1997), 182–84. In my view, the plurality opinion contradicts itself. See "Same-Sex Marriage?," 18-28, 78-87. In its first half, during its *due process* analysis, the opinion operates from the current view of marriage, and finds the existing male-female marriage statute constitutional. In the second half, engaged in its *equal protection* analysis, the opinion switches the unit of analysis from that of an individual entering a social institution, to that of "couples" entering a formal partnership status created by the State. Having redefined marriage as a "partnership," it then asks why some (opposite-sex) couples are included, but other (same-sex) couples are not. The answer. John can marry Jill but not Tom, because Jill is a woman and Tom is a man. Thus—so the logic goes—the marriage law is *sex* discrimination. Schwartz calls the reasoning in this second half of the plurality opinion "an affront to both law and language that well deserves its place on the list of worst decisions" (*A Book of Legal Lists*, 184).

13. The trial court's decision, *Baehr v. Miike*, Civ. No. 91-1394 (Dec. 3, 1996), was reprinted in 23 *Family Law Reporter* (BNA) 2001 (Haw. Cir. Ct. 1996). In addition to news stories about the trial in the *Honolulu Star-Bulletin* and the *Honolulu Advertiser*, I offered my own firsthand observations on the trial in two articles published by the *Hawaii Catholic Herald*: "Marriage on Trial: Leaving It to the Experts?" (Sept. 20, 1996), at 1, and "Marriage on Trial: Who is the Judge?" (Oct. 4, 1996), at 22. This decision is pending appeal before the Hawaii Supreme Court as *Baehr v. Miike*, No. 20371 (1997).

14. See, for instance, "Voters strongly oppose gay unions," *Honolulu Star-Bulletin* (February 24, 1997), A1. "Sentiments about legalizing same-gender marriage remain the same as a year ago, with 70 percent of respondents saying they were against it."

15. H.B. No. 117, S.D. 1, C.D. 1 (April 18, 1997). On April 29, 1997, the proposed Marriage Amendment was approved in the Senate 25-0, and in the House 44-6, with 1 excused; 1997 Senate Journal at 766, 1997 House Journal at 922 (April 29, 1997).

16. For an extended discussion of Alaska, from the perspective of opposition to the marriage amendment, see Peter Freiberg, "Mormons Pour Funds into Alaska," *Washington Blade* (Oct. 9, 1998), 1, 26. Liz Ruskin, "Limit on Marriage Passes in Landslide" *Anchorage Daily News*, (Nov. 4, 1998): A1. Detailed election results are located at <www.gov.state.ak.us/ltgov/elections>, the official website of the State of Alaska Division of Elections. On initial follow-up actions, see T.A Badger, "State Wants Gay Couple's Suit Tossed," *Anchorage Daily News* (Nov. 7, 1998), D1.

17. The County Court's decision is *Baker v. Vermont*, Superior Court Docket No. S1009-97Cnc, Opinion and Order (filed Dec. 17, 1997). The case has been docketed on appeal as *Baker v. Vermont*, No. 98-32 (1998), and both sides will submit briefs to the Vermont Supreme Court early in 1998. See "Couples appeal marriage ruling; Six seek right to same-sex unions," *Burlington Free Press* (Jan. 15,

1998), 1B, 6B. The article singled out the Roman Catholic Diocese of Burlington as the most prominent supporter of the Attorney General's position, quoting Bishop Kenneth Angell's statement, "I caution those who are in support of traditional marriages not to be complacent." *Id.*

18. "Clinton Signals He'd Support Curb on Same-Sex 'Marriage,'" *Washington Times* (May 23, 1996), A9. The White House contrasted the Defense of Marriage Act with the recent *Romer v. Evans* decision of the U.S. Supreme Court, calling that case "a separate issue." *Id.*

19. The official citation for the Defense of Marriage Act is Pub. L. No. 104-199 (1996). Section 2, which addresses Full Faith and Credit, is codified at 28 U.S.C. § 1738C. Section 3, which defines marriage for purposes of federal law, is codified at 1 U.S.C. § 7 (1996).

20. See, for example, the comments of one leading scholarly advocate of "same-sex marriage": "That Congress would even consider passing such an act and that the president would even consider signing such a bill into law are testaments to the willingness of many to codify the stigmatization of a disfavored group in exchange for votes." Mark Strasser, *Legally Wed: Same-Sex Marriage and the Constitution* (Ithaca, NY: Cornell University Press, 1997), 127. For contrasting views, compare these sources: Lawrence Tribe, "Toward a Less Perfect Union," *New York Times* (May 26, 1996), A11, and H. Jud. Rept. 104-664, at 26-29 (1996), in its analysis of section 2 (providing contrasting views on whether the provision on Full Faith and Credit Credit is constitutional). The House Report rebuttal of Professor Tribe draws heavily on the Prepared Statement of Professor Lynn Wardle of Brigham Young University, presented at the House Judiciary Constitution Subcommittee hearing on H.R. 3396 on May 15, 1996.

21. On February 7, 1997, the U.S. General accounting Office (GAO) released a follow-up report, agreed to as part of the legislative negotiations surrounding the Defense of Marriage Act. A copy of the report, GAO/OGC-97-16, can be found at <www.gao.gov>. The report identified over a thousand federal laws based upon marital status. GAO Associate General Counsel Barry Bedrick said, however, that the GAO lacked the time and resources to do a comprehensive analysis of the laws. "1,049 Laws Affect Married Couples, GAO says," *Washington Blade* (Feb. 21, 1997), 17.

22. In addition to Hawaii, which passed such legislation in 1994, these states include: Utah (1995); Alaska, Arizona, Delaware, Georgia, Idaho, Illinois, Kansas, Michigan, Missouri, North Carolina, Oklahoma, Pennsylvania, South Carolina, South Dakota, and Tennessee (1996); Arkansas, Florida, Indiana, Maine, Minnesota, Mississippi, Montana, North Dakota, and Virginia (1997), and Alabama, Iowa, Kentucky, and Washington (1998). To date, Massachusetts and Nevada are the only States in which no marriage recognition bills have been introduced. For regular updates on state legislation, see <www.pono. net> (the "In Defense of Marriage" page of the Hawaii Catholic Conference), and <www.ftm.org> (the website of the National Freedom to Marry Coalition).

23. Restatement (Second), Conflict of Laws, Sec. 283. All the issues related to the public policy exception—its meaning, extent, method of proof, and even its constitutionality—are now matters of increasingly intense debate, since they are crucial for the future of same-sex marriage. For contrasting symposia on these

questions, see 16 *Quinnipiac Law Review* 1 (1996) (predominantly in favor of "same-sex marriage" recognitino) and 32 *Creighton Law Review* 1 (1998) (predominantly in favor of recognizing only marriages between a man and a woman).

24. For contrasting assessments of these statutes, compare David Orgon Coolidge and William C. Duncan, "Definition or Discrimination? State Marriage Recognition Statutes in the 'Same-Sex Marriage' Debate," 32 *Creighton Law Review* 1 (1998), with Barbara Cox, "Are Same-Sex Marriage Statutes the New Anti-Gay Initiatives?," 2 *Nat'l J. Sexual Orientation L.* 194 (1996), and Andrew Koppelman, "Same-Sex Marriage, Choice of Law and Public Policy," 76 *Texas L. Rev.* 921 (1998).

25. By the end of 1997, 11 States (California, Connecticut, Hawaii, Maine, Massachusetts, Minnesota, New Hampshire, New Jersey, Rhode Island, Vermont, and Wisconsin) and the District of Columbia had adopted some form of "sexual orientation" antidiscrimination laws, primarily but not exclusively in the field of employment. On February 10, 1998, however, the voters of Maine repealed their statute. See "Maine Voters Repeal a Law on Gay Rights," *New York Times* (February 12, 1998), A1, A33. On the domestic partnership front, most of the action has been at the county and municipal levels. For a list of ordinances, see <www.hrc.org>. At the state level, Vermont and New York State also have policies of providing limited domestic partnership benefits to some of its State employees, as do some state universities. As discussed earlier, in 1997 Hawaii also passed a Reciprocal Beneficiaries law, although it is different than a domestic partnership statute. Ch. 383, 1997 Haw. Sess. Laws. The annual State of the States report by the National Gay and Lesbian Task Force <www.ngltf.org> reviews actions on a range of gay rights bills; similar reports are issued periodically by the Family Research Council <www.frc.org>.

26. Russell Shaw, "For Better or Worse or Not at All," *Columbia* (February 1998), 5.

27. I discuss the following models in greater detail in my article, "Same-Sex Marriage?" 38 *South Texas Law Review* 1 (1997), 28-42.

28. In this respect Commitment rejects the alleged neutrality of the liberal Choice model, which I discuss below. For an articulate critique of neutrality and a defense of same-sex unions, see Carlos A. Ball, "Moral Foundations for a Discourse on Same-Sex Marriage: Looking Beyond Political Liberalism," 85 *Georgetown Law Journal* 1871 (1997). Ball's work can be profitably contrasted with the work of Robert P. George, which also critiques liberal neutrality, but reaffirms the current law of marriage. See R. George and G. Bradley, "Marriage and the Liberal Imagination," 84 *Georgetown Law Journal* 301 (1995), and R. George, "Public Reason and Political Conflict: Abortion and Homosexuality," 106 *Yale Law Journal* 2475 (1997), 2495-2501 and Chai R. Feldblum, "A Progressive Moral Case for Same-Sex Marriage," 7 *Temple Political and Civil Rights Law Review* 485 (1998).

29. See the excellent recent narrative by John Witte, Jr., *From Sacrament to Contract: Marriage, Religion, and Law in the Western Tradition* (Louisville, Ky.: Westminster John Knox Press, 1997).

30. The archetypal expression of this point of view is David A.J. Richards, *Sex, Drugs, Death and the Law* (Lanham, Md.: Rowman & Littlefield, 1982).

31. Rochelle Gurstein's *The Repeal of Reticence* (New York: Hill & Wang, 1997) describes this conflict as a larger cultural struggle between "the party of reticence" and "the party of exposure." For more on this conflict, see Bruce C. Hafen, "The Legal Status and Definition of Marriage," 99-117 in Christopher Wolfe (ed.), *The Family, Civil Society, and the State* (Lanham: Rowman & Littlefield, 1998).

32. For a succinct and readable summary of these developments, see the first chapter in Glenn T. Stanton, *Why Marriage Matters* (Colorado Springs: Pinon Press, 1997).

33. The continuation of this trend among elites can easily be seen in the overwhelmingly negative portrayal of marriage which appears in textbooks. See Norval Glenn, *Closed Hearts, Closed Minds: The Textbook Story of Marriage*, a Report to the Nation from the Council on Families (Institute for American Values, 1997). IAV can be contacted at *iav@worldnet.att.net*.

34. One prominent example is Frank Browning, a frequent columnist for the *New York Times*. In his column, "Why Marry?" *New York Times* (April 17, 1996). His reaction to the push for "same-sex marriage" is this: "The problem is with the shape of marriage itself. . . . We homosexuals have invented richer alternatives." *Id.*

35. One bellweather of this change was the public response to Barbara Dafoe Whitehead's article, "Dan Quayle Was Right," in the *Atlantic Monthly* (April, 1993), 47-84. As one set of commentators has noted, "The article garnered a sensational response from American intellectuals, columnists, and political leaders." Don S. Browning, et al, *From Culture Wars to Common Ground: Religion and the American Family Debate* (Louisville: Westminster John Knox Press, 1997). This volume by Browning and his colleagues is itself a testimony to the reality of "Second Thoughts.

36. William N. Eskridge, Jr., *The Case for Same-Sex Marriage* (New York: Free Press, 1996).

37. Sullivan's central statement is his book, *Virtually Normal* (New York: Alfred A. Knopf, 1995).

38. See, for instance, the feature story on spirituality, "'Offerings' find acceptance: More and more, the contributions of Gay people of faith are accepted by the broader Gay civil rights movement," in the *Washington Blade* (December 26, 1997), 5-12. Lambda Legal Defense and Education Fund's Marriage Project in New York offers an online guide for organizing religious communities to support "same-sex marriage." It can be accessed at <www.lambdalegal.org>.

39. A recent UCLA poll illustrates this trend: While 34 percent of first-year college students believe there should be laws "prohibiting homosexual relationships," 50 percent believes that "same-sex couples should have the right to legal marital status." See "Students split on same-sex marriage issue," *Washington Blade* (January 23, 1998), 10. According to the *Blade*, "The annual poll includes 250,000 first-year undergraduate students at 464 colleges and universities around the country." *Id.* The poll was also widely noted in the mainstream press.

40. Philip Blumstein and Pepper Schwartz, *American Couples* (Morrow, 1983).

41. Ann Landers has addressed the issue of same-sex unions in at least eleven columns since 1989. In 1996, she declared that same-sex couples should have marital-type benefits, but not "same-sex marriage." "Ann Can't Give Her

Blessing to This Marriage," *Chicago Tribune* (July 21, 1996), Arts & Entertainment Section, 2. Deb Price, on the other hand, is perhaps the most prominent media advocate of "same-sex marriage." In 1996 and 1997 alone, she addressed the issue in no less than *fifty* of her syndicated columns. In her view, "Marriage can be the union of a man and woman, a man and man or a woman and woman. That's already the emotional reality." "Hawaii's Top Court Appears Willing to Legalize Same-Sex Marriage," *Detroit News* (Sept. 5, 1997), E2. Perhaps leaving well enough alone, she has never responded to Ann Landers.

42. Quoted in "San Francisco Celebrates National Freedom to Marry Day," a press release from All Our Families Coalition <www.Allourfamilies.org>, dated January 26, 1998.

43. Jean Bethke Elshtain, "Marriage in Civil Society," *Family Affairs* (Spring 1996), 4. *Family Affairs* is published by the Institute for American Values, which is based in New York.

44. *The Advocate* (Jan. 20, 1998), 49-58.

45. Ibid., 51.

46. Whenever critiques of promiscuity gain force within the homosexual community, they seem to generate a rapid and hostile reaction. This can be seen, for example, in the near-hysterical reaction to Andrew Sullivan, Larry Kramer, and Gabriel Rotello by the leaders of Sex Panic!, a new sexual freedom movement led by academics such as Michael Warner and Kendall Thomas. For dualing views of Sex Panic!, see any issue of *The Advocate* in 1997. A more critical report on the infighting, from a socially conservative point of view, can be found in "Gay Second Thoughts," *Heterodoxy* (Nov.-Dec. 1997), 1, 16-18. *Heterodoxy* is published by the Center for the Study of Popular Culture in Los Angeles.

47. David L. Chambers, "What If? The Legal Consequences of Marriage and the Legal Needs of Lesbian and Gay Male Couples," 95 *Michigan Law Review* 447 (1996), 490-91 .

48. Again, see John Witte, Jr., *From Sacrament to Contract: Marriage, Religion, and Law in the Western Tradition* (Louisville, Ky.: Westminster John Knox Press, 1997).

49. This theme is developed in A. Leon Higginbotham, *In The Matter of Color* (New York: Oxford University Press, 1978), Ch. 2, and *Shades of Freedom* (New York: Oxford University Press, 1996), Ch. 4.For more on the background of *Loving*, see the symposium in 41 *Howard Law Journal* (forthcoming, 1998). On the use the *Loving* analogy to advance the cause of "same-sex marriage," with particular focus on Hawaii, see David Orgon Coolidge, "Playing the *Loving* Card: Same-Sex Marriage and the Politics of Analogy," 12 *BYU Journal of Public Law* 201 (1998).

50. 388 U.S. 1 (1967).

51. Congressman Frank spoke these words to House Judiciary Chairman Henry Hyde on the House floor in 1996, during the debate over the passage of the Defense of Marriage Act.

52. Sullivan, *Virtually Normal*, 185.

53. See the discussion of these studies and their flaws in Lynn D. Wardle, "The Potential Impact of Homosexual Parenting on Children," 1997 *U. Of Illinois Law Review* 833 (1997).

54. For examples of how substantive assumptions inform the interpretation

of research, see these two excellent articles, both from the Summer 1997 Theme Issue on Christianity and Homosexuality of *Christian Scholars Review* (Vol. 26, No. 4): Mark A. Yarhouse and Stanton L. Jones, "A Critique of Materialist Assumptions in Interpretations of Research on Homosexuality," 478-495, and Heather Looy, "Taking Our Assumptions Out of the Closet: Psychobiological Research on Homosexuality and Its Implications for Christian Dialogue," 496-513.

55. This natural assumption is consistent with social-scientific data. See David Popenoe, "Modern Marriage: Revising the Cultural Script," in Popenoe et al, *Promises to Keep*, 247-70.

56. See Wardle, "The Potential Impact of Homosexual Parenting on Children," 844-52.

57. Ibid, 884-91 (on the use and abuse of social science in the *Baehr* trial).

58. One study often cited to this effect is D.P. McWhirter and A.M. Mattison, *The Male Couple* (Prentice-Hall, 1984), where the authors found that none of the couples who had been together for over five years had remained monogamous. The authors' solution was to distinguish between "emotional" and "sexual" faithfulness, in favor of the former. It can be argued, however, that this study was conducted before the height of the AIDS epidemic, and that things have changed. Eskridge, for one, contends that "Gay monogamy has greatly increased in the last decade, both in response to AIDS and to some social acceptance of committed relationships." Eskridge, *The Case for Same-Sex Marriage* (Free Press, 1996), at 53. To confirm this, he offers the following footnote, at 231: "See A.A. Deneen, et al, "Intimacy and Sexuality in Gay Male Couples," 23 *Archives of Sexual Behavior* 421, 429 (1994)." Yet according to Jones and Yarhouse, the Deneen study reported that "the majority of the partners in the couples (62%) had had sexual encounters outside of the relationship in the year before the survey, and that the average number of extrarelational sexual partners for each member of the gay couples in the year before the survey was 7.1." Stanton L. Jones and Mark R. Yarhouse, "Science and the Ecclesiastical Homosexuality Debates," 26 *Christian Scholars' Review* 446, 472 (1997). Jones and Yarhouse also report on a study of 1000 gay and 800 lesbian couples reported in P. Blumstein and P. Schwartz, "Intimate Relationships and the Creation of Sexuality," in D.P. McWhirter et al (eds.), *Homosexuality/Heterosexuality: Concepts of Sexual Orientation* (Oxford University Press, 1990), 319, 319 (footnote 9). The study "found a sexual 'nonmonogamy' occurrence rate across the life of the couple relationship of 79% and 19% respectively, and reported that only 36% of gay men and 71% of lesbians value sexual monogamy." Jones and Yarhouse, 572. It should be noted that none of these studies prove (or can prove) that gay male couples are incapable of monogamous relationships. They do suggest, however, two things: (1) that monogamous relationships are not the norm, and (2) that they are not *valued* as the norm. For a contrasting view, see Samuel A. Marcosson, "The Lesson of the Same-Sex Marriage Trial: The Importance of Pushing Opponents of Lesbian and Gay Rights to Their 'Second Line of Defense,' 35 *University of Louisville Journal of Family Law* 721 (1996-1997).

59. *Virtually Normal* at 202.

60. In his words, speaking of "Gay Couples as Models of Family Life," "And so monogamy (it appears) is not an essential component of love and marriage."

Richard Mohr, "The Case for Gay Marriage," 9 *Notre Dame Journal of Law, Ethics & Public Policy* 215 (1995), 233 . In his book this statement appears without the caveat "(it appears)": "Monogamy is not an essential component of love and marriage." *A More Perfect Union* (Beacon Press, 1994), 50.

61. On domestic partnerships, see above at note 25. On reparative therapy, see Joseph Nicolosi, *Reparative Therapy of Male Homosexuality* (New York: Jason Aronson, 1991).

62. See Martine Rothblatt, *The Apartheid of Sex: A Manifesto on the Freedom of Gender* (New York: Crown Publishers, 1995), who speaks of "five billion sexes."

63. Most liberationists contend that the reproductive character of sexual organs is no more than a biological "brute fact." It has no necessary meaning or implications for sexual behavior. The fact that some people see such meaning and implications only betrays their conventionality.

64. Eskridge ridicules this as the idea that "male-penis-in-female-vagina intercourse per se contributes to communion." *Case for Same-Sex Marriage*, at 96-98, 242 n.27. Stephen Macedo is similarly credulous in his "Homosexuality and the Conservative Mind," 84 *Georgetown Law Journal* 261 (1995). These characterizations of the view that sexual union creates a distinctive community miss the integral connection between sexual organs, embodiment, and personhood.

65. Instead, they make the following argument: (1) it is possible to procreate without marriage (or indeed without sex at all); (2) heterosexual Americans are permitted to do it; (3) procreation is a fundamental legal right, therefore (4) sex, procreation and marriage have no necessary relation, and any attempt to assert one would be interference with the fundamental rights of the individual. See, for instance, *Baker v. Vermont*, Plaintiffs' Memorandum of Law in Opposition to Defendants' Motion to Dismiss (filed Nov. 25, 1997), 72-75.

66. When one considers what has been written on marriage, past and present, by those who understand it as a unique sexual community, the idea that it is all "irrational" boggles the mind. For a creative recent philosophical reflection on these questions, see J.L.A. Garcia, "Liberal Theory, Human Freedom, and the Politics of Sexual Morality," in Paul J. Weithmann (ed.), *Religion and Contemporary Liberalism* (Notre Dame, In.: U. of Notre Dame Press, 1997), 218-51. One of the most eloquent and accessible scholarly writers on marriage is Professor Gilbert Meilander. See his recent articles, "The Meaning of the Presence of Children," in M. Cromartie (ed.), *The Nine Lives of Population Control* 149-60 (Grand Rapids, Mi.: Ethics & Public Policy Center/Eerdmans, 1995), "The Venture of Marriage," in C. Braaten and R. Jenson (eds.), *The Two Cities of God* 117-32 (Grand Rapids, Mi.: Eerdmans, 1997), and "The First of Institutions," *Pro Ecclesia* 6:4 (Fall 1997), 444-55.

67. For a discussion of this triad, see Hafen, in Wolfe, *The Family, Civil Society, and the State.*

68. Eskridge lists the States with "operative" consensual sodomy laws, in *The Case for Same-Sex Marriage*, at 135-136. He views these laws as unconstitutional invasions of privacy.

69. "I know in my heart of hearts that cannot be wrong." Quoted in Thomas H. Stahel, S.J., "'I'm Here': An Interview with Andrew Sullivan," *America* (May 8, 1993), 5-11; quote at 6.

70. *Virtually Normal*, 184.

71. "The Marriage Moment," 63.

72. For eloquent statements of these arguments, see Jeffrey Satinover, *Homosexuality and the Politics of Truth* (Grand Rapids, Mi.: Baker Books, 1995), John F. Harvey, *The Truth About Homosexuality: The Cry of the Faithful* (San Francisco: Ignatius Press, 1996), Thomas Schmidt, *Straight and Narrow? Compassion and Clarity in the Homosexuality Debate* (????: InterVarsity Press, 1995).

73. The influence of this ideology can be seen in remarks by Ritch Savin-Williams, author of the recent book, "...*And Then I Became Gay*" (1997). "'I'm 48,' Savin-Williams explained. 'The overwhelming number of Gay men of my generation had Gay sex before we identified as Gay. Now, an increasing number of kids identify as Gay prior to having Gay sex. It's a dramatic change, one that I sense will become increasingly apparent as kids see more positive Gay images.'" Greg Varner, "The kids are all right; Author says Gay teens are happier and come out earlier," *The Washington Blade* (Jan. 23, 1998), 33. Note also the capitalizing of "Gay".

74. See the resources referred to in the Satinover and Harvey books mentioned in note 8. In the words of Gerard van den Aardweg, "This picture is much more optimistic than emancipatory homosexuals—who have a vested interest in the dogma of the irreversibility of homosexuality—would make us believe. On the other hand, success is not so simple as some enthusiastic people from the ex-gay movement have sometimes contended." *The Battle for Normality* (Ignatius, 1997), at 12. In any case, as van den Aardweg maintains, "Marriage is not the direct goal of the battle for sexual normality; it should not be artifically or spasmodically set as a target." Ibid., 148.

75. *Baker v. Vermont*, Superior Court Docket No. S1009-97Cnc, State of Vermont's Motion to Dismiss (filed Nov. 10, 1997). Rather than burden the text that follows with numerous footnotes, the reader will find the State's reasons discussed in 52-65 of the State's Motion.

76. In Hawaii, as we observed earlier, some Justices found these kinds of arguments persuasive and others did not. In Vermont, the trial judge responded to the Attorney General's arguments by concluding that the law has a rational basis—the goal of maintaining a connection between procreation and child-rearing—and throwing out the case. In her decision, however, she dismissed all the other reasons offered by the State: *See Baker v. Vermont*, Chittenden Superior Court, Docket No. S1009-97CnC, Opinion and Order (filed Dec. 9, 1997).

CONTRIBUTORS

HADLEY ARKES is the Ney Professor of Jurisprudence at Amherst College.

GERARD BRADLEY is a professor of law at the University of Notre Dame Law School and vice-president of the American Public Philosophy Institute.

DAVID ORGON COOLIDGE is the director of the Marriage Law Project, a research fellow in the Interdisciplinary Program in Law and Religion, Columbus School of Law, Catholic University of America, and an adjunct fellow at the Ethics and Public Policy Center

PATRICK DERR is a professor of philosophy at Clark University.

RICHARD FITZGIBBONS is a clinical psychologist at Comprehensive Counseling Services.

ROBERT P. GEORGE is an associate professor of politics at Princeton University and a member of the United States Commission on Civil Rights.

WILLIAM KRISTOL is editor and publisher of the *Weekly Standard*.

RICHARD JOHN NEUHAUS is editor in chief of *First Things*.

JOSEPH NICOLOSI is a psychiatrist and the executive director of the National Association for Research and Therapy of Homosexuality.

MICHAEL PAKALUK is an associate professor of philosophy at Clark University.

GEORGE REKERS is a professor of Neuropsychiatry and Behaviorial Medicine, University of South Carolina School of Medicine, and the author of the *Handbook of Child and Adolescent Sexual Problems*.

JEFFREY SATINOVER is a psychiatrist and the author of *Homosexuality and the Politics of Truth*.

JANET E. SMITH is an associate professor of philosophy at the University of Dallas.

CHRISTOPHER WOLFE is a professor of political science at Marquette University and president of the American Public Philosophy Institute.

Appendix

Annotated Bibliographic Note on the AIDS Pandemic

For the most recent information on almost any aspect of the HIV pandemic, including epidemiological data, scientific and clinical developments, and the like, it is necessary to rely on electronic databases. Much of the material in these databases is never published in any other format, and most of what is published on paper is obsolete by the time that it appears. A select set of the most reliable and important such sources follows. Most of the information presented in the paper above was derived from these databases. The very latest data, which will supersede the grim data presented above, will appear on these sites.

Electronic Databases

Agency for Health Care Policy and Research (AHCPR)
http://www.ahcpr.gov:8o/

AIDS Education Global Information System (AEGIS) http://www.aegis.com/
The single most comprehensive online HIV-AIDS database in the world.

AEGIS News Digest
http://www.aegis.com/
A daily digest of approximately fifteen to twenty leading articles from government and other publications delivered directly to your email account.

ANANZI South African Search Engine
http://www.ananzi.co.za/
A powerful online search engine with especially rich connections to South African information sources.

Association Francois Xavier Bagnoud (FXB)
http://fxb.org/)
Very good international data on children and HIV.

CDC HIV/AIDS Surveillance Report (updated):
http://www.cdc.gov/ndhstp/hiv_aids/stats/hasrlink.htm
The definitive source for U.S. HIV-AIDS epidemiology.

Centers for Disease Control and Prevention (CDC)
http://www.cdc.gov

Centers for Disease Control and Prevention (CDC),
National Center for IV, STD, and TB Prevention (NCHSTP),
Division of HIV/AIDS Prevention (DHAP)
http://www.cdc.gov/ndhstp/hiv_aids/dhap.htm

Department of Health and Human Services (DHHS)
http://www.os.dhhs.gov/

Joint United Nations Program on HIV/AIDS (UNAIDS)
http://www.unaids.org/
The best place to start a search for international epidemiological data, although the official reports tend to be somewhat outdated. North Americans should use the mirror site at http://www.us.unaids.org

National Institute for Allergy & Infectious Diseases (NIAID)
http://www.niaid.nih.gov/

National Institutes of Health (NIH), Office of AIDS Research (NIHOAR)
http://www.nih.gov/od/oar/index.htm

National Library of Medicine (NLM), Internet Grateful Med (IGM)
http://www.nlm.nih.gov/databases/medline.htm
*The most powerful medical literature search engine on the web.

National Library of Medicine (NLM) (http://www.nlm.nih.gov/)
Panos Institute London
http://www.oneworld.org/Panos/)
Data for less developed countries.

The Pan American Health Organization (PAHO)
http://www.paho.org/

The World Bank
http://www.worldbank.org

US Food and Drug Administration (FDA), HIV AIDS Program (HAP)
http://www.fda.gov/oashi/aids/hiv.htm

World Health Association (WHO)
http://www.who.org/
Useful, but consult the UNAIDS site first.

XI and XII International Conferences on AIDS,
http://www.nlm.nih.gov/aidswww.htm
All of the thousands of abstracts from the XI conference, in computer searchable format; the abstracts of the XII conference should be appearing online here just as this book goes to print.

PRINT SOURCES

Several outstanding books can be consulted for historical discussions of the HIV pandemic. The most excellent are listed below.

Stine, Gerald J. *AIDS Update 1988*. Prentice-Hall, 1998.
The most comprehensive single volume on the pandemic, this book covers everything from the molecular biology of HIV and the human immune system to the latest therapeutic advances.

Shilts, Randy. *And the Band Played on: Politics, People, and the AIDS Epidemic*. Penguin Books, 1988.
Still, arguably, the definitive social history of the early years of the HIV epidemic in the United States.

Smith, James Monroe. *AIDS and Society*. Prentice-Hall, 1996.
An excellent complement to Stine's book: much less scientific material, but much more social, legal, and historical material.

Garrett, Laurie. *The Coming Plague: Newly Emerging Diseases in a World Out of Balance*. Farrar, Straus and Giroux, 1994.
A book which may do for public health concerns what Rachel Carson's *Silent Spring* did for environmental concerns. Chapter 14 includes a superb analysis of what has been learned about the origins of HIV.

Reamer, Frederic G., editor. *AIDS and Ethics*. Columbia, 1991.
The first, and perhaps still best, collection of important essays on the ethical and public policy problems raised by the HIV epidemic. Includes the superb "AIDS and the Obligations of Health Care Professionals" by Abigail Zuger, M.D.

Grmek, Mirko D. *History of AIDS: Emergence and Origins of a Modern Pandemic*. Translated by Russell C. Maulitz and Jacalyn Duffin. Princeton, 1990.
A superb scientific history of the pandemic.

Lapierre, Dominique. *Beyond Love*. Warner Books, 1990. Translated by Kathryn Spink.
Like Shilts' book, a social history, but from a very different social and national perspective.

INDEX

Abbott, Bud, 159
abortion, 23-24, 190, 194, 198
Acquired Immune Deficiency
Syndrome. *See* AIDS
ACT-UP, 242
adolescence, 87, 88, 90
adoption studies, 17
Advocate, 218, 219
affirmative action, 183
Africa, 108, 121, 125
aggression, 9-10, 52
See also anger
AIDS (Acquired Immune Deficiency
Syndrome), 14, 21, 22, 89-90, 93
in Africa, 109, 114, 115, 117, 118, 121
in Asia, 108, 111, 113, 124-125
epidemic exceptionalism and, 85,
122, 123
in Europe, 121, 125
incidence of, 107-108
liberation movement and, 214
orphans of, 108-109
in the United States, 118-119, 121
Alaska, 200, 204, 206
Alcoholics Anonymous, 95
alcoholism, 38-41, 48, 92, 97
Allen, Woody, 176

All Our Families Coalition, 217
AlphaI-Antitrypsin variant, 15
Amar, Akhil, 166, 170-72, 173, 175
Amendment 2. *See* Colorado
Amendment 2.
America, 179
*American Archives of General Psychia-
try*, 25
American Psychiatric Association
(APA), 19, 103
American Psychological Association,
84
androgenic hormones, 42
androgyny, 99, 100
anger, 92-96, 97
See also aggression
animal models, 9-10
anterior commissure, 13
anti-discrimination laws, 180, 183,
187, 210, 225
anti-miscegenation laws, 222
anxiety, 39, 40-41, 48
Apperson and McAdoo, 66
Aquinas, Thomas, 129-41
Archives of General Psychiatry, 24, 57
Aristotle, 138, 139, 159, 171, 176
Arkes, Hadley, 182

This book was designed and set into type
by Mitchell S. Muncy,
with cover art by Stephen J. Ott,
and printed and bound
by Quebecor Printing Book Press,
Brattleboro, Vermont.

❦

The text face is Caslon,
designed by Carol Twombly
and issued in digital form by Adobe Systems,
Mountain View, California, in 1989.

❦

The paper is acid-free and is of archival quality.

14